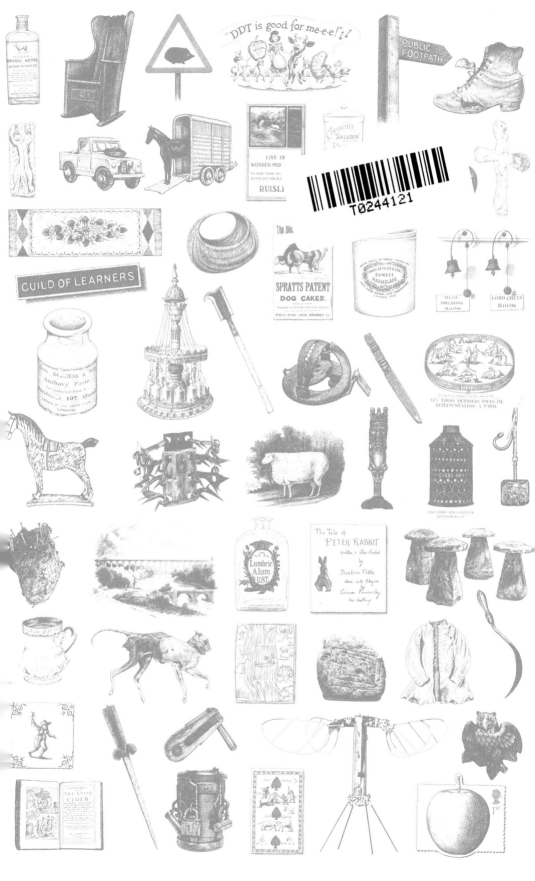

A Brief History of the Countryside in 100 Objects

A Brief History of the Countryside in 100 Objects

SALLY COULTHARD

Harper
North

HarperNorth
Windmill Green
24 Mount Street
Manchester M2 3NX

A division of
HarperCollins*Publishers*
1 London Bridge Street
London SE1 9GF

www.harpercollins.co.uk

HarperCollins*Publishers*
Macken House
39/40 Mayor Street Upper
Dublin 1
D01 C9W8

First published by HarperNorth in 2024

1 3 5 7 9 10 8 6 4 2

A catalogue record for this book
is available from the British Library

HB ISBN: 978-0-00-855942-7

Printed and bound in the UK using 100%
renewable electricity at CPI Group (UK) Ltd, Croydon

This book is dedicated to my rural ancestors. I am the product of generations of people who slogged through the centuries so I could sit in a warm house writing about them. It's a miracle none of my lineage scythed themselves in half or pitched headfirst into a well.

CONTENTS

Introduction   1

1. Deer Headdress (c. 9500 BCE)   5

2. Coracle Postage Stamp (c. 1920)   8

3. Clay Tablet (c. 3400 BCE)   11

4. Bone Necklace (c. 3200–2500 BCE)   14

5. Pig Jaw (c. 2800–2500 BCE)   17

6. Burton Agnes Drum (c. 3000 BCE)   20

7. Model of Servant Grinding Grain (c. 2400 BCE)   23

8. The Flute of Veyreau (c. 2500–2300 BCE)   26

9. Sigerslev Axe (c. 3000 BCE)   29

10. The Thames Beater (c. 3500–3300 BCE)   32

11. Bell Beaker (c. 1800 BCE)   35

12. Vösendorf Baby Feeder (c. 1200-800 BCE)   38

13. Drinking Straw (c. 3000 BCE)   41

14. Trundholm Sun Chariot (c. 1400 BCE)   44

CONTENTS

15. Tollense Figurine (c. 700 BCE)   47

16. Shoes of Damendorf Man (c. 300 BCE)   50

17. Hounslow Dog (c. 150 BCE)   53

18. Coligny Calendar (c. 1st Century BCE – 2nd Century CE)   56

19. Bronze & Iron Dagger & Sheath (c. 600–550 BCE)   59

20. Model of Oxen & Ard (c. 1800 BCE)   62

21. Corinium Cockerel (2nd Century CE)   65

22. Carbonised Orchard Apple (79 CE)   68

23. Slave Figurine (c. 3rd Century CE)   71

24. Water Newton Strainer (3rd to 4th Century CE)   74

25. House of Dionysus Mosaic (3rd Century CE)   77

26. Milestone (c. 120 CE)   80

27. Lead 'Pig' (c. 60 CE)   83

28. Roof Tile with Paw Print (1st Century CE)   86

29. Constans II Roman Coin (348–50 CE)   89

30. Jet Bear (3rd Century CE)   92

31. Shitterton Village Name (Anglo-Saxon)   95

32. Sutton Hoo Bucket (7th Century CE)   98

33. Cuddeson 'Bowl' (7th Century CE)   101

34. Axe-hammer (7th Century CE)   104

35. Falconry Finger Ring (c. 580–650 CE)   107

36. Month from a Farming Calendar (11th Century)   110

37. Wulfred Silver Penny (c. 810 CE)   113

CONTENTS

38. Benty Grange Helmet (7th Century CE)   116

39. Fish Brooch (5th–8th Century CE)   119

40. Galloway Bird Pin (9th Century CE)   122

41. Stone with Graffiti of Castle (c. early 13th Century)   125

42. Chew Valley Hoard (c. 1068)   128

43. Savernake Horn (c. 12th Century)   131

44. The Gloucester Candlestick (12th Century)   134

45. Village Stocks & Whipping Post on Wheels (date unknown)   137

46. Spitalfields Mass Burial (1258)   140

47. Whiteware Jug (13th–15th Century)   143

48. Cailleach (date unknown)   146

49. Bronze Steelyard Weight (Late 13th Century)   149

50. Stained Glass Roundel (c. 1340–45)   152

51. Lead Cross (c. 1348–49)   155

52. Owl Misericord (14th Century)   158

53. Wharram Percy Merrills Board (13th Century)   161

54. Spiked Dog Collar (15th Century)   164

55. Bollock Dagger (15th Century)   167

56. Boxwood Nutcracker (16th Century)   170

57. Woodcut From *De Arte Natandi* (1587)   173

58. Dried Cat (17th Century)   176

59. Delft Tile (1660)   179

60. Playing Card (c. 1670–85)   182

CONTENTS

61. John Worlidge's *Treatise of Cider* (1678)   185

62. Rush Nips (17th Century)   188

63. Knitting Sheath (Late 17th Century)   191

64. The Pitchford Hall Cup (1684)   194

65. Set of Staddle Stones (Early 18th Century)   197

66. Lumbric Alum (18th Century)   200

67. Coat From Quintfall Hill (c.1700)   203

68. Lancashire Lambing Chair (c. 1750)   206

69. Portable Strong Box (c.17th–18th Century)   209

70. Sheep's Heart Stuck with Pins and Nails (date unknown)   212

71. Tobacco Canister (1793)   215

72. Potato Rake (Late 18th Century)   218

73. Portrait of Robert Bakewell's 'Two-Pounder'
    (Late 18th Century)   221

74. Astley Circus Poster (1784)   224

75. Staffordshire Horse (c. 1780–90)   227

76. Pontcysyllte Aqueduct (1805)   230

77. Bird Scarer (Early 19th Century)   233

78. Kingfisher Trap (Mid 19th Century)   236

79. Jar from the Wreck of the *Katherine Shearer*
    (19th Century)   239

80. Dr Merryweather's Tempest Prognosticator (1850)   242

81. Keiller's Marmalade Jar (19th Century)   245

82. Spratt's Dog Food Advert (19th Century)   248

CONTENTS

83. Hen Basket (19th Century)   251

84. Canal Boat 'Castles & Roses' Panel
(Late 19th Century)   254

85. Leather Farm Boot (c. 1880)   257

86. Servant Bells at Dunham Massey (19th Century)   260

87. Peter Rabbit's 'Other Tale' (1901)   263

88. Women's Institute 'Guild Of Learners' Badge
(Early 20th Century)   266

89. Water Filter (Early 20th Century)   269

90. Commuter Transport Poster (1910)   272

91. Walker's Universal Mixture (Late 19th/Early 20th
Century)   275

92. 'DDT is Good for Me' Advert (1947)   278

93. Chicken Goggles (c.1930)   281

94. Public Footpath Sign (20th Century)   284

95. Land Rover with Horse Trailer Dinky Toy (1960)   287

96. Yorkshire Billhook (Early 20th Century)   290

97. Hedgehog Road Sign (2019)   293

98. Granny Smith First Class Stamp (2003)   296

99. Ach Valley Tusk (c. 36000–30000 BCE)   299

100. Robo-Bee (21st Century)   302

Acknowledgements   308

Index   309

INTRODUCTION

I grew up in a Yorkshire village called Calverley. Jostling for space between two northern behemoths, Leeds and Bradford, in the seventies it still retained much of its rural charm. Life was also deliciously self-contained in many ways: on my doorstep were the timeless pleasures that kept a fidgety, curious child occupied for hours – fields, woodland, stream, church, library, and, of course, sweetshop. But it was also a village in flux; one that was slowly being absorbed into urban, industrial sprawl. Change was afoot.

Now, as an adult, I can see how the village was, in many ways, a microcosm of the history of the countryside. Faint traces of a late Neolithic presence were left in the form of secret rock carvings, deep in Calverley's woodland, while tantalising hints of a Bronze Age burial ground next to a Norman church suggest an area that has held a special significance since prehistoric times. The village's name came from its Anglo-Saxon cattle farmers, people who were probably the first to make Calverley a significant settlement. It derives from the Old English *calfra* and *leah*: 'clearing in the woodland for calves.'

The village gets a brief mention in William the Conqueror's Domesday Book, that stock-take of his newly vanquished country and its assets. Described as property of the de Lacy family, French nobles from Calvados, Calverley would have been just one of many villages gifted by William to his most loyal supporters. Chillingly, by 1086, the village was also classed by Norman officials as 'waste', murderously razed to the ground under William's punitive 'Harrying of the North'.

Slowly rebuilt to become a thriving hub, Calverley became a busy farming community. From medieval times, families also wove and finished woollen cloth, and knitted stockings in their cottages to sell to middlemen. Extensive apple orchards surrounded the village and provided further employment, merriment and fruit. The lord of the manor bequeathed the village an almshouse in the eighteenth century, a common gesture of privileged benevolence. Just a few decades later, the effects of the Industrial Revolution, which would transform many northern towns beyond recognition, started to nibble at the village's edges. Mills and Methodist chapels sprang from the soil. Packhorse routes widened into new roads. Most significantly, the construction of a canal and railway finally connected the soft, undulating countryside to Britain's industrial might. And now, like many other villages, Calverley wrestles with busy traffic and high property prices while somehow managing to retain its quintessential rural character.

* * *

The countryside is not a meandering brook but a fast-flowing river. Our story begins around twelve thousand years ago, when families first permanently settled in Britain and started, albeit tentatively, to manipulate their natural surroundings. From that point onwards, the countryside has been in a state of constant mutability. Thanks to human intervention, landscapes have been an ever-changing canvas. Animal species have been exploited and revered, introduced and extinguished. Wildflowers and trees – both native and new arrivals – entwined themselves in our belief systems, medicine, food and craft. Rivers and marshlands, places of bounty and boundless danger, have both earned our respect and suffered our attempts to reclaim them.

The people who made the countryside their home have also changed dramatically, with immigration, migration and integration. New technologies and tools, religious beliefs, architectural styles, bureaucracy and food preferences – all these shaped our natural environment. Within all this change, however, also lies continuity. Spiritual places endure for thousands of years. The presence of water and woodland never lose their appeal. Wildlife is loved and loathed in equal measure. The seasons and lunar cycle always mark time, while the weather constantly frustrates. The countryside endures.

This is not *the* definitive history of the countryside. But it is most definitely *a* history of the countryside, told through the filter of someone fascinated by the courage, charm and occasional callousness of my rural ancestors. Material history is a brilliant way to bring the past to life; tangible objects are not only easy to relate to but they often tell many stories. A bottle of earthworm tonic unravels an extraordinary tale about our ancestors' skewed ideas concerning insects, soil and our own health. An ancient baby bottle reveals how risky but game-changing our switch to dairy was. A set of staddle stones says something about barn architecture and, more intriguingly, why farmers had to start lifting their buildings off the ground in the first place, faced with the threat of a new, fearsome foe. From sporting pastimes to rural poverty, or why parish churches are built where they are to the history of village punishments, every scrap of countryside history is absolutely teeming with fascinating details. There are some surprises too: local slavery, the history of booze, how we forgot to swim, and sinister rural superstitions.

This book focuses on the British countryside. Other nations have their own rural journeys. Some of the very first objects in the book, however, come from outside Britain. The story of the countryside and farming begins thousands of miles away. Only by understanding how and why we grow certain crops or raise particular animals can we make sense of the complete story. Above all, this book is designed to be a robust response to the impression that the countryside is frozen in time, a land of maypoles and quaint farm machinery. That could not be more wrong.

I still live in the countryside, albeit now in a more remote location in the limestone hills of North Yorkshire. Over the past two decades, even this traditional farming community has changed. From the crops that are being farmed to the social make-up of the village, nothing stays still for long. The area also faces many of the challenges experienced across the countryside, from hidden homelessness to plummeting biodiversity. New archaeological discoveries are also changing what we know about the ancient uses of the landscape. The history of the countryside is even to be found at my smallholding. Its farmhouse, barns, fields, hedgerows, middens and other rural features have slowly revealed their stories, many of which inspired the choices of objects in this book.

What hasn't changed, however, is my enduring passion for the countryside. I've made a life in many different places over the years, from capital cities to university towns, but feel most at home by far here, in my current rural surroundings. The British countryside is a wonderful place to live, full of fascinating, hard-working people, remarkable wildlife and gloriously complex history. A hundred objects was never going to be enough but, hopefully, those I have chosen convey some of the ingenuity, oddness and sheer graft of all our rural forebears.

But first, to a quiet stretch of farmland, where Yorkshire's rolling hills come to an abrupt halt just before the cliffs plummet into the North Sea …

1.

DEER HEADDRESS
C. 9500 BCE

People, or perhaps more accurately *Homo sapiens*, have been living in the British countryside for around forty-four thousand years. For most of that time, the landscape was in the grip of its last ice age. Over this tumultuous period, the climate fluctuated wildly. For long stretches, mild weather allowed hunter-gatherers to follow herds of animals across the terrain; at other times, ice and snow drove them back across the land that once connected Britain to mainland Europe.

Only when that ice age finally ended around 11,500 years ago could families wander back across from the continent and settle here permanently. The British countryside has never been uninhabited since. These small, tough communities were drawn to the woodlands and lagoons left behind by the melting ice. One such place was Star Carr, on the edge of Lake Flixton in North Yorkshire. Today, the lake is long gone, replaced by fertile fields, but just occasionally its claggy soils reveal traces of these extraordinary people.

It had always been assumed that these early pioneers were nomads, with no settlements to speak of. Sedentary life only began – or so it was thought – with the start of the Neolithic period around seven thousand years later.* And yet everything about Star Carr explodes

---

* Archaeologists often define periods in prehistory by the materials people used – such as stone, bronze and iron. The 'Stone Age' covers millions of years

that myth. Evidence of permanent structures – including the oldest timber building known in Britain – paints a picture of a community putting down roots, at least for part of the year. Families hunted creatures that lived on the fringes of the lake; their seasonal menu included everything from wild boar to hedgehogs. But, crucially, Star Carr's residents were also starting to think about their surroundings in a new way: as a landscape to be engineered in their favour.

Excavations at sites such as Star Carr show that pre-farming communities were beginning to clear sections of forest using fire and stone tools. Opened up to sunlight, these forest clearings sprouted useful plants – such as crab apples and hazelnuts – and lush regrowth, which in turn attracted grazing deer. This early form of environmental manipulation not only helped families exert some control over their prey, but also reduced the time they spent hunting and gathering, which in turn encouraged larger and more permanent settlements.

The most famous of Star Carr's treasures are its deer-skull headdresses. Over thirty have been found and yet their purpose remains a mystery. Were they worn as camouflage for hunting or used, perhaps, as some form of shamanic headgear in a long-forgotten ritualistic dance? Cross-cultural comparisons with both modern and historic hunter-gatherer societies suggest that both answers could be right; the antlers could be both a disguise and a means of connecting to the sacred spirit of an animal. By wearing the headdress, our ancestors may have felt some power over the deer's destiny or hoped to magically summon the herd.

The deer skulls were crafted with skill and attention. Experimental archaeology has revealed the process by which the antlers were carefully split, to make them lighter, and the fur painstakingly removed in one piece, to be dried and reattached. The skulls were also shaped with two openings pierced in the front, perhaps for eye holes or as a way of attaching them to people's heads.

---

so is subdivided into three phases: Palaeolithic (from *palaios*, old, and *lithos*, stone), Mesolithic (*mesos* – 'middle') and Neolithic (*néos* – 'new'). The Neolithic period is also when people transitioned from hunting and gathering to farming.

Remarkably, a deer ritual still graces Britain's countryside. The Abbots Bromley Horn Dance takes place every year in Staffordshire. Each September, a small troupe parades six pairs of antique antlers around the village, stopping to perform at houses and farms in the parish. During the dances, the performers clash horns before backing away, like rutting stags.

The earliest record of Abbots Bromley's celebration comes from Robert Plot's *The Natural History of Staffordshire*, written in 1686, but carbon dating has revealed the antlers used in the dance to be much older; 1065, give or take a few years, when the realm was still covered with forest and wild creatures. The people of Star Carr's first attempts to tame the land were imbued with ritual, seasonality and animal worship. Abbots Bromley's celebrations may not be quite as old. But strutting around with antlers is surely an echo of those ancient desires to make the landscape dance to our tune.

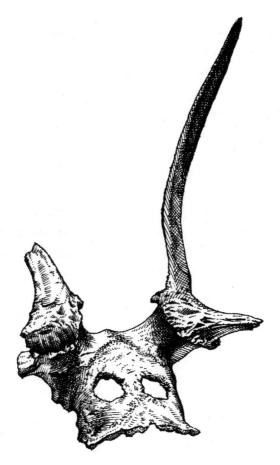

2.

CORACLE POSTAGE STAMP

C. 1920

While hunter-gatherers at Star Carr were locking horns, in the Near East people were starting to plant crops. In an area now known as the 'Fertile Crescent' – which stretched from Egypt to the Persian Gulf – communities had been attempting to cultivate and harvest wild cereals and pulses. Evidence suggests the earliest agrarian experiments may have begun some twenty-three thousand years ago. By 9000 BCE, trial and error had morphed into the widespread use of what archaeologists now call the 'founder crops', including wheat, barley and peas.

Within this vast region, disparate communities grew different crops, shifting from a largely nomadic existence to a settled one. Over time, these early farming communities expanded and spread out into new territories. People in Iran migrated east into India and Pakistan, for example, while those in Syria and Palestine headed south into Africa. And, around 6500 BCE, people farming in Greece and Turkey began to drift into the rest of Europe.

Although early farmers in the Fertile Crescent may have been the first to domesticate crops, other continents weren't far behind. The move from a hunter-gatherer lifestyle to a more settled existence appeared independently in at least seven different world regions.

Around 8000 BCE we start to see rice and millet cultivation in South-East Asia, for example, maize, beans and squashes in Central America, and potatoes in Peru.

For a long time it was debated, in academic circles, whether agriculture had spread like Chinese whispers, with communities sharing ideas with each other. Or had Neolithic farmers upped sticks and resettled, taking their skills and culture with them? Recent DNA analysis of ancient human remains revealed that, across Europe at least, farming was spread by the physical movement of people, not the dissemination of ideas. Scientists can trace the DNA of Neolithic farmers, over multiple generations, as they slowly made their way around the Aegean coast and into mainland Europe, mixing with local hunter-gatherer groups as they went. And, by around 4000 BCE Neolithic farmers had finally reached Britain.

This raises an intriguing question. Britain had been cut off from the rest of Europe two thousand years earlier. Around 6000 BCE, rising sea levels had swallowed the land bridge that once connected the British countryside to the continent. So how did farming men, women, children, livestock, fodder, crops and much more besides find their way across from the shores of the European mainland? The only logical way they could have arrived, it seems, was by sea.

Nautical archaeologists suspect that the first agrarians and their farmyard companions may have come by coracle. These shallow vessels, made from animal hides or canvases stretched over a thin circular frame, are usually thought of as small, one-man crafts. But across time and place, vast 'skin boats' have carried surprisingly large loads; traditionally, Iraqi coracles or *quffa*, as shown on this early twentieth-century postage stamp, could be large enough to take several tonnes of cargo or herds of animals.

And, far from being restricted to calm ponds and short river crossings, coracles are capable of astonishing feats of ocean endurance. In an epic 1977 voyage, led by historian and explorer Tim Severin, a coracle was navigated 4,500 miles from Ireland to Newfoundland. Severin wanted to prove that the journey made by the sixth-century monk St Brendan – which had always been attributed to a scribe's furtive imagination – was doable.

Severin and his team built an 11-metre replica, lathered it in sheep grease and, to everyone's amazement, bobbed their way into nautical history. Knowing that a simple craft could make such a heroic journey also helped British archaeologists understand the beginnings of the farmed countryside and how people and their animals might have first arrived.

A more recent piece of research, which translated a 3,700-year-old clay tablet from Mesopotamia (now modern-day Iraq), revealed the instructions for constructing a 70-metre-wide coracle – the equivalent of six London buses. The text was part of a wider story, a precursor to the biblical tale of Noah's Ark. Whether anyone ever built such a vast coracle and filled it with a menagerie of bleating and braying livestock, we'll never know. What is certain, however, is the courage shown by Neolithic farmers, with their panicky animals and piles of grain, as they launched off into a choppy English Channel.

3.

CLAY TABLET
C. 3400 BCE

The ancestor of all sheep is the Asiatic mouflon, a wiry, twirly-horned creature. It's an animal that bears little resemblance to the soft, marshmallow breeds of today's countryside. They're mountain-dwelling creatures native to south-west Asia, a region that also corresponds with the Fertile Crescent, that arc of land where farming first took hold. Around 9000 BCE, about the same time that crops were widely cultivated, people in the region also started to domesticate mouflon.

But it wasn't wool that early farmers were seeking. Mouflons' coats consist of dark, coarse hairs with only a short layer of wool underneath. Every spring, the mouflon sheds its coat, leaving fibres scattering in the breeze. Anyone who collected this hairy fleece would have found the fibres too brittle or itchy to use. These ancient sheep, thankfully, had plenty else to offer, including meat, milk and skin. Dung could be burnt as fuel or used as fertiliser, while bones and horns made materials for art and tools. Even mouflon lanolin and fat were useful.

By the beginning of the fourth millennium BCE, however, sheep farmers in the Fertile Crescent had managed to create a breed with soft, spinnable wool. Whether this was deliberate isn't known. Scientists believe that, early in the process of domestication, people started to select and breed from sheep with characteristics that made them easier to farm, such as calmness or the ability to fatten up quickly. Whether a thick woolly coat was also one of these desirable traits or a happy by-product isn't certain. More recent experiments, for example with wild foxes, show that deliberately breeding individuals for tameness also enhances ancillary traits such as floppy ears and white fur.

Wool fibre arrived in a cultural landscape primed for weaving and spinning. Evidence of textiles from the Fertile Crescent and surrounding regions reaches back thousands of years. Archaeologists sifting through a cave in Georgia, for instance, discovered flax fibres that were spun more than thirty thousand years ago. When wool came on the scene in the fourth millennium BCE, the skills people had honed working with other fibres – from hemp to rushes – really came into their own.

The development of wool sheep brought vast wealth and prestige. Living in the fertile valleys of the Tigris and Euphrates rivers (now southern Iraq), the Sumerians were the first large-scale farming civilisation and flourished between around 3500 and 2000 BCE. Being close to major watercourses allowed Sumer's inhabitants to irrigate crops, raise livestock and transport goods long distances. Sheep's wool formed a major part of Sumer's economy, and woollen cloth was one of its most valuable exports.

With commercial transactions, however, came the problem of how to document sales of agricultural produce and create binding contracts. And so, together with the development of a lively agricultural economy, came the emergence of the world's first writing system. At first, simple clay tokens were used to record numbers of livestock, a practice evolved from shepherds who used stones to count their flocks. In time, these tokens were replaced by clay tablets with more complex symbols called *cuneiform*. These tablets recorded not just numbers but descriptions of objects, locations and ownership.

This clay tablet from Uruk, one of Sumer's earliest cities, dates from around 3400 BCE. It's fascinating because of one particular symbol: a circle with a cross inside and a diamond-shape tacked onto the bottom. Meat sheep were represented by just a cross in a circle but the added diamond represents a tail. This is the sign for the 'fat-tailed sheep', a breed so useful for wool and meat that it now makes up around a quarter of the world's entire sheep population. This tablet records the ownership of seven fat-tailed sheep and is one of the earliest records of a farmer's flock anywhere in the world.

Western writing now uses the alphabet, each letter standing for a vocal sound. This allows us to emulate speech and use written symbols to express all aspects of the human experience, not just financial transactions. It's fascinating to imagine, however, that our first urge to write might have come not from the desire to convey an emotion or describe a beautiful landscape but from the need for plain old book-keeping. The story of writing started, it seems, with counting the countryside's sheep.

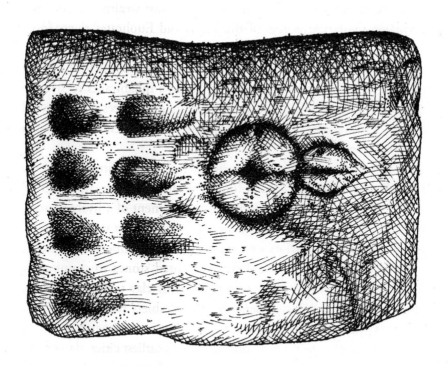

4.

BONE NECKLACE
C. 3200–2500 BCE

Partially revealed by a great storm in 1850, the prehistoric village of
Skara Brae is one of the most perfectly preserved Neolithic settlements in Europe. It sits on the western coast of Mainland, the
largest of Scotland's Orkney Islands. Thousands of artefacts have
been recovered over the years and some, like this handsome bone
necklace, tell us more about Neolithic life than first meets the eye.
The necklace is strung with thirteen small ivory beads, thirteen
made from bone, and two tusk pendants. These twenty-eight carved
discs and curved teeth make a fine accessory but, more importantly,
reveal plenty about the landscape on which these early farmers
relied.

When agricultural communities arrived from the European mainland, and settled far and wide across Britain's countryside, the land
didn't suddenly switch from wilderness to neatly farmed fields. For
centuries after, people continued to rely on both wild resources and
their newly domesticated crops and animals. Early agricultural life was
a hybrid of hunting, farming and fishing. From the bones in the Skara
Brae necklace, and other organic remains found at the site, archaeologists have been able to piece together the settlement's edible
menagerie. Red deer and boar roamed the island and were hunted as
wild game, while the ocean provided a smorgasbord of creatures

including walrus, seals, otters, dolphins and whales. Fish, crabs and seabird eggs were also part of the eclectic Skara Brae diet.

As well as these wild food sources, our early farmers were also keeping cattle and sheep, ancestors of animals first domesticated back in the Fertile Crescent. These useful bovines and ovines provided meat, dairy, wool and hides for the people of Skara Brae. The odd dog and cat bone has also been uncovered, although whether these animals found themselves curled up in front of the fire, or in a cooking pot, isn't clear. Climate scientists believe that, during the Neolithic period, the Orkney Islands experienced temperatures slightly higher than today. This, together with the region's rich soils, allowed migrating farmers with their cereal crops of wheat and barley to thrive.

The Skara Brae necklace gives us an insight into the mindset of its Neolithic owner. The introduction of agriculture and the creation of permanent settlements may have brought about a change in how people viewed themselves and their relationship to the countryside. Archaeologists have long associated the arrival of farming with a seismic social shift. Unlike hunter-gatherers, farmers needed to invest time and energy into improving their land; being connected to a particular plot or place brought with it the concept of ownership and the need to mark out and defend one's territory.

When farming societies began to generate surpluses, these were often unevenly distributed, creating inequalities between group members. Access to the best land, and the healthiest animals, would have been fiercely contested; generations of farmers would have passed on their fields and flocks to their offspring, reinforcing these disparities in wealth. High-status items, such as the Skara Brae necklace, were not only personal adornments but possibly a tangible symbol of this social differentiation. A rare item, or one that was costly in time or resources to create, was a way of advertising a person's rank, marital status, allegiances, or their commitment to certain values. Neolithic burials perhaps celebrated inequality, with grave goods mirroring the wealth of the living.

Across Europe, other Neolithic farming communities started to construct extraordinary monuments. Some were probably gathering places, where neighbouring communities could socialise, trade live-stock or exchange ceremonial gifts. Others were large communal tombs, spiritual sites where ancestors could be honoured and used to validate the living's claim on the land. These enormous earthwork henges, complex stone and timber circles, and monumental mounds still pockmark the countryside. Their purpose is often a mystery; the scale of construction and materials still leaves archaeologists aghast. Of these, our next object represents perhaps the best known of them all.

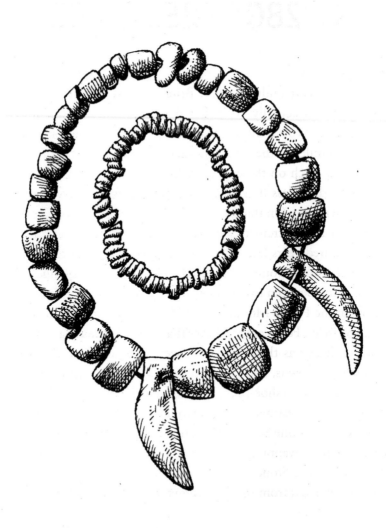

5.

PIG JAW
C. 2800–2500 BCE

Stonehenge wasn't built in a day. Britain's most famous prehistoric monument was actually constructed in stages, hundreds of years apart. Around 3100 BCE, as families were settling in at Skara Brae, six hundred miles to the south another community was excavating a vast, circular ditch on the edge of Salisbury Plain. Using only antler tools, these dauntless diggers created an earthwork more than 100 metres in diameter. On the flat ground within, fifty-six pits were hewn from the chalk and cremated human remains carefully placed inside.

Five hundred years later, the site was again the focus for colossal, communal effort. Around 2900 BCE, more than eighty bluestones, each weighing between two and five tonnes, were carried two hundred miles from the Preseli Mountains, in Wales, and heaved into place to form two circles. Four centuries after that, the enormous Sarsen stones – some as heavy as thirty tonnes – were dragged from the nearby Marlborough Downs, and raised to form a ring, topped with lintels, with a smaller, horseshoe-shaped stone circle inside.

Archaeologists estimate that it would have needed five hundred adults to pull just one Sarsen stone on a sledge, with another hundred souls constantly swapping the vehicle's wooden rollers from the back to the front. Once Stonehenge was erected, it seems that the purpose of the site changed from that of a cemetery. The stones were carefully aligned with points in the sky and framed two particularly important times of the year: sunrise at summer solstice and sunset at winter solstice.

In the countryside, the passing seasons are acutely important. Even now, people connected to the land experience the changing months not only as a practical challenge but as a cycle of continual rebirth, blossoming and senescence. And it's this experience that may have been behind the creation of Stonehenge, a place that could simultaneously mark time, venerate the ancestors, and connect to the gods of sky and land.

Collaborative spaces, such as Stonehenge, may have drawn together far-flung communities. With a population of only a quarter of a million people, Neolithic Britain must have felt a lonely place at times. Archaeologists suspect that large monuments would have been a focus for pan-regional feasting and rituals. Proving this, however, isn't easy. Thankfully, one object, or type of object, is proving remarkably revealing.

Durrington Walls, just two miles from Stonehenge, has yielded thousands of ancient pig remains, including this jaw bone. It is thought to have been the location where the families who built Stonehenge lived and took part in ceremonies and feasts. When porcine bones and teeth from Durrington Walls and similar sites nearby were analysed, scientists could establish where in the countryside individual pigs were raised. Chemicals in the natural environment where an animal lives leave a unique geographic signature in its skeleton.

It seems pigs were travelling great distances to Salisbury Plain, possibly from as far away as Scotland, north-east England and Wales. This geographic diversity suggests that Neolithic shindigs may have been Britain's earliest national celebrations – a way of uniting the countryside and its people. Furthermore, the age at which the pigs were slaughtered, at around nine months, perfectly coincided with midwinter and the time when Stonehenge's circle captured the solstice sunset.

Moreover, when the pigs arrived at Salisbury Plain, feasting wasn't the only collective activity. The discovery of pig bones with arrow injuries, or even with arrowheads still embedded, suggests that midwinter revellers held ritual killings, in which the poor creatures were first shot *en masse* and then devoured. Indeed, there seems to have been such a surfeit of porkers that archaeologists find discarded bones with plenty of meat still attached.

It seems astonishing that anyone would herd pigs, squealing and skittish, into vessels and sail down rivers and coastlines. Or coax a troop of porkers across miles of difficult terrain. And yet the sheer logistical effort of the task may have been part of its purpose. In the performance of a difficult, communal challenge – whether bringing bluestones from Wales or pigs from lowland Scotland – the journey may have been as important as the destination. Indeed, as we'll discover next, the process of creating a Neolithic megalith was as mystical as the monument itself.

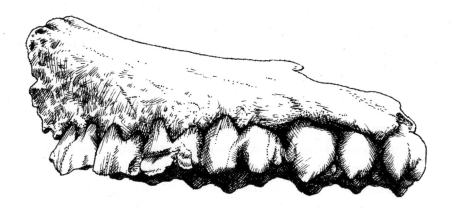

6.

BURTON AGNES DRUM

C. 3000 BCE

In 2015, a young archaeologist uncovered the grave of three children near the village of Burton Agnes in East Yorkshire. In death, they had been lovingly arranged in a close, comforting hug. The two youngest children had been laid, hands tenderly touching, while the eldest clutched them both in an embrace.

Just above the head of the first-born, the mourners had placed a small chalk 'drum'. This barrel-shaped, solid stone object was decorated with elaborate, intricately carved motifs. The drum bore a striking similarity to three others that had been found over a hundred years previously, in a village just thirteen miles away. This trio, dubbed the 'Folkton Drums', came in ascending sizes like Russian dolls and had also been found in the burial place of a young child. They too had been carefully arranged to touch the child's head and hip, as if protecting or watching over the body.

The Folkton Drums had long been regarded as beautiful but unique and inscrutable objects. Their striped designs mirrored those found on 'Grooved Ware' ceramics, a style of Neolithic pottery that has been found across Ireland and Britain, from Orkney to the south of England. Until recently, however, no other examples of these chalk 'sculptures' had ever come to light. The discovery of the Burton Agnes Drum, and another drum in Lavant in West Sussex in 1993 – both of which are noticeably similar to the Folkton collection – set archaeologists wondering. Were these strange objects being made to a common template? And, if so, what was their purpose?

In a brilliant piece of lateral thinking, archaeologists Anne Teather, Andrew Chamberlain and Mike Parker Pearson proposed that the chalk drums might be measuring devices. Previous studies had established that Stonehenge, and other circular Neolithic structures in the surrounding landscape, all had diameters that were evenly divisible by a standard measurement called a 'long foot', equivalent to 32.2 cm. Hundreds of miles away, two other Neolithic circular monuments – the Ring of Brodgar in Orkney and the Great Circle at Newgrange, Ireland – have similar diameters to the ditch at Stonehenge.

When the team measured the circumference of the smallest of the Folkton Drums, to everyone's amazement it too measured a 'long foot'. The other drums also fitted into the same mathematical pattern; the researchers took a rope the length of ten 'long feet' and found it wound around the smallest Folkton Drum exactly ten times, the Lavant Drum nine times, the medium-sized Folkton Drum eight times and the largest Folkton Drum seven times. All the drums date to a similar period, around 3000 BCE, when the first bluestones were being erected at Stonehenge.

The logistics of creating a large, ritual complex such as Stonehenge would have been taxing. Not only did its builders need to survey and accurately lay out the monument, they also had to find stones of the correct dimensions, in quarries or landscapes often miles away from site. 'Measuring drums' could have provided our Neolithic builders with an accurate and compact tool that could fulfil all these functions. It's mindboggling to think that Neolithic farming communities might have been using 'tape measures' to create henges, tombs and stone circles to a prescribed, reproducible format. And yet the similarities in the design of these monuments and the drums suggest an interconnected population across Britain and Ireland, one that was sharing ideas, artistic motifs and technology.

It's also interesting that both the Folkton Drums and the Burton Agnes Drum were found in children's graves. It's tempting to imagine these were the offspring of monolithic builders, sent to the afterlife with a parent's tool of the trade. Or that the measuring drums were so significant and valuable they were the perfect burial gift for loved ones taken before their time. Or, perhaps, is this an indication that children may have been involved in the mathematics and ritual of monument building as apprentices or even equals? If Stonehenge and other Neolithic monuments were places to celebrate ancestors and pray for future generations, it's hard to imagine an object more fitting.

7.

MODEL OF SERVANT GRINDING GRAIN
C. 2400 BCE

Thirty-two thousand years ago, in Puglia, southern Italy, a hungry hunter-gatherer bashed away with a makeshift pestle and mortar. Taking a small rock in one hand, they crushed seeds against a larger rock, slowly and methodically smashing wild oats, millet and acorns into flour. This is, so far, the oldest evidence of cereal processing anywhere in Europe.

Grains of all kinds need grinding to make them palatable. Kernels that have been pounded into a powder are more easily digested. Crushing the tough outer shell of a grain also makes its vitamins and minerals more accessible to our bodies. Using a pestle and mortar is long-winded work, however, and produces only modest quantities of flour at a time. With the introduction of cereal farming in the Neolithic period, and a greater reliance on grains of all kinds, it was clear something better was needed.

With the proliferation of crops, such as wheat and barley, came the stone 'saddle quern', so called because of its resemblance to the curved seat of a saddle. Some saddle querns were deliberately shaped into a shallow arc, others simply assumed their gentle concave form over years of wear. The miller would hold a sausage-shaped stone in both hands and push it to and fro on the saddle, grinding the grains into flour, which then fell off the end and the sides. By kneeling over the quern and sliding the 'rolling pin' with both hands, the miller could grind faster and with greater pressure than with a one-handed pestle and mortar.

From the Fertile Crescent to the Orkney Islands, when people shifted from gathering wild grains to plant cultivation, flour grinding became a key household activity. Saddle querns by themselves, however, can only tell us so much. This plaster model of a servant milling grain, made in Egypt around 2400 BCE, is particularly valuable because, unlike many other archaeological treasures, it shows a normal person working.

It instinctively looks like hard work but, until recently, the effort required to hand-grind grain into flour proved difficult to quantify. And, while this Egyptian model is probably a woman, it wasn't clear whether the task was gendered or unisex. A recent study at Cambridge University, however, seems to answer this question.

The effect on the human body of our switch from hunter-gathering to farming has long been debated. Studies suggest that, at least initially, early agricultural communities struggled to be as healthy as their nomadic ancestors. The intense physical activity of farming, and the unpredictability of harvests and access to animal protein, left early Neolithic agriculturalists with worse skeletal and dental health than their predecessors.

Once farming communities had got into their stride, however, an interesting physical change seems to have occurred, at least in women's bodies. Researchers at Cambridge University compared the bones of Neolithic and modern women and found that, while their leg bones were broadly similar, Neolithic women had arms like Popeye, even stronger than today's elite rowers. The Women's Boat Club at Cambridge, for example, clock up more than 100 kilometres on the river every week and have excellent upper-body strength. Neolithic women in the study, whose samples came from across Europe, had arm bones that were another 10–15 per cent stronger.

MODEL OF SERVANT GRINDING GRAIN

The gruelling, repetitive milling performed by Neolithic women left its trace in their bones. While everyone's skeleton is largely a product of their DNA, it's also moulded by the unique stresses and strains it experiences during life. Experimental archaeology shows us that it took around three hours, daily, to hand-mill enough flour to feed two adults. Hours of grinding cereals for an entire family, kneeling down and gripping a stone with two hands, left our female ancestors ripped. The newly agrarian countryside had transformed women's work, it appears, and not necessarily for the better.

8.

THE FLUTE OF VEYREAU

C. 2500–2300 BCE

Archaeologists spend a lot of time thinking about how the ancient countryside would have looked. And yet some of the most evocative objects tell us about what rural life would have sounded like. This is the Flute of Veyreau. It's a beautifully delicate instrument, about 18 centimetres long, made from the wing bone of a vulture. It was found in a burial cave in southern France, along with other artefacts and human remains, and has been dated to 2500–2300 BCE.

This is a type of instrument known as a 'fipple flute' and it was made to be end-blown, like a pennywhistle or recorder. Five finger-holes were carefully pierced into the bone; another, smaller hole was made on the side, probably so that the flute could be worn on a string. Similar examples of bone flutes appear across Europe, South America, China and many other regions.

To get into the mindset of the musician who made this instrument, experimental archaeologists have, over the years, crafted their own flutes following the same technique. Two things became immediately obvious: one was that the instrument didn't take that long to fashion – under two hours – and the other was just how melodious this ancient flute could be. The five fingerholes allow a range of one and a half octaves and produce clear, strong notes like a soprano recorder. With some deft fingering and tooting, the flute could also create variable pitches including musical 'slides' called *glissandos* (think of the opening to George Gershwin's *Rhapsody in Blue*).

Humans have been making bone whistles and flutes for a very long time. Some of the earliest in Europe go back forty thousand years. One found in Slovenia – the Divje Babe flute – has even been dated to around 50–60,000 BCE and was probably made not by a *Homo sapiens*, but by a Neanderthal. These instruments were carved from a wide variety of bones – vulture, swan, woolly mammoth, cave bear, reindeer – and their purpose has long been debated. Some of the oldest are simple one-hole whistles, made from the toe bone of a reindeer or other large mammal, and are thought to have been used as game-calls or a way of hunters signalling to each other during a chase.

The Flute of Veyreau, however, speaks of a different function. The sophistication of an instrument that can make not just sounds but music allows us to imagine our ancestors playing the flute for dancing, initiation, religious ceremonies, courtship rituals or funerals. Musical instruments and ability may have been reserved for 'special people', those allowed to communicate with the ancestors or spirit world. Or, perhaps, music was made by everyone just for the sheer pleasure of it.

The ancient acoustic world is one that has started to receive greater attention. Many scholars now suspect that our ancestors were only too aware of the auditory properties of different places in the landscape – especially caves – and would choose them for their ability to warp or enhance sound. Prehistoric cave paintings and musical instruments are often found together, suggesting perhaps that ritual, music and art developed together. Later Neolithic monuments are also thought to have been exploited for their musical potential. The stone circle at Stonehenge, for example, creates an acoustic chamber that magically amplifies the music and voices of those standing within it.

In a world where people lived in small groups, across a scattered landscape, music may have helped people feel part of a close-knit community. From lullabies to love songs, music between people breeds intimacy. Both listening and moving to music can also influence a group's moods and behaviour – think of the unifying experience of a rave or the stirring effect of a drumming band.

Researchers now suspect that early music played an integral part in community gatherings, ones that bound people into groups beyond their close blood relatives. These rituals would have also been the fore-runner to religious gatherings, events that affirmed common beliefs and a shared heritage. And, as ancient and rare as the Flute of Veyreau is, experts believe it would have been just one in a whole repertoire of instruments available to the 'countryside orchestra', including beating sticks, drums, clapping hands, stamping feet and, of course, hearty rural voices.

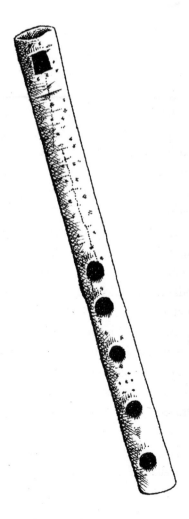

9.

SIGERSLEV AXE
C. 3000 BCE

Deforestation is often thought of as a relatively new problem. And yet we have been cutting down our woodland for millennia. As we already saw at Star Carr, hunter-gatherer communities were creating small forest clearings as early as 9500 BCE, but we can thank the arrival of farming for the world's first substantial man-made loss of its trees.

Pollen analysis or 'palynology' can help us reconstruct past environments. Pollen grains, thousands of years old, are often dramatically preserved in waterlogged soil, waiting for scientists to reveal their secrets. Studies that look at how our landscape changed with the arrival of farming reveal we lost about a fifth of Europe's forest between around 6000 and 1000 BCE. Communities were energetically clearing woodland for fields, timber and firewood.

While that's an alarming figure, it's also a strangely impressive one. Neolithic farmers used nothing but stone tools; the physical task of removing acres of woodland with a stone axe or adze must have been onerous.* In fact, archaeologists are so curious about this feat that many have tried to recreate the challenge for themselves. The most famous was the Draved Forest experiment, carried out in the 1950s in

---

* An adze is like an axe but with a blade mounted perpendicular to the handle rather than parallel, a bit like a pick-axe.

south Jutland, Denmark. Palynologist Johannes Iverson and his colleagues from the National Museum of Denmark took the unusual decision to use genuine Neolithic stone axe-heads as chopping tools. These were hafted to replica wooden handles copied from this rare survivor, the Sigerslev Axe, a Neolithic tool perfectly preserved in a Danish bog.

A number of important breakthroughs were made thanks to Iverson's lumberjacking efforts. Using the knowledge gained with blistered hands, Iverson's team concluded that it would have taken a Neolithic axe-wielder about 96 days to clear a hectare of woodland, or 10,000 square metres. Later experiments also revealed that, while stone axes were eminently useful for cutting trees with diameters up to 0.35 metres, anything over that, especially more than a metre wide, may have needed a different method, such as fire or girdling, where the tree is slowly killed by having a band of its bark removed.

Moreover, the team found that the care taken over the construction of the axe was critical to its usefulness. Not only was it important to have a well-constructed, razor-sharp blade but the axe-head also had to be hafted to the handle at just the right tension. Too tight and the stone would split with use. Too loose and the axe-head would fly off. Cutting technique, body position, and the rhythm of the chop also made the difference between triumph and failure.

The stone axe's role in shaping the landscape made it one of the most significant and useful objects in the Neolithic toolbox. The axe's centrality to the creation of productive farmland may have also imbued the tool with extra symbolic meaning. Archaeologists believe that some stone axes were kept as heirlooms and passed down through generations. Others were valued as sacred objects or buried with their owner. Some were even deliberately broken before being placed in a significant place, the act of 'killing' the axe putting it beyond the use of other mortals.

The finest, most beautifully crafted axe-heads often moved between communities, sometimes over hundreds of miles. More than a hundred jade axe-heads, for example, have been found across western Europe and as far north as Aberdeenshire. These remarkable tools were crafted from a green stone only found in the Italian Alps and would have taken dozens of hours to polish to a dazzling sheen. This prestige, in terms of both rarity and workmanship, may have given the axe-heads a special cachet – one that made them prized gifts among the elite, suitable for religious rites, or even as a form of international currency. Perhaps unsurprisingly, Neolithic tools could also be put to a much darker purpose …

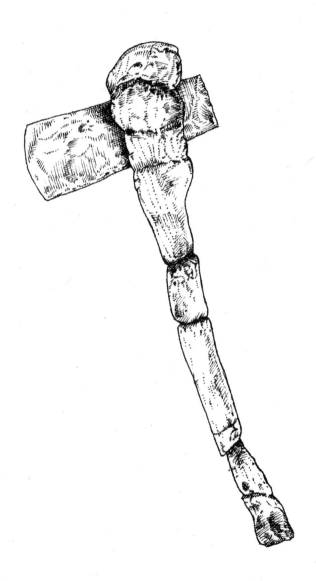

10.

THE THAMES BEATER
C. 3500–3300 BCE

In the 1990s, on the foreshore of London's River Thames, an archaeologist pulled a sodden object from the mud. About 65 centimetres in length and looking not unlike a cricket bat, this dramatic object was a Neolithic wooden club. This lethal-looking object, cheerfully dubbed 'The Thames Beater', turned out to be around five and a half thousand years old and made from alder. And, while some archaeologists initially identified it as a tool for beating flax, many others believe it to have a much darker purpose: to inflict lethal pain on a fellow human being.

The history of brutality is a murky one. In the absence of written records, evidence of murder and inter-personal fighting can be difficult to prove. The presence of objects such as stone axes isn't always conclusive. Such items were often used for everyday tasks like felling timber as well as serving as potential weapons, and so researchers are frequently left sifting through the gloomy remains of human skeletons to establish how people of the past died.

Some injuries on ancient skeletons, such as broken ribs, are difficult to interpret and may have happened after death. Skull fractures created by blunt-force trauma, however, produce patterns of damage that are more easily recognised. Modern analysis of Neolithic burials suggests that early farming life wasn't always a peaceful, rural idyll.

Indeed, there is growing evidence that one of the most surprising and depressing features of our switch from hunting and gathering to agriculture was a rise in aggression between countryside communities.

Assessment of the Neolithic skeletal records of both Britain and Europe shows that men, women and children often experienced fatal head traumas. Studies of skulls from Denmark and Sweden from this period, for example, found that nearly one in six people experienced severe head wounds. The patterns of injury also revealed some extraordinary insights. Men had a greater proportion of head injuries on the left side of their skull. Even taking into account right- and left-handedness, to forensic archaeologists these patterns suggested that males were mostly engaged in face-to-face fighting. Female injuries, on the other hand, were often found of the right side of the skull, a feature that indicated they were being hit in 'surprise attacks' from the back, possibly during raids.

A team of researchers at the University of Edinburgh also conducted experiments with a replica of the Thames Beater to establish its lethality; remarkably, blunt force trauma caused by the replica bore a striking similarity to many of the injuries found on Neolithic skulls.

With change comes uncertainty. The Neolithic period was one marked by a radical shift in many different facets of people's lives. New plants and livestock were domesticated, families began to settle down, social hierarchies emerged and people began to live in larger settlements. And, as we've already learned, settling in one location, rather than being on the move, meant vigorous competition over the best land, access to water and other vital resources.

Conflict may have also flared up when harvests failed or disease swept through animal and human populations, leaving a community looking to neighbouring territory for survival. A number of mass graves from the Neolithic period have come to light across northern Europe that shed light on the explosive violence that could rip through the countryside. At one site, in Hesse, Germany, around twenty-six individuals had been killed and thrown into a pit within their settlement. Of the dead, thirteen were children and babies, and thirteen adults, mostly men. The absence of young women suggests they may have been captured and taken elsewhere.

For a long time, it was thought that the Neolithic period was relatively peaceful. Few settlements from this time were heavily defended. Neolithic farmers also didn't seem to have any specific weapons; if they had to fight, they made do with the stone tools of their livelihood – axes, adzes and hunting spears. But 'The Thames Beater' expands this lethal repertoire, as a wooden weapon created with the intent to kill another human. On the face of it, a harder wood such as oak would have been a more obvious choice for a 'basher', but alder may have been chosen for its symbolic value; when alder trees are cut, their red sap appears to bleed. It appears that the Neolithic countryside was no bucolic refuge, but a place haunted by bloody upheavals. No amount of weapons, however, could have battled the threat coming over the horizon.

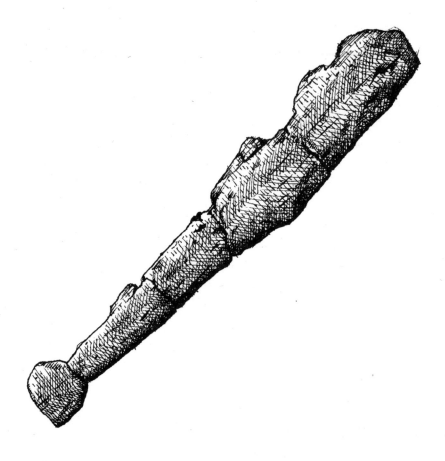

11.

BELL BEAKER
C. 1800 BCE

Sometime between 2500 and 2000 BCE, life in the British country-side dramatically shifted once again. Just as Neolithic farmers had crossed the sea and supplanted native hunter-gatherers two thousand years earlier, now it was their turn to be almost entirely wiped out. Genetic evidence shows that Britain experienced an almost total replacement of its population around this time. Over a relatively short period – perhaps as little as three to five hundred years – Neolithic farmers went from total domination to constituting just 10 per cent of the population, largely displaced by a new group who hailed from central Europe.

These migrants were later dubbed 'Beaker folk' and brought with them new technologies, such as metalworking, and eye-catching pottery beakers, hence their name. This is one such beaker, found in the soft, wet banks of the River Humber in north Lincolnshire. Unlike Neolithic farmers, Beaker folk also tended to bury their dead in individual graves, rather than communal tombs, a tradition we still follow today.

Around four and a half thousand years ago, this new style of pottery emerged in the Iberian Peninsula, an area now divided between Spain and Portugal. These new fashionable ceramics and other facets of Beaker culture spread quickly through Europe and parts of northern

Africa. Rather than being the result of any significant movement of people, however, Beaker culture seems to have become popular through social interactions, trade and the transmission of ideas. Britain, though, was different. A group of people living in central Europe, whose ancestors had previously migrated from the Eurasian Steppe, seem to have set their sights on Britain, bringing with them their fashionable new ceramics, metallurgy and other cultural practices.

How the existing Neolithic farmers were so rapidly erased from the British countryside isn't fully understood. But what's interesting is that there is little evidence of inter-personal violence or mass graves from this specific time. This leaves archaeologists with at least two possible theories. One is that Beaker folk were simply more advanced technologically and managed to marginalise the existing Neolithic farming population in Britain. With the Beakers came metalworking – copper at first, then bronze tools and weapons. This may have given them the edge over stone-tooled Neolithic communities, allowing Beaker folk to gain control of the best land and access to resources. Pushed into marginal areas, with poor land, it wouldn't take long for the Neolithic farming population to crumble.

A more dramatic explanation suggests that Beaker folk brought over a disease that wiped out Neolithic farmers. *Yersina pestis*, the bacterium that caused the catastrophic Black Death in the Middle Ages, was alive and well five thousand years ago. New evidence suggests it may have been endemic among Beaker populations, who had built up some genetic resistance to it, but devastating for any new groups they met. It's not difficult to find parallels in modern history. The arrival of Europeans on Australian shores during the late eighteenth century, for instance, had a similar effect on indigenous populations. Native communities were decimated by the double-whammy of new diseases such as tuberculosis and smallpox and the seizure of traditional land and water resources. Either way, back in Britain the people who had brought Stonehenge to life, colonised the wilds of Skara Brae, and carved the exquisite Folkton Drums, all but vanished.

Looking into the genetic profiles of hunter-gatherer, Neolithic and later Bronze Age populations, it's also possible to establish how the people of the British countryside might have changed in appearance. What emerges is not only an astonishing variety of hair, eye and skin colours, but that these physical traits changed over time. While hunter-gatherers are thought to have predominantly been dark-skinned, with dark hair and blue eyes, later Neolithic farmers brought olive-brown skin and brown eyes. When Beaker populations then migrated into Britain, everything changed again, and there's an increase in the frequency of genes for blonde hair, blue eyes and fair skin. As we'll see from our next object, however, one genetic trait that proliferated in the Bronze Age is proving difficult to pin down.

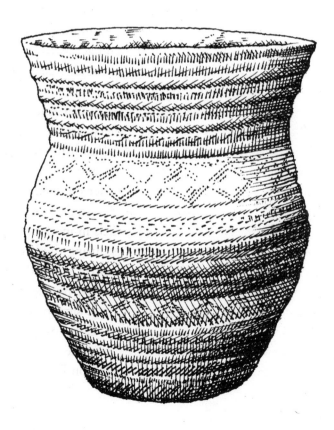

12.

VÖSENDORF BABY FEEDER

C. 1200-800 BCE

When humans first domesticated sheep, around eleven thousand years ago, shortly followed by cows, it was probably for both meat and dairy. Fat residues on ancient pottery, and tooth analysis of Neolithic individuals, certainly confirm that people have been consuming milk products for a very long time indeed.

This is a curious puzzle, however. Until relatively recently, all people were lactose intolerant. In other words, they couldn't drink milk without it giving them a thundering tummy ache or nausea. To digest milk properly, you need to produce an enzyme called lactase. All babies do this – it's how we tolerate breastmilk as infants – but for lots of people that ability stops at the age of about three.

'Lactase persistence' or LP is a genetic mutation that allows some of us to carry on producing lactase in adult life and, crucially, means we can enjoy lashings of milk well after childhood. It's a dietary super-power but one that emerged not that long ago, probably around 4700 BCE in central Europe, and only really became widespread in northern Europe about 2000 BCE. Many parts of the world remain largely intolerant of milk; in fact, two-thirds of the world's population don't have the LP mutation and manage perfectly well without it.

Which raises some interesting questions. There is a large stretch of six thousand years between the domestication of ruminants and the emergence of the LP mutation. How did early farmers use milk if they were intolerant to it? The answer is that they fermented milk into different products such as cheese, kefir and yoghurt. Fermenting transforms lactose into lactic acid, which is much more digestible. The process of fermentation also makes nutrients more available to the body and acts as a method of preservation. Ancient residues of this process show just how old this technique is. Archaeologists recently discovered the remnants of a remarkably mature 7,200-year-old feta, for instance, on pottery vessels in Croatia.

Fermenting dairy products allowed farming communities to access the nutrients in milk, so why did some communities go on to develop the LP mutation and others not? The short answer is we don't really know. There have been lots of theories: the ability to drink lots of milk may have helped farmers in northern latitudes to avoid rickets, a disease caused by low levels of sunlight and a lack of vitamin D; milk may have become more tolerated in cooler, wetter climates where people relied on pastoral farming – cows and sheep – rather than sun-reliant crops; or, perhaps, people who could digest raw milk had a better chance of surviving the crop failures and diseases that may have plagued early farming communities.

Luckily, because most babies produce their own lactase enzyme, they could tolerate ruminant milk whether they had the LP mutation or not. Objects such as this charming baby feeder, from 1200-800 BCE, demonstrate that young children were being given cows' or sheep's milk from a very early age. Pottery milk feeders from this date, and well into the Roman period, were often crafted to look like loveable creatures – birds, piglets, fish, mice – perhaps making them more tempting for an anxious child.

What we should take from this isn't completely clear. Archaeologists suspect they might have been used for weaning or feeding babies whose mothers were unable or unwilling to breastfeed. It's perhaps telling, however, that most Bronze Age baby feeders – including this object – were found in the graves of very young children. While ruminant milk was undoubtedly a valuable source of nutrition, the pathogens in raw, liquid dairy could have proved deadly. Of course, it wasn't only milk that Bronze Age people were glugging …

13.

DRINKING STRAW
C. 3000 BCE

In 1897, archaeologist Nikolai Veselovsky excavated a grave on the edge of Maikop, in the east of Russia's vast empire. It contained three adults and a treasure trove of Bronze Age artefacts. The Maikop culture, named by archaeologists after the city of their discovery, flourished between 3700 BCE and 3000 BCE. Successful farmers, these remarkable people were also skilled metalworkers, fashioning objects of breathtaking expertise.

Lying alongside one of the skeletons was a set of eight tubes made from gold and silver. Each tube was hollow, around a metre in length, but only one centimetre in diameter. Four of them also had a small silver or gold bull attached to their base. Unsure of their purpose, Veselovsky named the artefacts 'sceptres' while others argued they were poles to support a funereal canopy.

A more recent study, however, was undertaken by the Russian Academy of Sciences. There, archaeologists revealed traces of cereals on the inside of one of the tubes and suggested they were used for sucking up a grain-based ale. Far from this being a fanciful suggestion, long 'drinking straws' were already known in other contemporaneous cultures. Ancient carvings from Sumerian settlements, for example, 1,800 kilometres to the south of Maikop, showed people using similar straws to sup from communal bowls. It wasn't just men who were drinking ale either; Queen Puabi, an elite woman from the Sumerian city of Ur, was sent to the afterlife with her pure-gold drinking straw.

Straws are thought to have been used for drinking unfiltered ale by penetrating below the yeast and grain residues that floated on its surface. Most drinking straws would have probably been made from natural materials such as reeds or bamboo, but others, like the ones found in the Maikop or Puabi's grave, were clearly designed for special ceremonies.

It was long assumed that the invention of brewing was a rather nice, but accidental, side-effect of our transition to farming. Intoxicating brews only came about after we had settled down and started to produce a surplus of crops. This idea was challenged, however, by a recent discovery of fermented grains in a thirteen thousand year-old cave burial site in Israel. This is two thousand years earlier than the establishment of cereal farming. Archaeologists now suspect that grain-based booze, and its mood-altering effects, may have even kick-started communities to domesticate cereals. It's also curious that one of the first kinds of wheat to be 'tamed' – einkorn – produces great ale but terrible bread.

The purpose of ale may not have been simply the innate pleasure of being tipsy. It's interesting that much of the evidence for very early brewing comes from ritual contexts, especially burials. The prehistoric use of alcohol and plant drugs, such as opium, is thought to have been intimately entwined with belief systems and sacred rituals, especially communication with the spirit world.

When the Beaker folk first arrived in Britain around four and a half thousand years ago, they brought with them the skills to create their eponymous cups. There has been lively debate among archaeologists about the function of these vessels; one popular idea is that they were used for ale by high-ranking individuals, who used drinking as a way of cementing relationships and maintaining prestige. Evidence of Bronze Age 'micro-breweries' is also gaining momentum. Nursing a hangover one morning, archaeologist Billy Quinn decided to test his theory that one of the most ubiquitous Bronze Age structures in Ireland may have been used for brewing.

DRINKING STRAW

Fulacht Fiadh or 'burnt mounds' consist of a horseshoe-shaped pile of stones, often shattered by heat, around a central trough in the ground. Around five thousand *Fulacht Fiadh* dot the Irish landscape but their purpose was, until recently, a mystery. Quinn and his colleague Declan Moore demonstrated that Bronze Age brewers were probably heating the stones in a fire and then dropping them in the trough, which was already filled with water and milled barley. Warmed to the right temperature, in just three days Quinn's 'beer-bath' created over a hundred litres of frothy, eminently quaffable ale. What better drink to accompany an evening around a blazing, Bronze Age fire, cementing social relationships and telling ancestral tales?

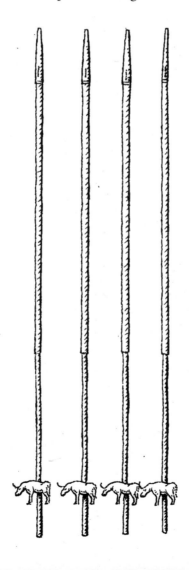

14.

TRUNDHOLM SUN CHARIOT
C. 1400 BCE

Just over a century ago, a farmer was ploughing a peat bog in Trundholm, southern Denmark. There, sticking out of the mud, he saw what he thought was a children's toy and took it home. We now know this object is one of the most important Bronze Age finds ever discovered. Named the 'Sun Chariot', this astonishing artefact is, in fact, nearly three and a half thousand years old. It gives us an insight not only into ancient belief systems but also into the arrival of one of the countryside's most beloved animals – the horse.

The Sun Chariot is thought to be the representation of a divine horse that pulls the sun across the sky. The journey is an eternal one, through day and night, the heavens and the underworld. Archaeologists suspect the model may have been used by Bronze Age priests to demonstrate the daily voyage of the sun across the skies, but also the transition from death to the afterlife.

Humans and horses have had a bumpy ride throughout prehistory. Evidence from horse bones and cave paintings show that, prior to their domestication, people energetically hunted wild horses for their meat rather than attempted to ride them. As a domestic creature and a useful farm animal, horses came rather late to the stable. The Botai people, who lived in what is now northern Kazakhstan, were the first to demonstrate any evidence of horse husbandry. Originally nomadic hunters, in the fourth millennium BCE they decided to put down roots and live in large, semi-permanent settlements. Excavations of these ancient sites have revealed extraordinary numbers of horse bones, almost to the exclusion of any other animal. Many of these reveal evidence of butchery, indicating that the Botai were eating horsemeat, and their pottery has yielded residues of mare's milk. Concentrations of manure and horse urine at Botai settlements also indicate that large herds were being kept in corrals.

This evidence led archaeologists to conclude that the Botai were the original domesticators of the modern horse. More recent genetic studies, however, show that the Botai were concentrating their efforts on Przewalski's horse, a now rare and endangered wild species that isn't directly related to domesticated horses. And while the Botai undoubtedly consumed equid meat and milk, they never truly tamed the horse.

The genetics of the modern horse have been traced, instead, further west of the Botai territory. In the lower Volga-Don region, which nestles between the Black and Caspian seas, DNA evidence has revealed the origin of all modern horse breeds. There, between 2700 and 2200 BCE, people started to manipulate wild horse populations, slowly selecting and breeding from animals that showed docility, endurance and the spinal strength to carry humans.

Once steeds became biddable, they completely transformed long-distance travel and warfare. Domesticated horses quickly spread into the Near East and western Europe, including Britain, by around 2000 BCE. While the tamed horse was initially used for riding, not draught, we soon start to see evidence of horse-drawn chariots and other wheeled vehicles. Our Danish object, resplendent in gold and an item of immense craftsmanship made around 1400 BCE, demonstrates just how rapidly and how far the 'horse revolution' travelled from its Central Asian beginnings.

The story of the horse has an interesting twist in its tale. The horse genus *Equus* first evolved in North America millions of years ago.

Horses then trotted over into Asia and Europe via the icy landscape that once connected Alaska to Siberia, called the Bering Land Bridge. With the end of the Ice Age, and the gradual warming of the climate, the Bering Land Bridge flooded and became the Bering Strait. While wild horses continued to thrive in Asia and Europe, they quickly vanished from North America. Why this happened isn't fully understood. Grazing land could have been reduced with the changing climate. Or horses, and other large beasts, may have been overexploited by hunter-gatherers who had migrated into America before the Bering Strait became unpassable. For millennia, the sound of hooves thundering across the American plains fell silent. It wasn't until Columbus made his second voyage to the New World in 1493, bringing twenty-five horses with him, that our four-legged friend finally returned to its ancestral homeland.

15.

TOLLENSE FIGURINE
C. 700 BCE

In 2020, a truck driver called Ronald Borgwardt was snorkelling in one of the many tributaries that feeds the Tollense River, in north-eastern Germany. There, in the soft belly of a flowing beck, Borgwardt stumbled upon a small bronze object. The Tollense figurine weighs about the same as a billiard ball and stands around 15 centimetres high. With stylised head and small looped arms, she also has glorious knobbly breasts, a vulva and childbearing hips: there is no mistaking her sex. This prehistoric find is just one of thirteen similar figurines to be uncovered around the Baltic region, all dating to the late Bronze Age.

The Tollense Valley, where our object was plucked from the silt, was a notorious one. There, around 1200 BCE, one of Europe's earliest large-scale massacres took place. In the late twentieth century, an amateur archaeologist spotted an arm bone sticking out of the riverbank. On closer inspection, he could see that the humerus had an arrowhead firmly embedded in its surface. Since then, excavations have revealed more gruesome evidence – at least 1,200 human remains, from about 145 men, women and children. Many had fractured skulls and all bore the hallmarks of blunt-force trauma.

At first, the site was hailed as Europe's oldest battlefield, a landscape where over the space of just one day, hundreds if not thousands of Bronze Age warriors – some on horseback – took a tribal feud to its deadly conclusion. The evidence didn't quite fit the scenario, however, especially the presence of older women and young children. Archaeologists were also puzzled by the large number of valuable objects among the dead, including gold rings, bronze cylinders, ingots and jewellery. New analysis of the human remains revealed two surprises: first, that the dead came from a wide geographical area; and, second, that some victims showed evidence of skeletal wear and tear indicative of a life of carrying heavy loads, rather like a porter.

A new picture has emerged, one that suggests a large caravan of merchants, their families, slaves and pack animals who were travelling through the countryside. Vulnerable to attack, this mobile band of traders also had a small party of armed guards with them, possibly on horseback. Despite this protection, the merchants' wares proved too tempting for robbers to ignore; in a surprise attack, it seems the caravan and its guards were ambushed and killed.

The idea that the countryside has always been a remote, insular place doesn't bear scrutiny. During the Bronze Age, long-distance foreign trade was afoot. Luxuries and raw materials travelled enormous distances by sea and land, remote regions swapping goods they lacked in their own territories. The south of Britain was rich in tin, for example, an essential ingredient for making bronze, while the Baltic had amber and the Steppes bred fine horses. Central Europe mined salt and copper, while Egypt and south-west Asia produced the finest blue glass.

Archaeologists now suspect that the Tollense victims were traversing a well-trodden trade route that conveyed amber, precious metals and other treasures between settlements in northern and southern Europe. Among the remains of the fallen were glass beads from Mesopotamia, a silk veil from the eastern Mediterranean, tools from southern Scandinavia, and bronze from Bohemia.

So where does that leave our Tollense figurine, an object made at least five hundred years after the massacre? One theory is that she was a ritual offering to commemorate the traumatic episode in the valley's history, a way of remembering the dead whose tale was passed down the generations. Oral history can transform countryside spaces into sacred places, to which people return time and again over the centuries. Our urge to tell stories turns natural landscapes into patchworks of collective memories. It's interesting, however, that the Tollense figurine was found in a watercourse. During this period, people's relationship with the countryside's rivers and wetlands took on a whole new, and sometimes shocking, significance.

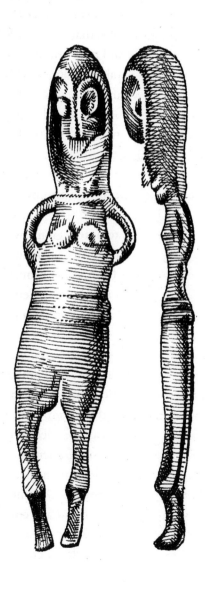

16.

SHOES OF DAMENDORF MAN
C. 300 BCE

About three hundred kilometres north-west of the Tollense Valley, in a museum in Schleswig-Holstein, lie some macabre remains. Among a vast array of prehistoric objects are five bog bodies and one bodiless head. Included in this unfortunate line-up is Damendorf Man, complete with his leather trousers, belt and these beautifully intact, lattice-like shoes.

Damendorf Man was discovered in a peat bog, not far away from the museum, at the turn of the twentieth century. Although he was flattened by the weight of the soil, it was still possible to make out that his body had been laid in the ground, face down, with his head resting on his arm. As with many other bog bodies, the acidic conditions of the peat had left our victim's skin and his clothing remarkably preserved. From his remains, it was estimated that he had died around 300 BCE.

Remarkably, he wasn't the only person found in this German peat bog. Just sixteen years before Damendorf Man had been pulled from the mire, the remains of a woman had also been uncovered, which were later dated to around 400 BCE. And, in 1934, the bog gave up yet another victim; this time the remains of a fourteen-year-old girl who had died even further back in time, around 800 BCE.

Bog bodies are some of northern Europe's most evocative finds. Over the years, dozens have been discovered across Britain, Germany, Denmark, the Netherlands and Ireland – places with generous swathes of bogland. At four thousand years old, Ireland's Cashel Man is the oldest, but most met their swampy deaths between 800 BCE and 100 CE. They're special for so many reasons. Not only is their preservation miraculous but they're also evidence of an ancient rural belief system that, in some ways, endures even today.

Most interments during this period were either cremations or 'dry' burials in tombs or pits, but those consigned to these bogs seem to have received unique and rather brutal treatment. Their resting places are wetlands, peat bogs and marshes. These soggy spaces were neither farmland nor open water, but peculiar, dangerous places that could trap the unwary traveller (though they also provided valuable peat for fuel and, later, iron ore). Furthermore, bog victims often met untimely deaths and were dispatched in methods that seem unimaginably barbaric. Many show signs of being hanged, garrotted, bludgeoned or stabbed, often in combination, in an act of deliberate 'over-kill' or ritualised violence. High-status weapons, tools, cauldrons, chariot fittings and jewellery also seem to have been cast into 'wet places' with enthusiasm.

Watery spaces meant something important to our ancestors and the practice of jettisoning valuable items, including people and animals, into bogs, rivers and lakes seems to have reached a peak in the Bronze and Iron Ages. Quite why, no one knows, but many suspect that our ancestors worshipped many different gods and goddesses of the countryside, including sky, earth and water deities.

Since our earliest beginnings, water has played a central role in spiritual and religious beliefs. It both sustains and destroys, a duality that has given it rich significance and focus for offerings and sacrifices to water deities. Watery sites of importance were also often used over many generations; Damendorf's victims, for example, cover a period of at least five hundred years. The practice of sacrificing objects by throwing them into water persisted over the centuries; even today, we still toss coins into rivers and wishing wells, hoping for good luck.

Structures, such as bridges or walkways, may have even been constructed to facilitate watery sacrifices. At Flag Fen, in Cambridgeshire, a one-kilometre wooden causeway was constructed sometime between 1400 and 900 BCE to carry its passengers across a large stretch of marshy ground. There, archaeologists have uncovered at least three hundred examples of Bronze and Iron Age metalwork, mostly weapons, many of which were deliberately broken before being pitched into the marshes. The people who crossed the causeway, over the centuries, also threw in many other valuable objects, items that represented a significant loss. These included jewellery, horse and vehicle trappings, joints of meat, and even several dogs. Not even man's most loyal countryside companion, it seems, could dodge its fate as a divine offering.

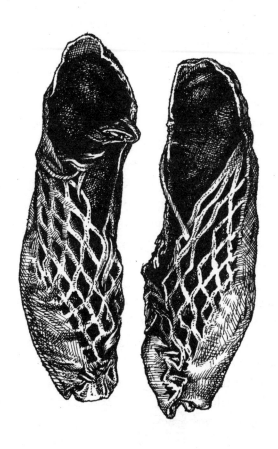

17.

HOUNSLOW DOG
C. 150 BCE

Dogs and humans have had a close relationship for at least fifteen thousand years. They have served us as sheep-herders and guardians, sled-pullers and lap-dogs, and our interactions have ranged from exploitation to deep affection. Perhaps no other animal has captured our hearts more than the canine.

While we know that dogs are descended from wolves, the story of domestication is tricky to unpick. The line between a wild beast, stealing the scraps from a human settlement, and a tame pet isn't always clear. In fact, wolves and dogs are classed as the same species and, if mated, produce healthy offspring. There are, however, key traits that separate a modern dog from its lupine ancestors, two of which are particularly interesting.

Wolves are predisposed to be fearful of people. The ancestors of the modern dog, however, may have had genetic mutations that made them less stressed when in contact with humans. This allowed them to move among hunter-gatherer communities, scavenging from carcasses and, in time, returning the favour with protection or helping with the hunt. Even before the advent of farming eleven thousand years ago, it seems that at least five different dog lineages had emerged across the globe, including the ancestors of the Australian dingo and America's native Carolina dog.

The second key trait of modern dogs is their ability to eat other food besides meat. While wolves are voracious carnivores, domesticated dogs are omnivorous and can tolerate significant amounts of starch. This ability to cope with a generalist diet, especially one that included cereals, rice and potatoes, allowed dogs to stay close to humans, and survive on our leftovers, even after our shift from hunting to farming.

From the moment of domestication, the human–dog relationship has been complicated. The archaeological evidence, from cave paintings to refuse pits, shows that people were as happy to eat dogs as to use them for hunting. The domesticated dog could find itself both a treasured companion and an object of sacrifice. Some communities used canines as a source of meat and skins, while others valued them as working animals, herders of livestock or guard dogs. Thousands of years' worth of burials, where humans are carefully interred with their pet pooches, also testify to a deep bond that has long existed between a dog and its owner.

For most of prehistory, the size of dogs doesn't vary that much. Across Europe, for example, during the first millennium BCE the average wither height of dogs – the distance between its paw and the highest point of its shoulder – is around 40–60 cm, about the same as a Border Collie or small wolf. There are, however, exceptions. Writing in the fourth century BCE, for example, the Greek philosopher Aristotle praises the *molosser*, a vast livestock guardian dog not unlike a mastiff. In contrast, a number of ancient sites across Europe have yielded bones of small breeds and dogs with shortened legs. Archaeologists digging at the pre-Roman settlement of *Calleva Atrebatum*, near Silchester, for example, found the burial of a tiny 'handbag' dog, possibly the pet of a tribal leader.

Our object, a model of a dog, also comes from this time and was found by farm labourers digging in a field in the rural outskirts of Hounslow, London, in 1864. (It's rather fitting that Hounslow derives from the Anglo-Saxon 'Hundes hlāw' or 'Hound's hill'.) Dated to around 150 BCE, it's unmistakably a canine with stumpy legs. Shortened limbs in dogs are caused by a genetic mutation known as chondrodysplasia. Far from being a modern phenomenon, it's possible that short-legged dogs became popular thousands of years ago with the emergence of pastoral farming. Little legs allowed dogs to dart amid the hooves of cows and nip at their heels, without being kicked. This one, with its sublimely bendy back and pointy ears, looks not unlike a corgi, a breed that may have been introduced to Wales from central Europe in pre-Roman times. With the advent of farming, the need to control livestock was just one of the many new challenges that faced people who lived in the countryside. The desire to tame the landscape, its plants and its animals, may have even changed how we viewed time itself.

18.

COLIGNY CALENDAR
C. 1ST CENTURY BCE – 2ND CENTURY CE

At the close of the nineteenth century, the remains of a bronze plaque were discovered in a field north of Coligny, in eastern France. The plaque had been smashed into dozens of pieces, some of which were missing, but when the shards were carefully pieced back together it became clear that this was no ordinary find.

The Coligny Calendar is an extraordinary object. It's a huge 1.5m² metal sheet covered with engraved letters and numbers. It's also a strange hybrid – the font is Roman but the language is Gaulish, the ancient Celtic 'mother-tongue' spoken in western and central Europe. Ironically, for an object focused on marking time, archaeologists can't quite agree on when it was made, putting it somewhere between the first century BCE and the second century CE.

The calendar is divided up into sixty-two months, with an extra two 'intercalary' months, the monthly equivalent of leap days. The calendar is lunar-solar, meaning it tracks the phases of the moon and the time it takes for the Earth to make one revolution around the sun. Each of the months on the Coligny Calendar consists of twenty-eight or twenty-nine days. The months are also split into halves, each fortnight marked as lucky (*matus*) or unlucky (*anmatus*), perhaps indicating auspicious dates for big events such as going to war or making a sacrifice.

From the remains of the Coligny Calendar, we can imagine how our ancestors might have viewed the passing of the seasons and the purpose of each month. Agrarian life, with its focus on cyclical crops and livestock, needed order to make sure things were happening when they should. This applied not only to practical tasks, such as sowing crops or culling animals, but also to religious events. Rituals marked the wheel of the farming year and gave communities valuable reminders to venerate the gods who made it all possible.

The months of the Coligny Calendar are named. Academics argue furiously over translations of the Gaulish words but the names can give us an insight into the rural preoccupations of our ancestors. *Equos*, for example, is usually taken to be June/July, and interpreted as 'horse time', perhaps the month when foals were born. *Cutios* is March/April, or the 'Time of Winds', an attribute we still give to those blustery few weeks. *Samonios* is read as October/November and is believed to relate to *Samhain*, a festival written about by later Celtic scribes. This is when autumn slid into winter and livestock were rounded up from the fields and either slaughtered or spared for breeding.

Samhain also marked the end of one fruitful year and embodied hope for the next. As it is now, late autumn was a time of rural reckoning, a counting of the year's successes and failures. *Samhain* is also thought to have been a strange, unsettling time. Archaeological evidence from many sites across northern Europe during the Iron Age indicates a rush of rituals at this time of the year. *Samhain* heralded in the darker months and was believed to be a moment when the barriers between the natural and the supernatural became more fluid, and spirits could move freely into the world of the living.

The idea of four seasons is central to many people's experience of the countryside. By the first century BCE, Roman writer Varro in *Rerum rusticarum libri III* (or 'Three Books of Rural Topics') had set down on paper the notion of spring, summer, autumn and winter, each with its own set of farming tasks, but the four-fold year may go back even further in time. The Celtic year is also thought to have been divided into surprisingly familiar quarters, the beginning of each marked by a significant ritual: *Samhain*, which kicked off winter, was characterised by culling and festive feasting; *Imbolc*, or spring, celebrated lambing time and new life; *Beltane*, at the beginning of summer, saw cattle turned out onto grassland; while *Lughnasa* focused on rituals that ensure the ripening of harvest grain. And, while the early summer celebration of *Beltane* may have faded away, it's curious that Christmas, Easter and Harvest festivals bear an uncanny resemblance to these ancient countryside rituals.

19.

BRONZE & IRON DAGGER & SHEATH
C. 600–550 BCE

Neolithic farmers in Britain were remarkably resourceful, creating tools out of stone, wood, antler and bone to perform a wide range of tasks. During the Bronze Age, weapons and objects of high status were often made from metal, but agricultural implements, which were used by ordinary people, changed little in terms of materials. When iron arrived around 700 BCE, however, nothing was ever the same again.

Bronze was expensive because its alloys – tin and copper – were both rare. As we've already seen, metals were exchanged over vast distances and circulated among the elite. Iron, however, was a different kind of material. Although it was labour intensive to mine and needed high temperatures to smelt, iron's greatest appeal lay in its ubiquity. Iron ore is absolutely everywhere.

By 1500 BCE metalworkers in the Fertile Crescent had worked out how to extract pure iron from ore found in sedimentary rock. Just three hundred years later, the technology had reached the Mediterranean and south Asia, and by the eighth century BCE, iron objects were found in Britain. At first, this strange new material probably reached the south coast as finished objects, traded or exchanged as gifts. By around 600 BCE, however, the country had started to smelt and forge its own.

There was no wholescale replacement of bronze, however. With its coveted buttery glow, bronze still outshone ferrous metal when it came to jewellery and prestige goods. Many objects from the first few centuries of the Iron Age often mixed the two. This dagger, crafted just as Britain was beginning to create its own ironwork, made the most of each metal. Found in Cookham, Berkshire, it dates from around 600–550 BCE, just as metalworkers were getting to grip with this new material. Its swirly hilt and sheath are both cast in bronze, which allowed greater intricacy, while the blade is worked from iron, giving it a strong, sharp cutting edge.

In fact, iron was so plentiful, it soon became the go-to metal for everyday objects, including farming implements. From iron plough-shares to sickles, saws to chains, many of the everyday metal tools we still use today were perfected in the Iron Age. Unlike bronze, which had to be melted and poured into moulds, wrought iron was heated in a furnace before being hammered into shape on an anvil. Archaeologists suspect the skills of smithing were probably highly guarded, and gendered, perhaps passed from father to son or via apprenticeships. In many ancient cultures, blacksmiths were often revered and feared in equal measure. Their work was viewed as alchemy, transforming an unpromising material into wonderous objects, using immense heat, skill and brute strength. It's telling that Iron Age communities across Britain and northern Europe believed in a similar blacksmith god: the Gauls had *Gobannos*, the Welsh worshipped *Gofannon*, and the Irish celebrated *Goibniu*.

Iron also attracted supernatural beliefs. Pliny the Elder, in his first-century work *Natural History*, dubbed it 'the most useful and the most fatal instrument in the hand of mankind', a metal so potent that it could create and destroy civilisations with equal force. He also thought it both cursed and capable of healing. Human blood made iron more apt to rust, he wrote, but burying iron under your thresh-old could prevent ill-spirits and nightmares. Iron was lucky too – if a circle was traced around a child with a sharp iron weapon, or carried three times around them, they were protected from evil. Folklorists believe we touched iron for luck centuries before we changed to 'touching wood'. The Italians continue to *toccare ferro* ('touch iron') and a lucky iron horseshoe still graces many a British pub and cottage.

The blacksmith held one of the most important occupations in the countryside. He was the person who made not only weapons and armour but also the stuff of everyday life. From cauldrons to chisels, he turned his hand to any number of objects. From the Iron Age onwards, most communities had a blacksmith in their midst, a trend that persisted well into the twentieth century. The importance and prevalence of this ancient occupation is still reflected in one crucial place; as we'll see later in this book, 'Smith' remains the most common surname across the English-speaking world.

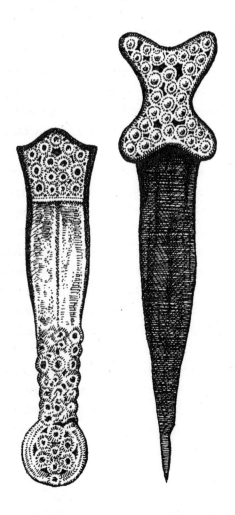

20.

MODEL OF OXEN & ARD

C. 1800 BCE

The cow was first domesticated around ten and a half thousand years ago. Farmers in the Fertile Crescent were, again, probably the first to turn wild aurochs into docile cattle, but soon after, and independently, agricultural communities in Pakistan, and central Africa, had also tamed the herd. At some stage during this process, farmers also twigged that castrated bulls, or 'oxen', made biddable beasts of burden and put them to work.

The earliest evidence for ploughing comes from the Czech Republic, around 3500 BCE, but many other cultures soon harnessed the oxen's potential. This painted wooden model, made around 1800 BCE in Egypt, shows a field worker guiding two speckly oxen and a wooden plough called an ard. The tool, which was essentially a wooden spike, worked perfectly on light, arid soil. By gently scratching the surface, it created a fine tilth and scraped a drill into which seeds were thrown.

Global temperatures throughout the Neolithic and Bronze Ages were slightly warmer than today. Around 750 BCE, however, north-west Europe including Britain slid into a period of wetter, chillier weather that didn't improve for five hundred years. This seems to have had two effects. British farmers abandoned fields in many marginal places, such as uplands, which had previously been productive. And the ard, which was suited to dry, crumbly soil, started to struggle with an increasingly soggier countryside.

By the time Roman rule reached Britain, in 43 CE, the ard had experienced a makeover. Two key improvements helped it move through wetter, claggier soil: one was a coulter, a knife that sliced through the ground ahead of the ard; and the other was an iron ploughshare, the tip of the ard that dug through the soil and pushed it to one side. These simple but crucial developments allowed Iron Age farmers to break up soil more easily, improve drainage, and open up more land for cultivation.

Arable farming seems to have been surprisingly productive in parts of Iron Age Britain, particularly in the south and east. Strabo, a Greek geographer who lived between the first century BCE and the first century CE, noted with some admiration that Britain 'produces grain, cattle, gold, silver and iron. These things are exported, along with hides, slaves and dogs suitable for hunting.'

During the Iron Age, there was also a proliferation of hillforts: fortified settlements in elevated positions. There are more than three thousand in the British countryside alone. While their raised position gave occupants a useful vantage point, many hillforts are thought to have been seasonal assembly places for farming communities. Others were possibly occupied all year round.

Most hillforts had grain storage pits. At Danebury, in Hampshire, for example, thousands were dug out from the chalk. These large underground holes were filled with the cereal harvest in late summer and sealed shut. This protected the grain from weather, vermin and violent raids from neighbouring tribes. The act of putting precious food resources into the ground also had a spiritual element – the gods of the underworld were being asked to protect it. Once the holes were emptied, come springtime, if the grain was edible many of the pits seem to have been 'thanked' in the only way Iron Age people knew how. With a thumpingly good sacrifice of livestock or unfortunate human beings.

One of the tricky things to convey about ploughing with an ard is just how toilsome it was. We can see it, however, in one of the topographical relics of the countryside, the 'Celtic field'. Most have been scrubbed away by intensive farming, but just occasionally these prehistoric fields survive. Celtic fields are unusually small and square compared to large, modern rectangular fields. They average only about 30 metres by 30 metres and, grouped together, create a chequerboard pattern across the landscape. Because ards don't flip soil over, like a modern plough, farmers had to cross-plough, first one way and then again at right angles, to properly break up the soil. This was such slow work, the Celtic fields' diminutive size probably represents how much an oxen could cultivate in a day. When the plough received another upgrade in the medieval era, field sizes completely changed. For the next millennia, however, ploughing remained jolly 'ard work.

21.

CORINIUM COCKEREL

2ND CENTURY CE

In 2011, archaeologists working in Cirencester, in south-west England, uncovered a child's grave. In it, they discovered the body of a toddler, wearing tiny hobnail shoes, buried in a wooden coffin. To accompany the infant, the parents had also lovingly placed a pottery feeding bottle, called a *tettine*, and the object pictured here: a captivating enamelled bronze cockerel.

Cirencester was once called Corinium, a settlement established not long after the Roman conquest of Britain in 43 CE. What began life as a military fort, built on land belonging to an Iron Age tribe called the Dobunni, soon became a lively settlement with shops, houses and marketplaces. Unlike some of the more combative tribes, the Dobunni quickly submitted to the imperial rule and adopted many aspects of the Roman lifestyle. Our deceased toddler was buried with distinctly Roman grave goods, a sign that his or her parents were perhaps expatriates or, as native Dobunni, had embraced some of the empire's cultural practices.

The cockerel represents more than just a touching gift from the bereaved. When Julius Caesar wrote about the Iron Age tribes of Britain a century before the Roman conquest, he noted with interest that 'They do not regard it lawful to eat the hare, and the cock, and the goose; they, however, breed them for amusement and leisure.' Zooarchaeologists, who study the ancient remains of animals, have dated the arrival of the chicken in the British countryside to around the fifth century BCE. Curiously, however, the chicken – which went on to become the world's most ubiquitous bird – wasn't initially valued for its meat.

The chicken's ancestor, the red junglefowl, was domesticated sometime between twelve and six thousand years ago in south-east Asia. From there, it spent the next few thousand years migrating with merchants and seafarers, both east into the Pacific region and west into the Near East and Europe. While the Egyptians and Greeks admired the male chicken for its fighting prowess, the Romans loved the bird for both its pugnacity and its culinary potential. The Romans were one of the first cultures to practise intensive chicken farming, for both meat and eggs, the latter not only for its food value but as a component of egg tempura paint.

What the Romans and British tribes had in common was a sense that the cockerel had ritual significance. The Romans believed in Mercury, a divine messenger and guider of souls to the afterlife. Mercury's symbolic animals were the crowing cockerel, which announced the dawn, and the virile, combative ram. Many Iron Age tribes also buried important people with chickens, with remarkable care and no evidence of butchery, leading many archaeologists to believe they viewed the fowl as sacred.

After conquest, the two cultures infused each other. Archaeologists call this period 'Romano-British' and the symbolism of the cockerel may have been a shared point of culture. During the three and a half centuries Britain lived under Roman rule, the bird continued to hold deep significance. Not only are chicken bones frequently represented in shrines and other ritual places, suggesting a key role in religion and sacrifice, but jewellery and valuable ornaments also feature the chicken, including our magnificent object from Corinium. Archaeologists believe the bereaved parents placed the cock-a-doodling cockerel in the coffin as a symbol of Mercury, to watch over their child's final, divine journey.

The early symbolism of the cockerel, as a heralder of the dawn, still graces the countryside in the familiar form of the weather-vane. With the arrival of Christianity came the story of 'The Denial of Peter'. At the Last Supper, Jesus predicted that his disciple Peter would deny all knowledge of him before the cock crowed the following daybreak. As foretold, Peter did disown Jesus but, realising his grave mistake, he went on to reaffirm his love for Christ and become a saint. The cockerel was adopted as St Peter's emblem and, in the ninth century, Pope Nicholas I decreed that all churches should be topped with a rooster to remind its followers of Peter's spiritual journey. It also symbolised the power of day over night, light over darkness. From town steeples to tiny parishes, many of the countryside's churches still have cockerel weather-vanes to this day.

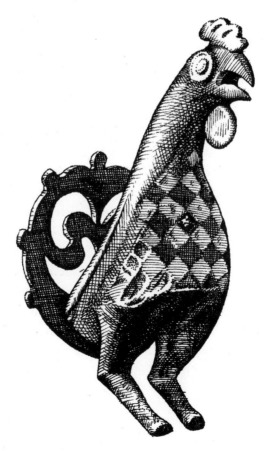

22.

CARBONISED ORCHARD APPLE

79 CE

In 79 CE, the bustling town of Pompeii was buried under millions of tonnes of volcanic debris. Nearly two thousand years later, the voids left in the ash by Pompeii's people and pets were filled with plaster to reveal their agonised bodies frozen in time. The heat of the eruption also carbonised organic objects in nearby areas, turning them to charcoal, including this remarkably preserved Roman apple.

The apple is a quintessential fruit of rural life, the orchard one of our most treasured spaces. From pies to roast pork, crumbles to cider, the apple is at the core of so many of our favourite rustic foods. Few of us know, however, where the apple originated and how it became such a stalwart of the countryside.

For all its homeliness, the apple is actually a deeply exotic fruit and hails from the Tian Shan mountains of Kazakhstan. There, some ten to four thousand years ago, the wild crab apple ancestor of the modern pome was first cultivated. Ancient trackways and, later, the Silk Road – which joined China to Europe – helped the new apple escape its Central Asian homeland. Thanks to herders, traders, and their four-legged pack animals, the apple was picked, munched and its seeds discarded along the routes that headed west.

New apple trees sprang up along these routes, which, in turn, were also scrumped and their seeds dispersed further along the way. This edible hopscotching across the landscape eventually brought the fruit to the Near East around 3000 BCE and Turkey by 1500 BCE. By the fourth century BCE, the ancient Greeks had embraced the apple with gusto and were the first to write down the secrets of successful apple growing and grafting. They also took the fruit to their hearts, turning it into a symbol of love and fertility.

The Romans, however, brought apple cultivation to the next level, creating new varieties with fabulous names. From the 'Pert Breasted' pome to the wrinkly 'Ragged Apple', the Romans loved growing sweeter, juicier, larger varieties. Roman physicians also believed the apple to be deeply efficacious for all manner of ailments. From morning sickness to sore eyes, it seems there was no end to their enthusiastically applied appley-cures.

When the Romans arrived in Britain, they found a country unfamiliar with the art of apple cultivation. Iron Age tribes had probably tasted sweet, orchard apples thanks to trade and contact with the continent, but they didn't seem to be growing their own. Native Britons did, however, make liberal use of the indigenous crab apple, a fruit they carefully dried to intensify its sweetness and preserve it over winter.

The Roman contribution to the British countryside came, as we shall see, in many forms. But one of its most enduring legacies was the introduction of apple growing and orchards. It's almost impossible to grow the same variety of apple by planting its pips. If you plant an apple seed, the resulting tree won't bear the same fruit as its sweet parent. In this horticultural lucky dip, some trees will bear fruit that is delicious, others will grow sour apples called 'spitters'. And, while these make excellent cider or vinegar, spitters don't make good eating.

The only way to reliably reproduce an apple variety is by grafting. Historians suspect that, for the Romans to successfully introduce their sweet apple varieties to Britain, they had to bring young apple trees in terracotta pots. Others believe they pushed apple cuttings into balls of wet clay, which were then wrapped in rags to keep them damp.

Remarkably, this technique was still being used by pome pioneers in nineteenth-century America. When the cuttings arrived in Britain, they were probably initially grafted onto native tree cousins such as crabs or hawthorn, before established orchards took root.

Once safely installed in British soil, many apple varieties were well suited to the countryside's cool winters and gentle summers. Roman cookbooks abound with different ways to appreciate the fruit – from apples steeped in honey to pork stewed with red apples, the pome opened up the culinary repertoire of those lucky enough to enjoy imperial favour. For others, as we'll see with our next object, life in the countryside under the Roman occupation wasn't quite so rosy.

23.

SLAVE FIGURINE
C. 3RD CENTURY CE

The Romans were the first people to create what we would recognise as 'country estates'. These were called *villae rusticae* and combined a large comfortable farmhouse with land and agricultural buildings, all serviced by a team of estate workers. Many of these villas were luxurious, with exquisitely mosaicked floors and underfloor heating. The estate would function not only as a residence for the local landowner and his family but also as place of worship, with a domestic shrine. Key to the *villa rustica*, however, was its role as a farm management centre, with its labourers, livestock, grain storage, workshops, wineries and other productive areas all in one place.

The *villa rustica* was as much a symbol of the Roman ideal as a practical way to organise a farm. Roman literature effused about the natural beauty of the countryside; the *villa rustica* embodied the ideal of healthy, rural life with its simple, wholesome pleasures. Roman high society longed for *otium*, 'quiet leisure time', as a balance to the excesses of busy city life, *negotium*. The countryside and the *villa rustica* provided the perfect setting for nature's restorative powers. It's a bucolic sentiment that hasn't lost its power today.

To function effectively, however, every *villa rustica* needed manpower. Slavery was common across the Roman Empire, slaves constituting as much as 10 per cent of the population. Men, women and children could find themselves enslaved for a number of reasons: as spoils of war; as the result of kidnap, abandonment or deliberate sale into bondage; or as punishment for a crime or debt. Newly conquered territories such as Britain also provided a ready supply of captives, as did snatch-and-grab raids into lands beyond Roman frontiers.

When it came to Britain, some Iron Age tribes were already experienced slavers, trading people captured in raids into neighbouring communities. And, as we already know, the Greek geographer Strabo listed slaves as one of Iron Age Britain's most lucrative exports. The discovery of ancient neck and wrist chains, feet shackles, and slave identity tags – the apparatus of slavery – also demonstrates how depressingly efficient the practice had become.

This object – a metal figurine of a captive – is particularly striking; it's one of a handful of miniature slave statuettes known from Roman Britain. It's not clear what they were for, or to whom they belonged, but from the distinctive hairstyle and features of the trussed victim, archaeologists believe the slave is a native Briton. The figurine also has a curiously flat back, and holes allowing it to be threaded onto a rope and worn. It's not clear whether the Romans were capturing slaves or acquiring enslaved Britons from 'friendly' Iron Age tribes, but choosing to wear such a figurine would send a clear message: there is glory in oppression.

Captives could find themselves spirited across the empire, to be bought and sold in slave markets or trafficked into private hands. Some slaves no doubt stayed within Britain and would have been forced to work at a *villa rustica*, where in some cases indentured labour made up almost the entire workforce. In one of the first farming manuals ever written, *De Re Rustica*, next to advice about how to care for livestock and crops, its Roman author Columella had plenty to say about slaves. For the farm to run properly, Columella advised that slaves with different qualities be given different roles. These traits still run through stereotypes of the countryside today. The isolated shepherd, for example, should be 'unremittingly watchful' rather than necessarily strong, while the ploughman must be a gentle giant, big in voice and bearing but kind to his oxen. Slaves employed in vineyards needed to be strong and quick-witted – vine-dressing involved specialist skills – and those who knew about viticulture cost three times more than an unskilled labourer.

A quick mind combined with physical strength, however, needed controlling. On a *villa rustica*, according to Columella, vineyards were commonly tended by slaves in chains. Under Roman rule, vineyards sprang up across the British countryside. Elites among Iron Age tribes had long enjoyed wine imported from the continent, a sign of their cosmopolitan wealth. After the Roman conquest, while some native British chiefs no doubt embraced the bacchanalian delights of the *villa rustica*, those who resisted Roman rule found themselves tending the vines in chains.

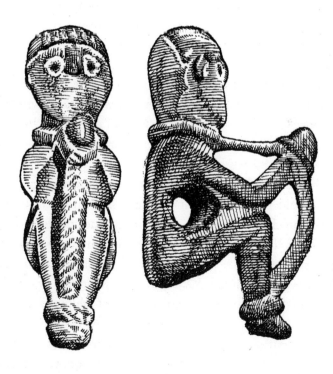

24.

WATER NEWTON STRAINER

3RD–4TH CENTURY CE

Archaeologists have had to work hard to find evidence of the Romano-British wine 'industry'. Using a winning combination of aerial photographs, ground surveys and pollen analysis, however, at least seven vineyards have been discovered so far. Their locations and sizes are surprisingly diverse – from Lincolnshire in the east to Buckingham in the south. At one Northamptonshire site, archaeologists calculate that the vineyard grew around four thousand vines, an enterprise that produced more than two thousand six hundred gallons of wine a year.

What kind of wine was produced isn't certain. Britain's temperatures improved from their Iron Age doldrums and between 250 BCE and 400 CE experienced what climatologists have dubbed the balmy 'Roman Climatic Optimum'. While this was a period warm enough for certain dry varieties of grapes to flourish, perhaps as far north as Yorkshire, Roman drinkers often preferred wines sweetened with honey and spices. Some speculate that white wine grapes, similar to the Bacchus variety that now grow well in southern England, would have thrived. Others suspect vineyard owners might have been cultivating an early version of Pinot Noir, a fruity red well suited to northern latitudes.

Red or white, Romano-British wines would have needed sieving to get rid of the sediment. This object, a silver wine strainer, was found as part of a magnificent hoard called the Water Newton Treasure. Discovered in Cambridgeshire in 1975, it's unusual not only for its survival, along with twenty-six other priceless silver vessels from jugs to chalices, but for what it represents.

The arrival of Christianity in Britain transformed both the cultural and physical terrain of the countryside. As we'll see later, church buildings eventually become a focus for rural life and one of the most prominent features in the landscape. The wine strainer tells us something about that critical moment in time. If you look closely, at the end of its handle you can see an engraved symbol. This is called *Chi-Rho* (pronounced 'Cairo') and is a very early Christian sign. It's formed by overlapping the Greek letters *Chi* (X) and *Rho* (P), which are the first two letters in the Hellenic word for Christ (ΧΡΙΣΤΟΣ).

Both native Britons and Romans were polytheists, meaning they worshipped many different deities and local spirits. Over time, Roman beliefs and those of Iron Age Britons sometimes merged, forming a pantheon of gods and goddesses of the natural world. When Christianity emerged in the first century in the Roman province of Judea, its rejection of all other gods but one deeply irritated the authorities. Its early followers were often brutally persecuted across the empire and forced to practise their faith in secret.

News of Jesus and Christianity may have reached Britain's shores almost immediately – the far-flung corners of the Roman world were remarkably well connected by merchants, soldiers and artisans. But few would have felt able to practise their new faith in public. For nearly three hundred years, until Emperor Constantine granted their freedom to worship in 313, Christians had to hide their beliefs and ceremonies.

The wine strainer, and the other objects from the hoard, are thought to be the earliest example of liturgical silver found anywhere in the Roman Empire, not just Britain. Archaeologists believe they were used during the third century by a local Christian group for communion, or baptism, and may have been hastily buried during one of the waves of persecution that often washed across the country. Only a decade before Constantine finally allowed Christians to practise their faith, Saint Alban had been beheaded and became the first British Christian martyr for refusing to renounce his belief.

The wine strainer, and the rest of the hoard, represent a moment in history when Britain's faith began to shift away from multiple gods to something altogether new. Its secret symbols and concealment in the ground also demonstrate how uneasy that transition was. It took another four centuries for everyday people to embrace Christianity as their core religion, but, as we'll see later in this book, old habits die hard. Although pagan and Roman gods may have slipped into the ether, belief in dark magic and capricious otherworldly beings still haunted the countryside for hundreds of years afterwards.

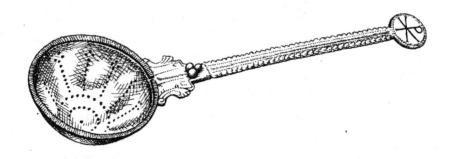

25.

HOUSE OF DIONYSUS MOSAIC

3ᴿᴰ CENTURY CE

When the Romans arrived in Britain, they decided to expand the country's culinary repertoire. The Iron Age larder offered some key basics – beef, mutton, pork, dairy, wheat, oats, barley, peas and beans – but the native menu lacked a little sparkle for people more used to pomegranates than porridge.

Many of the plants and animals we think of as native to the British countryside were, in fact, Mediterranean imports. The Romans introduced a huge range of edible flora and fauna, either through trade or conquest. Among these new foods, we can thank the empire for figs, grapes, pears, sour cherries, plums, damsons and mulberries. Keen to get their five-a-day, the Romans also introduced cucumber, celery and fennel, and new, cultivated varieties of cabbage, turnip, spinach beet and asparagus. Herbs that now define the quintessential cottage garden – rosemary, mint, parsley, marjoram and lovage – similarly arrived at this time.

The Romans brought their animals too. These included wild creatures, destined for the hunt, such as pheasants, guinea fowl and fallow deer, as well as 'working' pets such as cats and ferrets. Some animals were introduced as delicacies – from edible dormice to snails – while others hitched a ride without being spotted or were gifted to friendly Iron Age tribes. It seems we also have the Romans to thank for the black rat, the granary weevil, and fish tapeworms, the last of these perhaps encouraged by Rome's passion for *garum*, uncooked, fermented fish sauce.

Of all the countryside's creatures, however, the trickiest to pin down in archaeological terms is the rabbit. A native to France and Spain, the European rabbit features on many Roman mosaics from across the empire. This one, showing a bunny beginning to burrow, comes from the House of Dionysus in Cyprus, and was made around the third century. Pliny the Elder highlighted both the problems and the potential of farming rabbits; in his *Naturalis Historia*, published just before the eruption of Vesuvius in 79 CE, he described rabbit farming or 'cuniculture' in Spain. There, he explained, the rabbit is eaten as a newborn or foetus, a delicacy called a *laurice*. The creature had also, however, become 'extremely prolific' and destroyed many a farmer's harvest. The Roman author Varro, scribbling instructions to his wife a century earlier, mentioned keeping rabbits in her *leporarium*, to fatten them up for eating.

It was long believed that the rabbit had been brought to Britain for food and fur after the Norman Conquest in the eleventh century. A more recent find, however, has pushed back the introduction of the rabbit by a thousand years. An animal bone, from Fishbourne Roman Palace in Sussex, had been sitting in a box for decades until a keen-eyed zooarchaeologist recognised it as the leg bone from a rabbit. Later analysis revealed the tibia to be almost two thousand years old but, curiously, it showed no signs of butchery or gnaw marks. This opened up the possibility that the first rabbits brought to Britain were kept not for the pot but as exotic pets.

While the rabbit was known in Britain from Roman times, it doesn't seem to have proliferated until after the Norman Conquest. Now seen as an agricultural pest, it was initially a luxury, prized for its strokable, soft fur and gamey meat. Rabbits were housed in artificial warrens, with low, pillow-like mounds of banked earth. The right to own a warren or 'coney' was strictly controlled, however – a privilege jealously guarded by the rich. Some warrens even had their own warrener, whose job it was to keep his charges safe from predators and catch rabbits for the table. And while medieval warrens have left little trace in the landscape, their existence lives on in corners of the countryside. Place-names with Coney, Conigre, Warren, Burrows and Clappers (the breeding area of a warren) reveal their rabbity past. Ironically, Bunny in Nottinghamshire, whose name appears in the Domesday Book, has nothing to do with our furry friends and instead means 'island where reeds grow'.

26.

MILESTONE

C. 120 CE

People have always travelled through the countryside for food, ritual and trade. Hunter-gatherers followed the seasonal movements of herds, visited sacred spaces and wandered beyond the horizon in search of new resources. Neolithic life was no less mobile in many ways, with communities traversing huge distances to feast, exchange gifts and worship at communal monuments. Trackways have long criss-crossed the countryside, creating local networks and plugging into long-distance routes.

Following the Roman invasion of Britain, however, its army built a vast web of roads across the countryside. Between 43 and 150 CE, an astonishing 10,000 miles of Roman roads were laid down, stretching from England's south coast to Scotland's Firth of Forth. This new network linked together key places, from seaports to military forts, existing Iron Age settlements to unruly frontiers. Troops could now march across the landscape with deadly efficiency, but the roads also facilitated trade, communications and the movement of livestock and other farming goods.

Tracks made from flat, beaten earth quickly become impassable in heavy rain. The Romans solved this issue by covering the surface with stone – a technique called metalling – and gently cambering the resulting road so water flowed away. Well-engineered roads, however, weren't a Roman invention. Archaeologists recently discovered the remains of a metalled, cambered road in Shropshire that dates to the first century BCE, suggesting that wheeled traffic and thriving trade were already whizzing between Iron Age settlements. Interestingly, the presence of animal dung tucked under the Shropshire track indicates that the road may have been even more ancient, perhaps a drovers' route for cattle.

The Romans, however, built roads on an unprecedented scale. They also introduced many of the features we now associate with a journey across the countryside, including a unit of measurement they invented called the *mille passus*, or a thousand paces. We still use 'miles' today. The word 'street' also comes from the Latin *strata*, meaning road. The Romans introduced milestones, such as that pictured here, to mark distances along routes. Stone pillars displayed helpful information for the weary, including the distance to the next town and the year the milestone was erected. This milestone sat eight miles outside of Canovium, a military settlement near the Conwy river in Wales. It reads: 'The Emperor Caesar Trajan Hadrian Augustus, head priest, in his fifth year of tribunician power, father of his country, thrice consul: from Canovium 8 miles' and would have reassured travellers their journey was nearly over.

The Romans also had their equivalent of motorway service stations. Archaeologists find evidence that larger roads had facilities about twenty miles, or a day's journey, apart. There, travellers could bathe, sleep and eat, and rest their horses. These were called *mansio*, which is where we get the word 'mansion'. Interspersed between these stopovers were smaller staging posts, every four miles or so, where people changed horses and grabbed a quick drink or bite to eat. These were called *mutatio*, meaning 'changing', and were spaced at the maximum distance a horse could gallop before needing a sustained rest.

The Romans also introduced two-lane roads. Most were built so that a cart, pulled by oxen or horses, could comfortably pass another vehicle coming the other way. The standard width of these two-way roads was about 6 metres. Remarkably, single carriageways with two lanes are still roughly the same size, averaging between 5.5 and 7.3 metres. Some of these Roman roads, such as the Fosse Way and Ermine Street, are well-used traffic routes today.

Along with roads came the first true road map – the *Tabula Peutingeriana* – sometime in the fourth or fifth century (although it was probably based on an earlier first-century map). It marks the Roman Empire's entire system of public roads from the Atlantic Ocean to Sri Lanka. And, just like the modern glove-box favourite, the AA road map, the *Tabula Peutingeriana* highlighted handy places to stop, as well as sites of local interest including rivers, mountains and forests. As we'll see from our next object, however, sometimes road travel wasn't the best way to cross the countryside.

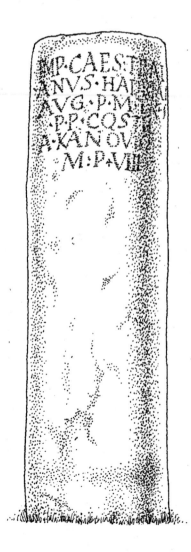

27.

LEAD 'PIG'
C. 60 CE

The British countryside was a rich seam waiting to be mined. Indeed, many historians believe that the country's mineral resources were the impetus behind the Roman invasion. Wales, western England and south-west Ireland were already well known for their metal extraction. From as early as 2000 BCE, local Bronze Age men, women and children had recovered copper and tin from the ground using little more than antler picks and stone tools. During the Iron Age, mining for non-ferrous metals continued apace but native communities also began to dig for iron and lead.

The Roman Empire consumed metals – gold, silver, tin, lead and iron – with insatiable greed. Of these, lead was perhaps the British countryside's greatest treasure waiting to be plundered. The Romans used it for everything from cosmetics to coins, serving platters to water pipes; even the word 'plumber' comes from the Latin for lead, *plumbum*. From sewage channels to statues, slingshot to sweetening wine, the demand for lead was insatiable.

By 49 CE, only six years after the invasion, the Romans had begun to extract lead from existing Iron Age mines in the Mendip Hills in Somerset. Over the next three decades, new mines in north Wales, Shropshire, Derbyshire and Yorkshire were opened for business. At first, Britain's lead mines were controlled by the Roman army under the command of the Emperor; this lead ingot, or 'pig', comes from a Somerset mine during this early period of extraction. The words are abbreviated – NERONIS AUG EX K IAN QUARTUM COS BRIT – and have been transliterated as: 'British [lead] [property] of the Nero, from 1st January in his fourth consulship'.

By the beginning of the second century, control was handed over to private companies that were granted mineral rights in exchange for a hefty cut of the mines' revenues. Lead was heavy to transport, however, and many of the ingots discovered over the years have been found near navigable rivers. Waterways were used to transport heavy or precious goods of all kinds across the country; writing in the sixth century, the monk and historian Gildas singled out two of Britain's rivers for praise: 'the Thames and the Severn, arms as it were, along which of old, foreign luxuries were wont to be carried'. These, and other major waterways, would have kept Roman Britain's population – which may have comprised as many as four or five million people at its height – supplied in building materials, metals, coal and life's other necessities.

While some of this lead undoubtedly helped to build and service Roman settlements across the countryside, British-mined lead pigs have also been discovered on shipwrecks and archaeological sites in the Mediterranean. Indeed, Britain was so abundant in lead that to prevent prices dropping and protect other mines across the empire, laws were imposed designed to curb excessive extraction.

It's not clear who worked in the mines of Roman Britain. Examples from other parts of the empire show that most were fed by a constant supply of slave labour, prisoners of war and criminals. Sentencing for minor crimes could involve hard labour; the lucky few might receive a quick spell of community graft, such as road building or cleaning sewers, while those less fortunate could find themselves on the receiving end of *damnatio ad metalla*: 'condemnation to the mines', a punishment also meted out to Christians during periods of state-endorsed persecution.

Roman lawmakers knew the severity of the sentence. While some mines were less brutal than others, Roman texts suggest life expectancy in them could be alarmingly short. Condemned criminals at one copper mine in Jordan, called Phaeno, were only expected to live a few days. The threat of mining was also enough to send some native Britons into battle. Just half a century after the Roman invasion, the historian Tacitus described a stirring speech made by Calgacus, chieftain of the Caledonians, the last unconquered tribe in Britain. Facing the Roman army, Calgacus gave his men the option of fighting or facing a life of servitude: 'On the one side you have a general and an army; on the other, tribute, the mines, and all the other penalties of an enslaved people.' Stuck between a rock and a hard place, the Caledonians charged into battle.

28.

ROOF TILE WITH PAW PRINT
1ST CENTURY CE

Of all the countryside's animals, the cat is the odd one out. It occupies a strange niche: both pampered pet and untamed creature. While some cats have submitted themselves to their owners, living a life of captive luxury, most moggies retain a wild streak, walking a tightrope between full domesticity and feral freedom.

Genetic studies suggest that the domestic cat (*Felis catus*) first emerged as a distinct species from its ancestor, the African wildcat (*Felis silvestris lybica*), about twelve thousand years ago. From its origins somewhere in the Fertile Crescent, the tame tabby slowly worked itself across Europe, hitching rides on boats or keeping close to human communities as it ventured into new territories. Between 4000 and 3000 BCE the domesticated cat finally sauntered into Egypt, where it went on to become one of their most revered animals. The ancient Egyptians treated cats with great respect, both as an incarnation of the goddess Bastet and as a valuable rodent-killer. Over in China, a slightly different species of feline had also been domesticated around 3000 BCE, a relative of the Asian leopard cat. This glamorous, spotted feline's career didn't last long, however. Today, all domestic cats in China are the Western *Felis catus* and may have been introduced by ancient Greek or Romans traders travelling along the Silk Road.

The archaeological evidence for cats in the classical world is fairly sparse and paints a mixed picture of their relationship with humans. Roman mosaics occasionally depict felines but they're usually scuttling around in the background, catching birds or being mischievous. Texts sporadically refer to cats but mainly in the context of pest-control; both felines and, more often, weasels were kept as house pets for their vermin-catching skills. Carvings, however, give us the odd brief glimpse of a more affectionate relationship. A second-century tombstone found in Rome features a wonderfully chubby cat, no doubt a pun on the owner's name, *Felicla*, or 'Little Kitty'. On a funeral statue from the same date, found in Bordeaux, we see a little Roman girl lovingly clutching her pet kitten with both hands.

It was always thought that the Romans first brought the cat to Britain, one of their many introductions of Mediterranean flora and fauna. And yet new evidence suggests this wasn't the case. Whether the cat was imported into Britain as an exotic pet or snuck in on a ship as a stowaway, it had already leapt ashore at least three hundred years before the Roman invasion. The discovery of a number of feline remains at Gussage All Saints, an Iron Age Dorset hillfort, including a litter of five newborn kittens, suggests that farming communities and domestic cats were already living side by side by 250 BCE.

Like a *Tom and Jerry* cartoon, new studies into the domestication of the cat, and the remarkable success of the house mouse (*Mus musculus*), show the success of the two species is closely linked. The house mouse is originally from Central Asia. Its domination, however, is now worldwide – a feat we can attribute almost exclusively to the rise of grain farming and long-distance sea trade. When scientists track the spread of the house mouse, through time and across continents, they find the domestic cat hot on its tail. Once agricultural communities started to store large quantities of grain, rodents moved in, closely followed by the introduction of the domestic cat. It's telling that current evidence indicates that the house mouse first scampered onto British soil not too long before our Dorset hillfort welcomed its first litter of kittens.

Even throughout the Romano-British period, however, the domestic cat remained on the periphery of human affection. This indifference, it seems, was mutual. Our object, a cat's paw print on a Romano-British roof tile, captures a moment in time; a free-roaming feline wandering through a Nottinghamshire tilemaker's yard just as their clay was drying in the sun. For anyone who owns a moggie, it speaks volumes. Even two thousand years ago, unlike the faithful dog or the biddable horse, the cat was resolutely following its own path.

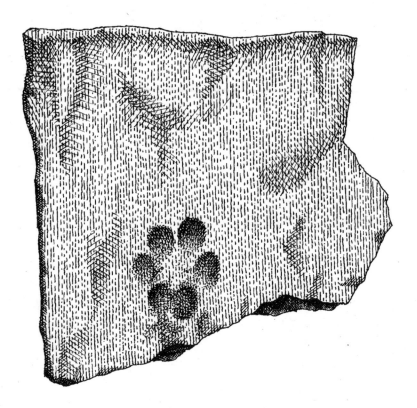

29.

CONSTANS II ROMAN COIN

348–50 CE

Few things give us a time-travelling connection with our ancient past. And yet, tucked away in almost every village are buildings that represent one of the countryside's most enduring traditions. Thatched, wattle and daub cottages have become a timeless symbol of rural life and yet their survival is down to more than just nostalgia.

It was once thought that permanent buildings only arrived in Britain with the arrival of Neolithic farmers. More recent discoveries, including at Star Carr in North Yorkshire and Howick, further up the coastline in Northumberland, now paint a different picture. At both sites, archaeologists have found remains of small roundhouses, circular structures made from timber posts and roofed with thatch or turf. These functional, beautiful constructions show that, even as early as 9000 BCE, hunter-gatherers knew how to craft a home.

Thatch continued to be used throughout the Neolithic period. Archaeologists aren't certain what kinds of homes these early farmers built. Excavations indicate the presence of large rectangular buildings, big enough to accommodate at least a dozen people; one example, found in Balbridie in Aberdeenshire, was an impressive 26 by 13 metres. This is larger than most village halls today. Other Neolithic sites, such as Durrington Walls, near Stonehenge, have yielded smaller, 'one-family' thatched homes. Some communities may have also used yurt-like structures with thatch or hide roofs, which, although robust, haven't survived in the archaeological record.

The Bronze Age saw a return to the roundhouse. These were constructed out of timber posts, with woven willow or hazel panels, called wattle, in between. The wattle would then be liberally smeared with daub, a render made from mud, dung, straw and animal hair that dried to a remarkably durable surface. For all its rustic simplicity, the beauty of daub is in its performance. Unlike modern cement, which is rigid, daub could flex with the natural movement of the building's timbers. It offered excellent insulation and acted like blotting paper, absorbing moisture without letting it penetrate the fabric of the building, and then quickly allowing it to evaporate again with the wind and sun.

Thatch as a roofing material was also ubiquitous and more than fit for purpose. As is true today, the materials used for thatching differed depending on where you lived. If cereals were abundant, straw could be used, but resourceful thatchers might also craft a roof from grasses, sedge, bracken, reeds, rushes, heather and even gorse. Differences in climate, topography and local tradition would have resulted in subtly varied vernacular styles across landscapes.

The Roman invasion brought with it novel foods, animals and customs, but also new architectural styles. The desire to create a 'home from home' in the British countryside – with rectangular, Mediterranean stone buildings and terracotta roofs – led to a huge upsurge in demand for pottery roof tiles. Kilns and tilemakers, including the maker of our last object, the paw-print tile, sprang up across the landscape to supply both garrisons and growing settlements.

It's not clear how many roundhouses were abandoned in favour of new Roman homes. In busy urban settlements and *villa rustica*, people undoubtedly lived in Roman-style buildings, but archaeologists also suspect that most native Britons probably stuck to their age-old building traditions and lived much as they had always done. Indeed, as this object shows, even as late as the fourth century, the roundhouse was seen as the barbarians' building. This coin, from the reign of Emperor Constans, shows a Roman soldier yanking a submissive native, possibly a child, from his thatched hut – a symbol of the might of the empire versus the 'backward' savage. Constans was the last emperor to visit Britain in 343. Contemporary sources suggest he made a quick trip, during winter, a risky journey possibly prompted by a local insurrection. The Roman presence didn't last, however. Only four decades after Constans' flying visit, Roman troops began to withdraw from Britain.

Tilemaking, and many other rural industries that fed the Romanised way of life, struggled to continue. Thatched, wattle and daub buildings doggedly persisted, however, and although altered in shape and size, remained little changed in terms of building techniques into the twentieth century. Welcome an Iron Age farmer into a thatched country cottage and they'd probably feel right at home.

30.

JET BEAR
3RD CENTURY CE

One of the most striking features of our modern countryside, even its hidden corners, is the lack of wild beasts. But we haven't always lived a life free from apex predators. Britain and Ireland have lost more large native mammals than any other European country. Of all the magnificent creatures we have driven out of existence, however, three are particularly notable: the lynx, the wolf and the brown bear.

The lynx once had the run of the British countryside, its ancient bones turning up in archaeological excavations from the south coast to Scotland. A forest creature at heart, its desire for solitude would have soon clashed with the interests of early farmers, who chopped down woodland for livestock and arable land. Deprived of its ecological niche, the lynx had little alternative but to prey on domesticated sheep, a strategy that made it deeply unpopular. By the seventh century CE, it had been hunted and marginalised into extinction, with pockets perhaps surviving in the Highlands until medieval times.

The wolf's extermination was no less catastrophic. Medieval chronicler Hector Boece wrote about a Scottish king, Dorvadilla. Reputed to have reigned in the second century BCE, Dorvadilla decreed that anyone who slayed a wolf would be rewarded with an ox. Successive bounties offered by kings and landowners pushed the beast further into the last bastions of wilderness. By the end of the tenth century, it had been largely expunged from the Welsh countryside and in the 1600s it had all but vanished from England. Scotland's wolves survived in penny numbers, eking out an existence in the forest shadows, but by the end of the seventeenth century, they too had gone.

The brown bear's story, however, is slightly different. *Ursus arctos* emerged as the largest British carnivore at the end of the most recent ice age and was widespread across Europe. Quite how many brown bears roamed the countryside isn't known. Three bone fragments recovered at Star Carr, in North Yorkshire, suggest the community there possessed at least one bear's head, perhaps for rituals, but on the whole it seems that hunter-gatherers and bears kept each other at a safe distance.

During the Neolithic period and the advent of livestock farming, however, bears and humans came into conflict. The striking paucity of bear remains from this time, and throughout the Bronze and Iron Ages, suggests bears may have all but disappeared from the British landscape by around 2000 BCE, hunted to a handful of survivors. Unlike other fearsome creatures, such as boars and wolves, the bear as a motif on weapons and other artistic treasures is also conspicuous by its absence.

In a strange turn of events, however, we may have the Romans to thank for reintroducing the brown bear back to British soil. Or, at least, boosting their numbers. The creature held a strange place in the empire's affections as an animal worthy of torment but also a symbol of guardianship. The object pictured here, a third-century jet bear, was found in a child's grave in Malton, North Yorkshire. Jet was an enchanted gemstone for Roman society; it produces an electric charge when rubbed vigorously, which was thought to infuse it with protective magic. The double symbolism of a guarding bear, crafted from such a potent material, wouldn't have been lost on its owner.

Sadly, most of the skeletal evidence for brown bears in Roman Britain comes from urban settlements. The Romans enthusiastically traded live animals across the empire; it seems the brown bear returned to the country shackled, destined for baiting, dancing and other execrable pastimes. Whether any of these poor creatures managed to escape and return to the wild isn't known, but a recent discovery offers the tantalising possibility. At Kinsey Cave in North Yorkshire, the vertebra of a brown bear was discovered and dated to between 425 and 594 CE. This makes it the last specimen ever found in the wild. Whether this isolated bear was a descendant of a Roman import, or a native bear that had somehow survived in an ecological refuge, it had managed an amazing feat. Its presence, however, wasn't to last. With the end of the Roman occupation and the beginning of a new chapter in Britain's countryside, the days of *Ursus arctos* were numbered.

31.

SHITTERTON VILLAGE NAME

ANGLO-SAXON

Have you ever wondered how places in the countryside got their names? Britain prides itself on having some of the most bewildering and curious. From North Piddle in Worcestershire to Great Snoring in Norfolk, place-names can actually reveal a wealth of information about the history of an area, its chequered past or its most redeeming features.

As we've already learned, Britain's story is one of folks arriving, staying and settling. Each wave of different people left its traces not only on the physical appearance of the countryside, but also in the names we use for its landmarks and locations. From forts to settlements, rivers to mountain-tops, place-names often add colour to our historical understanding of an area and give us clues about who lived there and what it was like.

During the Iron Age, people in Britain spoke a number of broadly similar Celtic languages. These are thought to have had a common root but were different enough to divide into two branches – Irish, Manx and Scottish Gaelic (called the Goidelic languages) and Welsh, Cornish and Breton (called the Brittonic languages). Some of our oldest geographical names come from these ancient tongues. Many of our rivers – the Avon, Derwent, Ouse, Severn, Tees, Trent and Tyne are thought to have Celtic names. The Thames, for example, probably comes from Tamesas, meaning 'dark river'.

Some county names also have their origins in Celtic languages – Devon, from *Dubona* or 'black river', Kent from *canto*, 'border land', and Cumbria, derived from the Brittonic word *kombroges*, meaning 'fellow countryman'. Aberystwyth and Abergavenny include the ancient Welsh word for river mouth, *aber*. *Pen*, which meant hill or promontory, can still be found in Pendle, Penryn and Penzance. And *combe* or *coombe*, as in Salcombe or Ifracombe, comes from *cym*, meaning 'valley'.

While it's telling that these Celtic words were applied to natural features, the Roman contribution came in a different form, most notably in man-made places such as *castra* (military fort) – as in Chester – and *portus* (port) – as in Portgate. Some places even combined both Celtic and Latin words – Manchester, for example, is thought to be a delightful marriage of *castra* and the Brittonic *Mamucion* or 'breast-like hill', while Lincoln combines the Celtic *lindo*, 'pool', and the Latin *colonia*, or colony.

Following the collapse of Roman rule in 410 CE, a number of different tribes from northern Europe – including the Saxons, Angles and Jutes – invaded and settled in Britain. How chaotic or complete this transition was isn't clear but many of the countryside's most commonly used place-names come from this period. Some counties kept the names of their settlers – Sussex or 'South Saxons', Middlesex or 'Middle Saxons', and Essex or 'East Saxons'. Equally, the Angles gave us East Anglia and even the name England, 'land of the Angles'. The depth of this conquest is also reflected in place-names. The various tribes that we now lump together as the 'Anglo-Saxons' first landed and settled in eastern England, before moving west and northwards, but the places where they failed to make as significant an impact – such as Wales and Cornwall – retained more of their Celtic place-names.

The great majority of place-names, however, have Anglo-Saxon roots. These include *burh*, *burg* or *borough* meaning 'fortified place', *tun*, 'enclosed settlement', and *ham*, 'home or village'. Some are reassuringly familiar – such as *ford* – while others can be deceiving; *barrow* means forest, *burn* a stream. Many give away their agricultural history: *feld*, a field; *wic*, a farm or dairy, or *appel*, an apple orchard. The jigsaw pieces of a place-name soon come together when you know the key elements: Swinton, a pig village; Oxford, a ford for oxen; and Hartham, a deer home.

Some Anglo-Saxon place-names have been delightfully skewed over the centuries, hiding their original meaning. Badger in Shropshire probably means 'ridge belonging to Bacga', Piddle in Dorset was a marsh or fen, and Loose in Kent denotes a place with *hlose* or pigsties. But spare a thought for poor Shitterton, a hamlet in Dorset, whose name meant exactly what it said. Thought to originate from the Anglo-Saxon *scite*, or 'shit', its moniker pulled no punches. Shitterton was, unfortunately for its residents, a settlement defined by its stinking stream used as an open privy.

32.

SUTTON HOO BUCKET

7TH CENTURY CE

Many place-names in the countryside have the ending *ley* or *leigh*. This comes from the Anglo-Saxon *leah*, a name broadly translated as 'woodland clearing'. As we already know, both Neolithic and Bronze Age farmers had a significant impact on the nation's trees. By the Iron Age, it's thought that only half the land was still covered in pristine 'wildwood', a contraction that continued apace throughout the Roman period. Then, many of its new settlements and industries relied on timber for construction, shipbuilding and fuel. Woodland was also cleared to make way for animal pasture and arable farming.

It's not known just how many trees the Anglo-Saxons inherited from the Romano-British landscape. What's interesting, however, is that many scholars believe that the total area of woodland may have actually increased after the Roman withdrawal. Archaeology can give us some clues – abandoned 'Celtic fields' and the remains of Roman villas both appear within the boundaries of later woodland, suggesting that at least some agricultural land reverted back to forest.

What we do know is that the Anglo-Saxons understood the economic value of woodland. The King of Wessex between 688 and 726 left a body of legislation, the *Laws of Ine*, which included legal protection for forests: anyone caught cutting down trees without permission was fined 30 shillings, about £3,000 in today's money. The forfeit doubled for deliberately setting fire to a tree. Carefully managed and harvested, the countryside's native woodland proved a rich resource. Archaeologists recreating Sutton Hoo's spectacular longship, for example, worked out its Anglo-Saxon boatbuilders would have needed to fell between a dozen and twenty mature oaks to create the impressive 27-metre-long vessel. A modest 8- by 4-metre timber-framed Anglo-Saxon hall would have needed five times this quantity just for its beams, posts and planks.

Other areas were 'wood pastures': grazing land with trees. Unlike dense forests, these were semi-open landscapes. Widely spaced, large trees could accommodate animals such as cattle and sheep browsing in between them. The trees were also 'pollarded', a practice of cutting off the branches about three metres above ground to encourage new shoots to grow. This fresh growth was out of reach of nibblesome cattle and sheep but easily harvested for firewood and crafts. The new branches could also be pruned at the end of summer, when the tree was in full leaf, and then dried and stored for animal fodder. Making 'tree hay' was a countryside skill that continued well into the twentieth century but is now largely forgotten.

Dense woodland was perfect for pigs, who were fattened up on 'mast' – the acorns, beech nuts and fruits of the forest. The term 'mast year' is still used to describe a bumper crop of wild berries, seeds and nuts. Other areas of woodland were ripe for coppicing. Ash and hazel, for example, were heavily utilised for roof timbers and wattle panels and would be cut on a five- or ten-year cycle, producing an ever-replenishing crop.

Woodland and its timber, however, wasn't just appreciated for its practical uses. This object, a carefully staved wooden bucket also found at Sutton Hoo, hints at how trees and belief systems could become entwined. The bucket, one of over three hundred found in Anglo-Saxon burials, is made from yew. It's a curious timber to have chosen, largely because almost all parts of a yew tree are toxic and the bucket could have poisoned any liquid it held. The Roman writer,

Pliny the Elder, noted a number of deaths caused by wooden wine flasks made from yew, while its berries were well known for their deadly toxins.

Yew trees enjoy preternatural longevity. Many can live for hundreds or even thousands of years. The Fortingall Yew, in Perthshire, for instance, is thought to be at least two thousand years old. Some academics believe the yew's heady blend of toxicity and long life, combined with its robust evergreen nature, encouraged ancient cultures to associate it with immortality and access to the Otherworld. Burial sites may have also been chosen for their proximity to established yew trees. These weren't, of course, the only magical plant in the Anglo-Saxon countryside …

33.

CUDDESON 'BOWL' 7ᵀᴴ CENTURY CE

When this bright, peacock-blue glass beaker was pulled from the Oxfordshire soil in the middle of the nineteenth century, its colour was as flamboyant as the day it was made. This Anglo-Saxon drinking vessel, crafted in the early seventh century CE, would have enchanted anyone who supped from its rim. The Anglo-Saxons were skilled glassmakers, their craft directly influenced by Roman techniques that preceded them. Indeed, some objects were even made by melting down broken Roman glass and mosaics and refashioning them into new, luminous jewellery and drinking cups.

As seductive as Anglo-Saxon glass is, however, it's also fascinating to think about its purpose. High-status cups such as these would have probably been used for rituals and ceremonies involving alcohol. It's also likely that lavish vessels were used in medicinal cures and charms, many of which relied on the countryside's pharmaceutical bounty. One such example, from the medical text *Bald's Leechbook* compiled in the tenth century (but probably written a century earlier) recommended the following treatment 'against elf-kind and nightgoers, and the people with whom the devil has intercourse': 'Take eowohumelan [hops], wormwood, bishopwort, lupin, ashthroat [vervain], henbane, harewort, haransprecel [viper's bugloss], heathberry plants, cropleek, garlic, hedgerife grains [cleavers], githrife [corncockle], fennel. Put these herbs into one cup, set under the altar, sing over them nine masses; boil in butter and in sheep's grease, add much holy salt, strain through a cloth; throw the herbs in running water. If any evil temptation, or an elf or nightgoers, happen to a man, smear his forehead with this salve, and put on his eyes, and where his body is sore, and cense him [with incense], and sign [the cross] often. His condition will soon be better.'

This remarkable prescription, which demonstrates the mingling of pagan and Christian practices, reveals our long-standing reliance on *flora Britannica* and their healing properties. People have long turned to the countryside for therapeutic plants, many of which we still use today. Another medicinal spell, called the 'Nine Herbs Charm', written down sometime around the tenth or eleventh century, invoked the use of some reassuringly familiar ingredients, including nettle, chamomile, plantain, lamb's cress, chervil and crab apples.

Of all the curative plants, however, mugwort was revered by the Anglo-Saxons as the *yldost wyrta* ('oldest of herbs'), a claim not entirely without merit. In the grave of an Iron Age healer, dated to 40–60 CE and discovered on land once belonging to the Catuvellauni tribe, archaeologists discovered an extraordinary array of medical items. The 'Druid of Colchester's' burial site included an amazing selection of magical and surgical items, including a jet bead, divining poles, forceps, needles, a scalpel, surgical saw, and a cup containing traces of mugwort. Throughout history, mugwort has been used for gynaecological and gastro-intestinal problems, but also taken to promote lucid dreaming. The countryside's herbs weren't simply a first-aid cabinet, it seems, but a means by which people attempted to connect with the supernatural or steel themselves against dark forces.

Historians often like to focus on the 'eye of newt' tone of Anglo-Saxon medical texts, highlighting the bizarre rituals and incantations that accompanied many treatments. And yet it's clear that many herbalists had a practical understanding of the curative properties of the countryside's plants. Anglo-Saxon remedies included eminently sensible prescriptions such as nettle ointments for muscle pain, leeks and wild garlic for bacterial infections, chamomile for skin complaints, and sneezewort – a herb that numbs the mouth when you chew it – for toothache and facial pain.

It's also interesting to consider the kinds of ailments Anglo-Saxon country dwellers might have had. 'Spring fever', which is now believed to be malaria, troubled the marshlands of eastern and southern Britain, while viral infections or 'the flying venom' and intestinal worms thrived in crowded, communal spaces. Plague and leprosy, battle wounds and burns, could be calamitous, but it's strangely reassuring that most herbal remedies in Anglo-Saxon texts focused on those niggling ailments – coughs, colds and those weird rashes that appear from nowhere – that still vex rural GPs today.

34.

AXE-HAMMER
7TH CENTURY CE

Sometime in the first half of the seventh century CE, a bereaved community placed an incredible array of objects within the central chamber of a ship, carefully laying them out in a meaningful way. Today, one and a half thousand years later, the burial site of a powerful East Anglian leader at Sutton Hoo remains one of the most extravagant graves ever found in Europe.

Grave goods of all kinds aren't just treasures for the afterlife; their placement in a burial is often deliberately designed to convey a message about the person who died. Objects such as this axe-hammer, from Sutton Hoo, not only reveal the blacksmithing skills of a culture but also say something about the status of the deceased and his or her place in the world of the living.

For many years, archaeologists thought the axe-hammer was a weapon. New research, however, suggests that, at three times the weight of an average battle-axe from this period, the Sutton Hoo chopper would have been too unwieldly to be used for fighting. It was also found in an unusual place in the burial chamber, away from the stash of weapons, nestled among a selection of banqueting objects including cups, bowls and knives.

A new theory put forward has suggested that the axe-hammer is, in fact, a tool for slaughtering cattle. Killing a formidable beast such as an ox is not an easy job. Most cultures that eat large domesticated animals stun their animals with a heavy blow before delivering the final cut to the throat. Cattle skulls from other Anglo-Saxon sites, which show evidence of heavy fractures, indicate this was indeed a common method for dispatching beef cattle.

But why would a king be buried with a butcher's axe? To understand this odd object, we must get inside the Anglo-Saxon mind, and a culture that valued cattle above all other domesticated creatures. The cow could do it all: provide meat and milk, fertiliser and immense pulling power. Ards and, later, ploughs, carts and sleds all relied on the sheer brute strength of the ox. Anglo-Saxon society also used bovine leather with cheerful abandon, not only for clothing and shoes, but also for practical kit such as saddles and bridles, ropes, bags, armour, book bindings and shield coverings among many other things.

The value of cattle in Anglo-Saxon society was reflected in its laws and language. Wealth and, therefore, status were often measured by how many cattle you owned. The Old English *feoh* (from which we get 'fee') meant 'cattle wealth', while *chattels* – now a legal term for personal property – comes from a time when transactions were based on trading heads of cattle: chattel literally meant 'head'.

Cattle were also used to pay fines and tributes. The *Laws of Ine* asked for two adult cows as annual payment for ten hides of land (one hide was a unit of land sufficient to support one family). Other texts take great pains to detail the value of cattle compared to their farmyard friends; in the tenth century, for example, the laws of King Æthelstan rated the value of oxen at thirty pence each and female cows at twenty, compared to a modest ten pence per pig. Sheep, at just five pence, ranked the lowest. Cattle theft was so serious it was treated as a crime comparable with homicide, while the laws of Æthelberht, King of Kent, specified that if a man bought a maiden with cattle, he was entitled to a full refund of livestock if she didn't live up to her side of the bargain.

Anglo-Saxon kings had to be more than just protective leaders. Their role was viewed as sacred, their job being to act as an 'intermediary' between the spiritual and human realms, especially through communal ritual. *The Old English Martyrology*, compiled in the ninth century CE, looked back at Anglo-Saxon traditions from earlier centuries. Of November, the *Martyrology* recalled: 'The month is called *Novembris* in Latin, and in our language *Blotmonath*, "sacrifice month", because our ancestors [...] always sacrificed in this month; that is, they took and devoted to their idols the cattle which they wished to offer.' Only a community deeply embedded in farming life, with its immensely valuable cattle, could understand the weight of this gesture. For the Sutton Hoo king, the axe-hammer, for all its grisly, slaughter-house connotations, was possibly one of his most sacred objects of all.

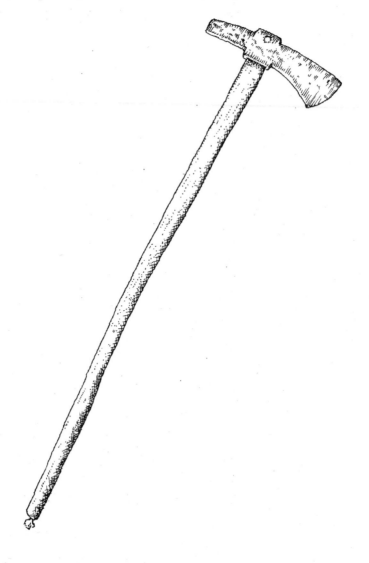

35.

FALCONRY FINGER RING
C. 580–650 CE

There are some things about the countryside that seem to have enjoyed an enduring charm. The Anglo-Saxons were keen 'twitchers', fascinated by both wild and domesticated birds and their idiosyncrasies. In a world where man-made noise rarely threatened nature's soundtrack, they were particularly taken with bird song and gave many species onomatopoeic names we still use today.

The Anglo-Saxons had two words to describe bird song, a distinction now lost in the cacophony of modern life. While the Old English word *sang* was generically used to describe the noises birds made, *winsum* was reserved for those avian melodies that were deemed particularly pleasing to the ear. Anglo-Saxon descriptions of birds often focused on their aurality. Similar-looking birds were defined not by their looks but by their voices – the rook (*hroc*), crow (*crawe*) and chough (*ceo*), for example, all named after their various shrieking cries. *Finc* (finch), *cyte* (kite) and *hraga* (heron) are also thought to be imitative names, while the particularly lovely Anglo-Saxon *ule*, from where we get the word 'owl', perfectly mimicked the tawny owl's nocturnal 'woo-woos'. The Anglo-Saxons also had a different word for owl, *ufe*, which may have described the short, explosive 'ooof'-like cries of either the short-eared or long-eared owl, both of which were common during this period.

Some Anglo-Saxon bird names encapsulated a particular bird's singing habits – the *stangella* ('bird that shouts from the rocks') described the kestrel, for example, or the *pipere* 'the piper'. Equally, the *nihtegale* or 'night-singer' was named after the nightingale's sweet, nocturnal melodies. The names of some domesticated birds also came from their familiar calls – the goose (*gōs*), the chicken (*cycen*) and the cock (*cocc*) are all thought to be titled after their hisses, clucks and cock-a-doodle-doos. Even the word *hen*, which now is only used for the female chicken, comes from the Old English word for cockerel (*hana*), and meant 'bird who sings'. We also have the Anglo-Saxon language to thank for the avian titbits 'chirp', 'cluck' and 'gaggle'.

Surroundings, and sense of place, were clearly important, and birds often feature in Anglo-Saxon place-names, especially in conjunction with a description of the landscape. Knowing this, places such as Raveley (ravens' wood), Ravenscar (ravens' rock) and Ravensden (ravens' valley) suddenly come alive in the imagination; equally, Cranwich (cranes' meadow), Cranham (village where the cranes are) and Cranborne (cranes' stream) help modern readers conjure up the ancient countryside and its wealth of wild birds.

Two birds, in particular, piqued the Anglo-Saxon imagination: the raven and the eagle. These redoubtable creatures, along with the wolf, formed a formidable trio – the 'Beasts of Battle' – and were thought to be ever-present at times of warfare. The Anglo-Saxons were both horrified and fascinated by these three animals, all of which scavenged on carrion, including the flesh of fallen warriors. Anglo-Saxon poetry often described the three animals appearing in anticipation of a battle, as presagers of doom. In one poem, *Elene*, 'The trumpets sang out loudly in the presence of the troops; the raven rejoiced in the word; the dewy-feathered eagle watched the march [...] the wolf raised its song, co-spoiler of the grove.'

Predatory birds clearly fascinated the Anglo-Saxons, and this glistening object – a recent archaeological find – suggests a culture that may have also learned to tame them. Discovered by a metal detectorist near Saffron Waldon in Essex, the buttery gold ring shows a person holding a raptor in their hand, while a larger bird of prey flies overhead, and has been dated to around 580–650 CE. It's thought to have been crafted in the same workshops that produced many of the treasures at Sutton Hoo, suggesting that falconry may have initially been a sport of elite warriors or aristocracy. Burials from other Germanic-speaking territories indicate falconry was known from the sixth century CE. The grave of a warrior in Rickeby, near Stockholm in Sweden, for example, included an entire mews of dead raptors, including a sparrowhawk, goshawk, eagle owl and two peregrine falcons. This impressive flock was also accompanied by the warrior's four faithful hunting dogs, preserving his favourite countryside pursuit for eternity.

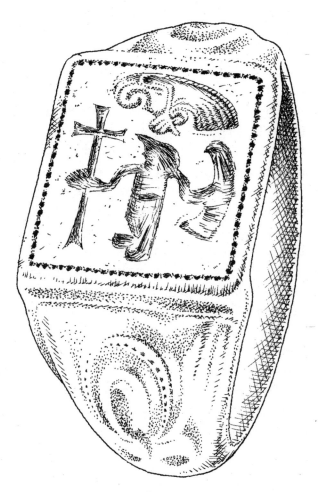

36.

MONTH FROM A FARMING CALENDAR
11TH CENTURY

Have you ever wondered why an *acre* is called an acre or a *furlong* a furlong? These rural measurements, on the face of it, might not seem to tell us much about the history of the countryside. And yet, their very existence can give us a window into the working lives of our Anglo-Saxon predecessors.

Take the *acre*, for example, an area now standardised to 4,047 square metres. The word comes from the Anglo-Saxon or 'Old English' *æcer*, meaning 'field where crops are grown', and is thought to have started life as the average plot that could be ploughed in one day using a 'yoke' or team of oxen pulling a wooden plough. Whereas modern acres can be any shape, during the Anglo-Saxon period the acre was long and thin – roughly 20 metres wide by 200 metres long. This length became known as the *furlong* – 'furrow long' – and was probably the distance the oxen could plough in a straight line without needing a rest.

Which begs the question: why were oxen pulling in long, straight lines rather than working in smaller, square sections like the 'Celtic fields' of the Iron Age? One of the most radical changes of the Anglo-Saxon farmed landscape was the adoption of the 'heavy plough'.

The Iron Age ard was a useful farming tool, capable of stirring up and breaking the soil. The heavy plough, on the other hand, with its addition of the curved mouldboard, could flip the soil over to one side, burying weeds, digging in manure, and creating useful ridges and channels. On waterlogged soil, farmers could then plant their crops in the drier, raised ridges, while the channels facilitated drainage. This allowed Anglo-Saxon farmers to grow cereals such as bread wheat and rye that had previously only flourished in lighter, drier soils. Only spelt, an ancient cereal, could stand being waterlogged for any length of time.

The heavy plough, however, had one disadvantage. Like a slow cruise liner, the plough and its pairs of oxen needed plenty of space and time to turn about at the end of a furrow, making it more practical to go in a straight line for as long as possible. Farming calendars from this period, such as this one by a late Anglo-Saxon scribe from Canterbury, show a plough team in action. One man guides the plough, one broadcasts seeds and the third spurs on the beasts with a sharp long stick known as a *goad*. We still use the word to describe metaphorically prodding someone into action.

The period between the ninth and thirteenth centuries saw a shift in farming practices so dramatic that many describe it as an 'agricultural revolution'. Alongside the adoption of the heavy plough, we see the introduction of something called 'three-field rotation'. Up until that point, farmers had simply divided their land into two, planting half with crops and leaving the other fallow to recuperate. Under the three-field system, one field could be planted with crops such as rye or winter wheat, which would be immediately followed by spring oats or barley; the second field could grow legumes such as peas or beans, which also boosted the soil's fertility, and the third field rested as fallow. Every year, the crops would be rotated. Cultivating the same area using the three-field system, instead of two, boosted a farmer's productivity by nearly a fifth.

Changes in agricultural practice may have also helped to shape the countryside's settlements, especially in lowland regions. In order to share valuable resources, such as a team of oxen, people had to live and farm near each other. This led to the development of places we now recognise as villages – small clusters of houses around a focal point such as a road, village green or a church. Settlements would be surrounded by two or three very large fields, in which the inhabitants had their individually allotted strips of land. Villagers also worked together to bring in harvests, mend fences, and agree rotas for stock grazing, as well as managing shared resources such as water or woodland. It's likely we have the Anglo-Saxons and their cereal crops to thank for another icon of the countryside – the barn – a building that gets its name from the Old English *bere* ('barley') and *aern* ('a place for storing').

37.

WULFRED SILVER PENNY

C. 810 CE

When did the village church become such a countryside landmark? Earlier in this book we learned that Christianity was introduced to Britain during the Roman period but believers could only practise their faith in safety from the fourth century onwards. After the Roman withdrawal from Britain in the early fifth century, Christianity faced a new threat. The invading Anglo-Saxons were enthusiastic devotees of pagan worship – every week, we still inadvertently invoke their polytheistic beliefs: Sunday (*Sunnan-dæg*) and Monday (*Monandæg*) honoured the deities of the sun and moon, while their gods *Tiw*, *Woden*, *Thunor* and *Frig* provided names for the rest of the week. Saturday, *Sæternes-dæg*, borrowed its title from the Roman god Saturn. Christianity wasn't entirely extinguished under early Anglo-Saxon rule, however, clinging on in remote locations in Wales and the south-west of England. During the fifth and sixth centuries, Ireland had also been converted to Christianity, becoming a stronghold of the faith.

In the 590s, Rome's Pope Gregory the Great chose a monk called Augustine to lead a band of missionaries on a special assignment. They were dispatched to England with the onerous instruction to convert the Anglo-Saxon kingdoms. King Æthelberht of Kent was the first to succumb, helped in no small part by the fact that his continental queen, Bertha, was already a Christian. Just three years later, King Æthelberht founded an abbey at Canterbury, with Augustine right at its heart as the first Archbishop of Canterbury.

Christian missionaries had also begun to arrive from Ireland with the aim of converting Scotland and the north of England. Their first monastery was founded on the island of Iona, in the 560s, but more sites soon followed including the ill-fated monastery on Lindisfarne, on the Northumberland coast, in 635. Despite several setbacks, by the end of the seventh century Christianity had become Britain's exclusive faith.

While monasteries were often self-sufficient communities acting as centres of scholarship, art and spirituality, smaller religious buildings also sprang up across the landscape. Some of these were minsters, 'mother churches', that covered a wide area and employed a group of priests who would go out into the community to evangelise, while wealthy nobles also built their own small manorial churches served by a single priest, a precursor to the parish system still in use today.

The idea of tithes or church taxes also developed during this time. The word comes from the Anglo-Saxon, *teotha*, 'tenth', and villagers were expected to give 10 per cent of their agricultural produce to fund the church and its priest. The *Laws of Ine* mention *ciricsceat* or 'church money' in the seventh century, a due probably paid in grain, while later Anglo-Saxon ecclesiastical taxes included 'light-dues' (payment for church candles), 'Peter's Pence' (a penny taken from every household to go directly to the papacy), and 'plough-alms' (a penny from each plough team). A penny would have been worth around £20 in today's money.

This coin, featuring Wulfred the Archbishop of Canterbury in the early ninth century, demonstrates how powerful Christianity had become. Coins, throughout history, had long been one of the most tangible and visible ways an emperor or monarch could demonstrate their wealth and influence. The symbolism of a face or name on a coin wasn't lost on those who either exercised power or were subjected to it. While a tiny number of early Anglo-Saxons coins had featured the king on one side, and a bishop on the reverse, Wulfred the Archbishop felt important enough to mint just a portrait of himself. Look closely and you can see his 'tonsured' head, the iconic shaved hairstyle of a monk.

The location of some village churches can seem arbitrary, but there is often a very good reason they are where they are. Some were built on sites of pagan ritual significance or Roman occupation, a clever way of encouraging continuity with locals. Carbon dating of a wooden post, recovered from a dig at the Church of the Holy Fathers in Sutton near Shrewsbury, revealed it was first placed in the ground in 2033 BCE. The medieval church had been built over the remains of an Anglo-Saxon church and, it now appears, even earlier structures. At over four thousand years old, it is the earliest, and probably least well-known, sacred site still in use in Britain today.

Churches were sometimes built on ancient burial sites in the hope that these could be absorbed into the Christian faith; the presence of millennium-old yew trees, natural springs, standing stones, and earthen circles can all indicate that a cemetery predates its church. Sometimes church locations were simply practical, making use of existing materials; St Peter on the Wall in Essex was deliberately built on the ruins of an old Roman fort, for example, reusing many of its old stones and bricks. Some Anglo-Saxon churches even survived after villages were deserted; Wharram Percy's church, for instance, now stands eerily alone, a ghost in a once bustling Yorkshire village.

38.

BENTY GRANGE HELMET

7TH CENTURY CE

First domesticated in the Near East around 8500 BCE, pigs were introduced to southern Europe with early agricultural communities. As the tame swine trotted north, however, their genetics changed. DNA analysis has shown that, around 4000 BCE, farmers in northern Europe allowed their domesticated pigs to breed with wild boars. Quite why communities did this isn't clear – wild boars may have been introduced to boost numbers or create new strains of pig better suited to local conditions. Such was the level of interbreeding, however, that the DNA of modern European pigs is mostly derived from its wild boar population, not its Near Eastern ancestor.

Unlike the cow or sheep, the pig is only kept for its meat. What swine lack in secondary products, however, they more than make up for in their adaptability. Pigs are omnivores, and unfussy ones at that, happy to munch on a wide range of organic matter. In the wild, boars will snuffle out roots, fungi, bulbs and other plants, but also devour insects, birds' eggs, small mammals and carrion. Throughout history, pigs have coped admirably with the pressures of life in human settlements, surviving on food scraps and detritus. From brewers' grains to rotten vegetables, human faeces to whey, domesticated pigs have greedily gobbled up many of the things folk discarded. This frugal diet, combined with the ease with which pork could be preserved by smoking or salting, made pigs popular among all sections of society.

Lard was also extremely useful. In the *Laws of Ine*, pigs were rated as 'three-finger', 'two-finger' or 'thumb' swine, a reference to the depth of the animal's fat. Lard was chock-full of valuable calories and a versatile cooking ingredient. It was also invaluable for protecting and sharpening blades (using a *strickle*, a piece of wood smeared with fat and sand), and a useful ingredient in poultices, soap and polishes.

In larger settlements, pigs were most likely confined to pigsties, or expected to scavenge in middens, while smaller rural communities made use of local grazing. Villages with nearby woodland or wood-pasture allowed pigs to browse there during the day, to be brought back home in the evening. *Hisperica Famina*, a collection of Irish Latin poetry from the seventh century, painted a particularly bucolic image: at the crack of dawn, 'the bristly crowd of swine leave [their] huts, the swine dig sandy soil with their snouts, they eat the solid bracken roots, and taste the grassy juice'. Then, as the sun goes down, 'the bristly swine go back to their familiar sties'.

Allowing pigs to fatten up on the fruits and nuts of the forest, between late August and the end of the year, was a lifeline for Anglo-Saxon villagers. Mast or *den-bera* feeding (later renamed 'pannage' by the Normans) was an inexpensive way of fattening up pigs for winter slaughter and helped to remove the acorns that were poisonous to horses and cattle. Key to its success, however, was the swineherd. His or her job was to not only drive pigs to woodland, but also knock the mast from the trees. Many an illuminated manuscript features a swineherd thwacking acorns from a branch or clambering up a trunk to shake the entire tree. Certain properties in the New Forest still hold the right of 'Common of Mast'. Place-names that end in *den* or *denn* – which meant swine-pasture – are also widespread in Kent and Sussex, both places with a rich heritage of mast feeding.

While domesticated pigs provided easy meat, the wild boar was regarded as prestigious, challenging game. Wild boars were infamous for their aggressive strength and hunters were often injured, a risk that added to the thrill of the chase. Our object, a reconstruction of a boar-ridged helmet, shows just how respected and feared a creature it was. The slightly battered original was discovered in Derbyshire in 1848. That, and its handsome bristling reconstruction, are now in the safe hands of Weston Park Museum in Sheffield. Further archaeology and literary analysis have revealed that the boar was a key Anglo-Saxon motif. In *Beowulf*, the epic Anglo-Saxon poem, for example, boar-adorned helmets are mentioned five times. Few lines so vividly evoke the brutality of battle as 'when the hefted sword, its hammered edge and gleaming blade slathered in blood, razed the sturdy boar-ridge off a helmet'.

39.

FISH BROOCH
5TH–8TH CENTURY CE

The countryside's rivers and shores have long been exploited. And yet whether a group of people choose to hunt and eat certain foods can depend on a wide range of factors. While some are practical, like seasonality or location, the decision to exploit a natural resource can be more complex. Beliefs, knowledge, tools, and other cultural factors can play a huge part in deciding whether an animal makes it onto the menu.

It's tempting to imagine that, throughout time, our desire to eat aquatic creatures has been consistent. And yet the evidence tells us something different. When looking at ancient diets, archaeologists have a number of leads they can follow. Coprolites (ancient poo) are a great place to start, but isotopic analysis of human remains can also tell us something about what people were eating and where these foods originated. The presence of tools can show us how people procured their food, while place-names may indicate a site's historic purpose.

Evidence suggests that the hunter-gatherers who moved around the countryside relied heavily on aquatic food sources, making seasonal camps by rivers and other wetland sites. During the Neolithic period, and the introduction of farming, fishing seems to become less important, perhaps as part of a broader shift away from wild resources towards crops and domesticated animals. Fish were not particularly popular in the Iron Age either, a trend some experts link to belief systems about the ambiguous or sacred nature of watery spaces. With Roman contact, however, came a radical shift. The Roman diet in Britain was rich in fish and shellfish, both fresh and preserved. The consumption of fish also said something about who you were. Villa owners and local dignitaries might build expensive fishponds and serve rare and unusual catches such as cod or sturgeon. In contrast, small freshwater fish, oysters and imported *garum* (fermented fish sauce) sustained both rich and poor alike.

Historians and archaeologists have tried to piece together what happened to fishing after the end of Roman occupation. Fish bones from early Anglo-Saxon sites (410–650 CE) aren't particularly common, and half of all those that do exist come from just one species: eels. This tallies with Bede, an English monk, who wrote that the South Saxons (in Sussex), at the end of the seventh century 'only had skill in fishing for eels', while laws from the same era demanded, among other things, 100 eels as rent for ten hides of land.

Such a sweeping dismissal of Anglo-Saxon fishing skills is no doubt an exaggeration, and the period between 650 and 850 CE does see an increase in the quantity and range of fish consumed. Archaeologists find not only the remains of lots of different freshwater and marine species dating from this time but also remnants of ancient fishhooks, weights and weirs or fish traps. Anglo-Saxon place-names add detail to the picture: *wer*, *waru* or *war* can denote a weir (as in Wareham), for example, while prefixes such as *fisk/fish* or the species-specific *trout* and *el* (eels) (as in Ely) are also revealing.

It's not certain why fishing picked up pace. Some scholars link it to the spread of Christianity during this period, with its fasting and monastic rules that forbade the consumption of meat. Others suggest that sea fishing, with all its inherent dangers and costs, became a status symbol for growing elites, while freshwater fishing remained a more prosaic but popular endeavour. In *Ælfric's Colloquy*, from the tenth century, a peasant fisherman tells us: 'I board my boat and cast my net into the river; and throw in a hook and bait and baskets; and whatever

FISH BROOCH

I catch I take [...] Eels and pike, minnows and turbot, trout and lampreys and whatever swims in the water.'

Of this watery list, the pike held a special place in the Anglo-Saxon mindset. A number of high-status objects, including this pike-like brooch found in Kent, celebrate predatory fish or 'wolves of the water'. Aggressive and voracious by nature, but elusive to catch, these wild river monsters represented everything an Anglo-Saxon warrior could want to be. And, as we'll see from our next object, a wave of mettle-testing trouble was about to come crashing ashore.

40.

GALLOWAY BIRD PIN
9TH CENTURY CE

The year 793 didn't get off to an auspicious start. The *Anglo-Saxon Chronicle* described with a creative flourish how 'immense whirlwinds, flashes of lightning and fiery dragons were seen flying in the air'. A famine soon followed but a lack of food was to become the least of the country's problems. On 8 June, on the north-east coast of England, Viking raiders unleashed hell. Landing at a sleepy monastery, 'heathen men wretchedly destroyed God's church on Lindisfarne, with plunder and slaughter'. This blood-splattered attack on a quiet religious community sent shockwaves through the land. Relationships between Scandinavia and Anglo-Saxon Britain had been largely peaceful until that point, but this marked the beginning of a new, turbulent phase.

Treasure and glory were the goals of the Lindisfarne raid, and subsequent Viking attacks around the coastlines of England, Scotland and Ireland. Isolated, undefended monasteries were particularly easy targets, with their stashes of ecclesiastical booty and holy relics. With few other options, religious communities often buried their treasures in the ground. This object, a gold cloak pin of breathtaking quality, was just one of over a hundred items, including sacred relics, ritual equipment and silver bullion, discovered by metal detectorists in Scotland. New research suggests this stash of booty, the 'Galloway Hoard', was hidden to prevent it falling into Viking hands, possibly by a local bishop from a major religious centre nearby. Few things convey the terror and uncertainty of the Viking raids more powerfully than the desperate concealment of this once-in-a-lifetime treasure trove.

By 865, however, the tone of the attacks had changed. With a considerable army behind them, the Vikings had launched all-out warfare. England at this time wasn't a united country but consisted of various kingdoms, including Mercia, which covered most of central England, Northumbria, a region that stretched across the north, East Anglia, and Wessex in the south-west. By the late 870s all but the kingdom of Wessex, ruled by Alfred the Great, had fallen to the Vikings. A peace agreement followed that sliced the country in two, roughly taking the line of the modern A5 road between London and Chester. Alfred's territories sat to the south and west while the Vikings held lands to the north and east, an area that subsequently became known as 'Danelaw'.

In these areas that once lived under Viking rule, rural communities still use linguistic relics of the ancient Norse presence. Regions such as Lancashire, Lincolnshire, the north Midlands, the Lake District, Yorkshire and northern Scotland – which all share a Scandinavian heritage – often have similar Viking nuggets hiding in their dialects. A *beck* is a stream, a *dale* a valley, a *tarn* a lake, a *fell* a hill. Similarly, a *foss* is a waterfall, a *ghyll* a ravine, and a *scar* a rocky outcrop. Local words for countryside objects and farm animals also reveal the Viking presence; a *skep* is a woven basket or beehive, a *gimmer* a young ewe, a *gilt* an immature pig, *ling* another word for heather, a *midden* a rubbish heap. Place-names that end in -*by* such as Whitby or Wetherby denoted a Viking farm, while -*thwaite* meant an area of forest cleared for tillage or habitation. Hamlets and villages ending in *thorpe* are Norse too, and probably meant a small or secondary settlement.

The peace agreement wasn't to last. By the early tenth century, descendants of Alfred the Great had begun to recapture Viking territories and in 927 they consolidated most of England under a single king, Æthelstan of Wessex. The stability was fragile, however, with some territories falling in and out of Viking hands, while other

Anglo-Saxon kingdoms struggled to contain their own internal rivalries. In 1013, the Vikings, led by Sweyn Forkbeard, grasped their moment and attacked; in 1016 his son, Cnut, became King of England.

The kingship of England eventually passed back into Anglo-Saxon hands in 1042, with Edward the Confessor, but decades of toing and froing, royal intermarriages and changing allegiances had left his succession in crisis. In 1066, Edward died childless, leaving no direct heir and four ambitious men believing they had the claim to the throne: Harold Godwinson, the Earl of Wessex; William, Duke of Normandy; Harald Hardrada, King of Norway; and Edgar Ætheling, Edward's great-nephew. It was all about to get very unpleasant.

41.

STONE WITH GRAFFITI OF CASTLE

C. EARLY 13TH CENTURY

In the final weeks of 1065, Edward the Confessor slipped into a coma. After suffering what many now believe to be a brain haemorrhage or stroke, the king briefly rallied, but by early January 1066 he was dead. Harold Godwin, Earl of Wessex, was immediately crowned his successor but within seven months William, Duke of Normandy, with the Pope's approval, had assembled an army of 7,000 men and their horses, and was intent on seizing the throne.

In late September 1066, William landed at Pevensey, on the south coast. Having only just defeated Hardrada's Viking army at Stamford Bridge, near York, King Harold route-marched his exhausted troops 250 miles south to tackle William. Few people don't know the outcome of the subsequent Battle of Hastings; in less than half a day, King Harold, his brothers and around four thousand English soldiers had perished. Triumphant, William was crowned King of England on Christmas Day 1066.

Peace would be harder to win. With a population of roughly two million to subdue, most of whom lived in rural areas, William was going to have to tame the countryside if he was ever going to secure lasting rule. One of the first tasks he undertook after his victory was to begin a programme of rapid castle-building, strongholds that his troops could ride out from and retreat to if under attack. Designed to dominate the terrain, these extraordinary structures also served as political statements, exclamation marks of power writ large. Unlike the stone fortresses that came later, these early castles were built of earth and timber. A simple wooden tower or keep would be constructed on top of a raised mound of earth called a *motte*. At the foot of the *motte*, a large fenced or walled area contained a number of ancillary buildings, including stables, workshops and food stores. This was called the *bailey*.

Timber castles had one key advantage – they were quick to build, sometimes taking only a matter of months. In the first twenty years of Norman rule, around seven hundred 'flat-pack castles' were hastily erected across England and Wales, including many in key strategic towns. Anglo-Saxon dwellings were often swept away to make room for Norman strongholds. The Domesday Book, for example, records that over six hundred homes were flattened across York, Lincoln, Norwich and Shrewsbury to make way for the new fortifications.

The perishable nature of timber, and the fact that many wooden castles went on to be rebuilt in stone, can make it difficult to imagine what these early motte-and-bailey structures looked like. Our object, however, offers a rare opportunity to get a first-hand view. This early thirteenth-century graffiti, a lively sketch scratched into a stone, was found during an excavation of the keep at Caen Castle, in Normandy. This remarkable image shows, in elevation, a Norman timber palisade atop a *motte*, very like the ones built in Britain by William. The artist added some fascinating details, including a timber bridge, a gate tower with wooden cross-bracing, and even a builder's hoist, suggesting the graffiti may have been doodled as the castle was under construction.

While motte-and-bailey castles peppered the countryside as far north as Aberdeenshire, all of which were either subsequently ruined or rebuilt in stone, perhaps the most famous is now Windsor Castle. William the Conqueror began construction just four years after his invasion, in 1070, and built a timber keep with a deliberate vantage point over the River Thames. Over the following centuries, subsequent monarchs replaced the wood with stone and began to add royal apartments, turning a defensive site into a palace fit for a king. It's now the oldest occupied castle in the world.

The record, however, for the most castles per square mile in Europe goes to Wales. Its concentration of castles is indicative of centuries of invasion, infighting and attempts to subdue feisty locals, particularly between the eleventh and thirteenth centuries. But Wales is also a landscape perfectly suited to elevated forts. With its numerous mountains and deep valleys, serviced by rivers and coastal links, it's no coincidence that many motte-and-bailey castles were erected on sites once occupied by Roman, Iron Age and even Bronze Age defensive structures. It's still a timeless truth that defensive strength is greater than offensive intent.

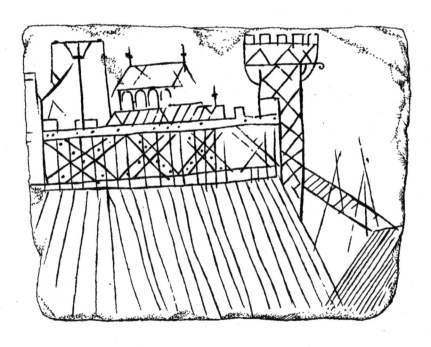

42.

CHEW VALLEY HOARD

C. 1068

On a freezing cold day in January 2019, metal detectorists discovered a bright silver coin in a Somerset field. In no time at all, one coin had turned into three, then thirty. After five hours of scrabbling through the soil, over 2,500 coins had been recovered. The 'Chew Valley Hoard' is thought to be one of the largest and most valuable medieval stockpiles ever found.

The hoard is exceptional not only for its £5 million valuation. It consists of two types of coins – half the hoard was minted to celebrate Harold Godwinson's brief stint as monarch, while the other half features the new king, William the Conqueror. The Chew Valley Hoard also tells us something about what was happening in the immediate aftermath of the invasion. Some of William's coins feature poorly spelled Old English words, a sign that Norman moneyers were perhaps struggling to understand the native language. A few pennies are also 'mules' – rare hybrids with William's logo on one side and Harold's on the other. Historians think these may have been a deliberate ploy to avoid tax. Every time a new coin was minted, the moneyer had to pay a tax to acquire the new die, which applied the logo and inscription to the metal. The moneyer was clearly banking on the fact that most people using coins couldn't read and wouldn't notice the mistake.

The fact that the hoard was hastily buried tells us about the political climate. The first few years of William's reign were particularly turbulent, with Anglo-Saxon uprisings across the country from Kent to Northumbria, East Anglia to Exeter. Harold's sons Godwin and Edmund, who had fled to Ireland after the Battle of Hastings, launched a raid against south-west England. This event may have persuaded the hoard's owner to bury his or her wealth, an amount significant enough at the time to purchase the equivalent of five hundred sheep.

William, however, crushed all insurrections. The most famous of all was his 'Harrying of the North', William's scorched-earth reprisals across vast swathes of northern England. Over the winter of 1069–70 William's men systematically razed villages to the ground and slaughtered their inhabitants. For good measure, farms and food stores were also destroyed, leaving survivors to starve. Writing just a few decades afterwards, English chronicler Orderic Vitalis recorded that William 'made no effort to restrain his fury and punished the innocent with the guilty. In his anger he commanded that all crops, herds and food of any kind be brought together and burnt to ashes so that the whole region north of the Humber be deprived of any source of sustenance.' Such was the ferocity of the harrying that tens of thousands of people are thought to have died and, sixteen years later, a third of the land in Yorkshire was still classed as *vasta* or wasteland.

In 1085, William was once again under threat of attack, this time from Denmark. War was an expensive business and William needed to establish just what kind of financial resources his new country held. At Christmas, he commissioned a countrywide survey to gather detailed information about the value of land, its rental potential, and to assess what he could raise in tax. This data was pulled together into a work later dubbed the Domesday Book, comprising two volumes: the Little Domesday Book, which covered Essex, Norfolk and Suffolk, and the Great Domesday Book, which encompassed the rest of the country.

The Domesday Book was much more than a fiscal reckoning. It helped set in stone a new system of land ownership. In Anglo-Saxon society, the vast majority of the population were peasants, who farmed land they didn't own, but about 10 per cent of Anglo-Saxon society consisted of *ceorls* (freemen who owned a small area of farmland in return for military service) and *thegns* (wealthy warriors who held large estates). Underneath the king sat his most powerful lords, the *earls*, five or six royal advisors who similarly owned huge areas of land. With William's conquest, a hierarchical system remained but with one key difference. For the first time in the countryside's history, one man – the king – owned it all.

43.

SAVERNAKE HORN
C. 12TH CENTURY

In return for their loyalty during the Conquest, William rewarded his supporters with English land. But, crucially, they didn't truly *own* it. These 'tenants-in-chief' answered directly to the king and were expected to provide well-trained knights or money in lieu of this obligation. Broadly speaking, tenants-in-chief then parcelled out villages and land to their knights in return for their military service. The knight then allotted parcels of land to his villagers so they could grow their own food. Depending on their status, these peasants had to provide labour, produce or cash payment as a form of rent.

William's new system concentrated land into a small number of hands; the thousand or so tenant-in-chiefs recorded in the Domesday Book now held half of all the countryside. The Church was allotted a quarter of the land and William kept a quarter for himself. In instituting this, the king had played a masterstroke. Lands could be removed if a tenant-in-chief didn't live up to his side of the bargain, and by dispersing landholdings across the country, William ensured that no one person got powerful enough to challenge his throne. The Domesday survey showed just how sweeping the transfer of land was; by 1086, just 5 per cent of tenants-in-chief were Anglo-Saxon.

The Domesday Book also adds vivid brushstrokes to our understanding of the countryside. From its records, we can see how significant agriculture had become. Over eighty thousand plough teams are mentioned, an astonishing figure that represented about six hundred and fifty thousand individual oxen, roughly one beast for every three people. Historians have calculated that as much land was 'under the plough' in 1086 as in 1914, at the outbreak of the First World War. Water-mills for grinding flour were also ubiquitous, central to a society that relied heavily on bread. William's survey recorded over five thousand water-mills in England, which would have allowed most households access to a local miller, although there were undoubtedly some regional differences. Peasants were obliged to have their flour ground at their lord's mill and paid a proportion of their grain, called *multure*, for the privilege.

Although not the purpose of the Domesday Book, a number of interesting occupations are also recorded and give a unique flavour of eleventh-century life. Falconers are recorded in dozens of entries, two jesters are mentioned – one male, one female – as are four foreign-language interpreters. Beekeepers, swineherds, cowherds, dairymaids, brewers, bakers, shepherds, millers, smiths, priests and slaves also pop out from the pages.

It's estimated that around 15 per cent of the land in the Domesday Book was woodland. Entries make note of how many pigs an area of trees could fatten with mast. Small thickets might support just a handful of swine, but a number of wooded areas named in the survey supported hundreds and even thousands of pigs in pannage season. The Domesday Book is also the first document to make a legal distinction between woodland and forest, the latter being specifically designated for royal hunting and enforced by often brutal physical punishment. The *Peterborough Chronicle*, written in the years after the Norman Conquest, recorded that 'He made great protection for the game, And imposed laws for the same, that who so slew a hart or hind, Should be made blind.'

Forest wardens were nominated by the king, their 'sign of office' a horn that they carried and blew at key moments during a hunt. This object, the Savernake Horn, belonged to the warden of Savernake Forest in Wiltshire. A hunting horn or 'oliphant' made for export in the twelfth century in southern Italy from elephant ivory (and embellished with silver two centuries later), it was not only a practical instrument but a key symbol of royal prestige. African ivory was a coveted luxury in medieval Europe, a material fit for a king. Such a valuable, cosmopolitan object spoke volumes about elite power and its place in the forest. The Domesday Book also greedily classified woodland for its other useful products, mentioning coppice, brushwood, fence material, fuel and even payments of honey collected from wild nests. In fact, as we'll see from our next object, medieval society was about as fond of bees as one could possibly be.

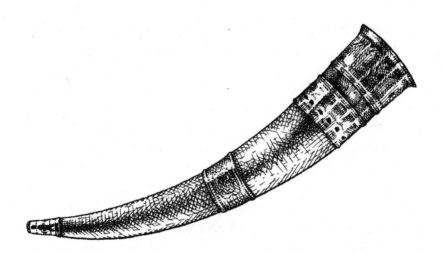

44.

THE GLOUCESTER CANDLESTICK

12TH CENTURY

Roman agricultural writers waxed lyrical about the art of beekeeping but the earliest documentary evidence for apiculture in Britain comes from the Anglo-Saxon period. Early hives were called *skeps* and were domed or conical structures woven from willow or straw, a design that changed little until the introduction of wooden-framed hives in Victorian times. By the time of the Domesday survey, beekeeping was widely practised, as was taking honey from wild woodland nests. Such was the value of wild honey, charters made explicit note of what people should do if they stumbled upon a feral swarm. One, dating from 1155 in Shropshire, noted that 'if a servant finds a swarm of bees in his wood, he shall give up one half of it [its produce] or he can keep the whole if it is not wanted'.

Unfortunately, beekeepers had to kill their bees to collect the honey and beeswax from a skep, as there was no way of easily removing either without damaging the other. At the end of the season, the bees would be destroyed, either by dunking the skep in water or by smothering the colony with fumes. Beekeepers, however, would leave a selection of colonies alive with a supply of honey, so they could expand and occupy new skeps the following late spring or early summer.

It's almost impossible to overstate just how important bees were to the medieval way of life. In the absence of sugar, not only was honey a much-loved sweetener but it was also a valuable ingredient in medicines and the production of mead, an alcoholic drink made by fermenting honey. In the centuries preceding the Norman invasion, epic battles and celebrations had been rocket-fuelled by mead. The eighth-century saga *Beowulf* sloshes with the stuff, including references to mead-halls, mead-benches and mead-bowls: 'Nor in all my life saw I, Under heaven's vault, among sitters in hall, More joy in their mead.'

One of the more overlooked reasons for beekeeping in medieval times was the huge demand for wax from the Church. Bees were powerful symbols in medieval Christianity; without a scientific understanding of the life cycle of bees, medieval writers regarded the insect as a virtuous, pure animal. Quite how bees reproduced remained a mystery – Isidore of Seville, in his seventh-century work *Etymology*, asserted with confidence that pollinators somehow emerged from the decaying flesh of animals: 'bees originate from oxen, just as hornets come from horses, drone bees from mules, and wasps from asses'. Critically, however, they weren't thought to reproduce sexually.

This chaste behaviour had an important consequence, namely that beeswax became the go-to choice for church candles, as opposed to cheaper animal fats. By the early thirteenth century, there were around nine thousand parish churches and hundreds of monasteries, all reliant on vast quantities of beeswax for lighting and ceremonies. Accounts from this time show that, apart from repairs to the fabric and bells, beeswax candles were the biggest cost a parish church incurred. Candles not only helped mark key celebrations in the liturgical calendar but were also needed for rituals and burials. Wealthy people often left 'gifts of wax' in their wills, while some beekeepers bequeathed their hives to provide their local church with an ongoing supply of candles. Royal households also burnt through beeswax. One record, from 1291, showed the queen's household was getting through 26 lb (roughly 12 kg) every day.

Christian teachings about the symbolic nature of light and darkness also found expression in the ceremonial use of candles. This object, the Gloucester Candlestick, illuminates the point. Not only is it a masterpiece of twelfth-century English metalwork, probably used to light up a shrine or relic on an altar; it was also a shining symbol of God's light. The gilt-bronze candlestick is decorated with a menagerie of fantastical beasts and humans, each either striving towards the lighted candle at the top or threatening to tumble into the darkness below. An inscription around the drip pan reads: 'This flood of light, this work of virtue, bright with holy doctrine instructs us, so that Man shall not be benighted in vice.' Unfortunately, as we'll find out from our next gruesome item, it wasn't always easy to be good.

45.

VILLAGE STOCKS & WHIPPING POST ON WHEELS

DATE UNKNOWN

Village greens and town market squares are quaint reminders of a communal past – places where people would congregate, chat and trade with convivial ease. And yet, nestling in the heart of many of these ancient gathering places are reminders of something altogether more sinister. Instruments of punishment still litter public spaces in the countryside, reminders of a system of justice that gathered pace after the Norman Conquest and prevailed well into Victorian times.

Stocks, pillories and whipping posts were designed to restrain people. Stocks clamped the feet in a sitting position, while pillories usually secured the head and hands and forced the miscreant to stand. The whipping post shackled a criminal while they were being flogged, and many places combined two or all three methods of punishment. Other ancient public humiliations included *thews*, neck rings attached to a post (a punishment often reserved for women, the name deriving from an Old English word meaning moral teaching or tuition), *prangers* (or chains) and cucking stools (also called *tumbrels*).

Public punishments are barbaric and yet their visibility has always been their *raison d'être*. Humiliation was viewed as the perfect way to deal with certain offences, especially those that were deemed crimes against the community rather than against a specific individual. Public chastisement has a long history; the Bible mentions four different methods – *mahpecheth* (pillories), *sad* (stocks), *tsinoq* (stocks for the hands and feet) and *ekes* (ankle chains).

In Britain, instruments of retribution seemed to proliferate from the eleventh century. The reasons behind this aren't clear but it's interesting to think about what kinds of crime were punishable by civic shaming. Most of the misdemeanours involved incidents that threatened to undermine public confidence – faulty craftsmanship, serving short measures, forgery, impersonating a public official, gossip, and, in particular, deceptive trade practices such as selling rancid meat or adulterated bread.

Between the eleventh and fourteenth centuries, trade fairs and markets flourished. While the Domesday Book recorded just sixty regularly held markets, by 1349 there were well over a thousand. As farming techniques improved and produced more food, this surplus could be traded. If fewer people were needed to grow food for a community, it also allowed others to engage more fully in non-farming occupations such as weaving, metalwork and tanning, the products of which could be bartered or bought at market.

Markets also meant revenue: the granting of Royal Charters for regular markets and fairs began in the twelfth century and allowed nobles, including local clergy, to charge tolls to those using the market and stop rival markets setting up nearby. Some historians believe that an increase in public, humiliating punishments and the proliferation of such markets went hand in hand, as more opportunities arose for people to be short-measured or defrauded. Authorities began to see public marketplaces as particularly suitable places for legal chastisement. Seeing someone sitting in the stocks or being pilloried not only acted as a deterrent, in theory, but also destroyed the reputations and future livelihood of those individuals. The punishment was meaningless if it was carried out in private.

Indeed, some market charters were only granted on the proviso that a pillory or stocks would be provided: the abbot at St Mary's, York, promised to erect a pillory and tumbrel in return for the right to hold a fair and a market. If a permanent device couldn't be erected, nobles might put a set of stocks on wheels, like this set that now sits redundantly in St Leonard's Church, Shoreditch. Or, even better, dignitaries could borrow each other's. Records show that the abbot of Cirencester lent his good friend, the abbot of Pershore, implements of punishment if one of his villages had none of its own. It's nice to share.

46.

SPITALFIELDS MASS BURIAL

1258

Volcanos tend to appear in the history books only when things have gone catastrophically wrong. Most of us have heard of Vesuvius, which erupted in 79 CE. Or of, more recently, Krakatoa's 1883 explosion, a blast so violent it spewed debris fifty miles into the atmosphere and could be heard thousands of miles away. And yet few people know about a volcanic event that puts most others in the shade, one so powerful it led to a global disaster and may have even triggered the Little Ice Age, a period of climate cooling that lasted well into Victorian times.

Sometime between May and October 1257, the Samalas volcano on the Indonesian island of Lombok erupted. Everything in its near vicinity was obliterated by hot gas and volcanic matter. The explosion forced millions of tonnes of sulphur, chlorine and bromine into the atmosphere on a scale unrivalled in the past two thousand years, sending the climate spiralling into a volcanic winter.

Over in sleepy St Albans, Hertfordshire, Matthew Paris – a Benedictine monk – was doing what English people do best: obsessing over the weather. What had started out as a poor year was rapidly turning into a disaster. The weather was behaving in a distinctly odd manner, he wrote: 'a fierce whirlwind, accompanied by a violent hailstorm, disturbed the atmosphere and obscured the sky with darkness like that of night'. This strange happening, he continued, was followed by weeks of 'sickly unseasonable weather'. Weeks then dragged into months, giving rise to 'mortal fevers' and failed harvests.

Grain, which usually cost two shillings a measure, rocketed to fifteen. 'Apples were scarce, pears more so, figs, beechnuts, cherries, plums—in short, all fruits which are preserved in jars were completely spoiled.' Cows and calves perished, sheep and lambs too. More than a year after the original eruption, England's villages and towns were still living through its terrifying repercussions. According to Paris, so many people had died from hunger and disease, 'the dead lay about, swollen up and there was scarcely any one to bury them'. Those few who did survive dug 'large and spacious holes [...] and a great many bodies were laid in them together'.

For such a significant event in the countryside's history, however, historians have struggled to find any physical proof of its effects. For all Paris's detailed descriptions of bodies, 'swollen and livid, lying by fives and sixes in pigsties, on dunghills, and in the muddy streets', the evidence was lacking. Until now. This object isn't an object, as such, but rather a burial. Three decades of excavations at a medieval priory near Spitalfields in London have uncovered thousands of bodies and mass grave pits. Originally, these victims were thought to be from the Black Death of 1348, but radiocarbon dating places three thousand of them a century earlier. Osteologist Don Walker, from the Museum of London, made the brilliant connection between the dates of these victims and the famine caused by the Samalas eruption; such tragic committals reveal the urgency and abandonment of social conventions that accompanied the crisis. In good times, people were often segregated in cemeteries by wealth, faith, family or sex. Mid-disaster, everyone was chucked in together.

While some of the dead may have been London residents, many of those who perished came from the surrounding countryside in search of food but died on or soon after their arrival. The 1258 *Chronicles of Mayors and Sheriffs* recorded that 'In this year, there was a failure of crops […] a famine ensued, to such a degree that the people from the villages resorted to the City for food; and there, upon the famine waxing still greater, many thousand persons perished.' Interestingly, Paris wrote of other abbeys, including that of Bury St Edmunds, where the famished were buried in their thousands. Medieval chronicles from across northern Europe also talked of the calamitous weather that followed the eruption but were at a loss to explain it. Even today, across the peaceful countryside, there must be thousands of victims from one of the world's least-known medieval tragedies still waiting to be uncovered.

47.

WHITEWARE JUG

13TH–15TH CENTURY

Over 80 per cent of Britain's population live in towns and cities. So it's interesting to think about why so many of us have surnames that are absolutely nothing to do with urban life. Why are there so many Bakers, Millers, Smiths, Wrights and Walkers?

We have the Norman Conquest to thank for the introduction of the family name. With the Normans' arrival came a passion for administration, the cataloguing of individuals and places for tax purposes, legal documents and the transfer of property. Norman landholders and their households became increasingly referred to not only by their 'given' name, which we would call their first name, but also by a surname. This could indicate a person's place of origin, usually denoted with a *de* or *d'* such as *Henry de Ferrers* (after Ferrières-Saint-Hilaire in Normandy), or be a nickname based on a personal trait, such as the waggish *Gernon* (moustache) or *Giffard* (chubby-cheeks). Others were given a surname based on their high office – *Sheriff*, for example, or *Mareschall* (now Marshall).

During the twelfth and thirteenth centuries, as more people began to adopt surnames, most still lived and worked in the countryside. Only a dozen or so towns had more than a few thousand inhabitants and many people who did live in urban areas continued to farm fields and wasteland outside a town's boundaries. The place where someone lived or worked often became a surname – local landmarks such as *Green*, *Wood*, *Sallow* (willow), *Lane* and *Kirk* (church) and directions such as West or East (as in *Westerby* – west in the village) were commonly adopted. Prepositions such as 'under', 'at' or 'atte' (at the) were added to words describing landmarks to distinguish between local people, creating surnames such as *Underhill*, *Atwood* and *Byford*. Feudal titles from this time also survive in modern surnames, while *Freeman* and *Franklin* were commoners with special privileges. The rare family names *Villan* and *Cotter* are relics of a lower status of peasantry.

Rural occupations also provided a useful way to mark out a person's identity. *Smith*, for example, was a well-regarded trade and is still the most common surname in Britain along with other stalwarts such as Taylor, Wright (a carpenter or joiner) and Clark (cleric). Sadler, Glover, Butcher, Baker, Miller, Shepherd, Fletcher, Chandler (candle-maker), Tanner and Turner are also wonderfully recognisable as jobs, but less obvious are delightfully obscure surnames such as Skipper (basket maker), Kellogg (pig butcher), Pinder (person in charge of the village livestock pound or 'pinfold'), and Hoggard (guardian of young sheep or pigs). Long-forgotten rural trades also live on in people's surnames such as Arkwright (someone who makes chests), Clower (a nailmaker) and Palfrey (someone in charge of saddles).

The craft of weaving has provided a particular wealth of surnames, with a name for pretty much every stage of the textile process. From Web, Webster and Webber (all meaning 'weaver'), to Spinner, Carder, Comber, Kemp and Kempster (also combers), Fuller and even Walker, the last of which was a job that involved fulling or shrinking cloth by trampling it in water. Dyer, Dexter and Lister all refer to the same occupation. Interestingly, medieval ceramics left less of an impression on the country's surnames. During this period, it seems that pottery making was viewed as a low-status skill and one that many peasants performed as a side-hustle to other seasonal work such as farming, woodland crafts or peat digging. Potters would use locally dug clay and build simple kilns to create rustic jugs, bowls and cooking vessels for themselves and other working people.

This object – a whiteware jug – was made in Cheam, now a suburb of London but once a busy rural village. Fourteenth-century legal documents from here give a direct example of how peasants were identified and named by their occupations. Records of misdemeanours include a 'Walter Potter', the master potter, and his two assistant 'Nicolas Walterservant' (i.e. servant of Walter) and 'Richard Walterservant'. Another of Walter's assistants – 'John Shepherde' – combined sheep husbandry and making pots. Brought as witnesses are 'John Carpenter' (no clue needed to his occupation) and a 'Ralph atte Rithe' (Ralph 'At the Small Stream').

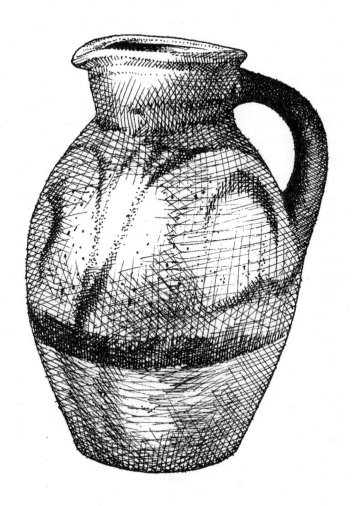

48.

CAILLEACH
DATE UNKNOWN

Harvest time is a critical moment in the countryside year. The gathering in of cereal crops is always a heart-stopping event, a brief window when the forces of nature must dance in perfect synchronisation. For the medieval peasant, the stakes must have been worryingly high. In the absence of weather forecasts, villagers looked to superstitions and weather lore for guidance. St Swithun's Day, 15 July, was particularly significant. Folklore held that if it rained on that day, over a month's worth of bad weather would follow. If St Swithun's Day was fair, however, 'for forty days, twill rain no mair'. Other presages of rain were keenly watched; frogs croaking, sheep bleating or playing, swallows flying low, and even church bells heard further away than normal.

How the harvest chores were divided up in the Middle Ages isn't entirely understood. Most of the population were peasants – at least 85 per cent – but within that structure lay a subtle hierarchy. Some peasants were freer than others and farmed their own plots, as well as working on the lord of the manor's fields. Serfs, on the other hand, were legally tethered to a plot of land with very few rights or agency. Manorial records show that both free and unfree peasants – men, women and children – were expected to help on 'boon days', the hay and corn harvests that required large numbers of people at short notice. Illustrated medieval manuscripts show busy villagers cutting with scythes and sickles and tying the sheaves with tightly twisted stalks – a technique known as *scramping*. The sheaves would then be stacked upright in small piles called *stooks* and left in the field to dry out or 'cure', this process helping the grains to harden ready for milling.

It was unrelenting, back-breaking work and the cutting of the last sheaf was hugely significant. Across farming cultures, similar rituals are thought to have accompanied this crucial moment. The last sheaf in the field was believed to contain the 'corn spirit', an idea whose origins may be as old as agriculture itself. The corn spirit was responsible for the fertility of the crop, and to ensure her survival, and therefore secure next year's harvest, the last sheaf would be cut with great ceremony and then plaited into a figure or shape. This harvest amulet was then kept safely indoors until spring, when it would be ploughed in or fed to livestock to return the spirit back to the soil.

The earliest written record of a straw figure dates to the sixteenth century but many believe the skill to be much older. Over time these intricate straw sculptures have attracted different names such as corn dollies, kern babies, ivy girls and mell dolls. Vernacular styles also emerged in various counties – Cambridgeshire has the handbell, for example, Worcester a crown, and Yorkshire an intricate spiral. In both Ireland and Scotland, harvest trophies were known as *cailleach*, a word that connects them to their Celtic past. In Gaelic mythology the Cailleach (meaning 'veiled one') was an old woman, a personification of the physical landscape and the forces of nature.

When all the hard work was finished, it was customary for the lord of the manor to provide a 'boon supper'. In some counties, these harvest feasts were called 'mell suppers', a delightful nod to their Anglo-Norman roots. Mell came from the Old French *meller*, which meant to mix together or mingle. Boon suppers might be taken in the landlord's home – one record from the thirteenth century shows haymakers at Ferring, West Sussex, being invited to 'eat in the lord's manor house' but only after they'd 'mowed all that meadow'. Bread, cheese and ale, and sometimes meat, would be laid on or money provided for the harvesters to purchase it for the feast. Harvesters at Warboys in Cambridgeshire, for example, got six pence 'from the abbot's purse' for *sythalis* or scythe-ale. Celebrations were rarely allowed to go on for too long, however. Revellers would be asked to leave as dusk fell or, if the feast had been given a small tallow-candle allowance, when a length the equivalent of a *shaftment* had burnt down. It's a now obsolete word but just one of many long-forgotten ways that medieval peasants measured the things around them.

49.

BRONZE STEELYARD WEIGHT

LATE 13TH CENTURY

When people buy or sell things at a market, they need to know what they're getting. The countryside has long been a place where animals, food, cloth and other commodities have been bartered or traded for money. To avoid disputes and disappointment, it's always been important to quantify the transaction. While modern life deals with metric certainties, standardised by the state, the medieval peasant relied on values now lost in time. Far from measuring things by some abstract concept, many medieval measurements are wonderfully anthropomorphic. Measurements become tactile, tangible moments in time – the width of a fist around a coppice hazel rod, for example, or counting a fidgety horse in hands, as it struggles to stay still.

The *shaftment*, for example, has been in use since at least the tenth century. It defined the width of the fist with an outstretched thumb, a 'thumbs-up' hand that was perfect for measuring lengths of timber such as poles or staves. The measurer could grip the base of a pole and count hand over hand up the stick; the word literally translates to 'shaft hand'. Lots of things could be measured by using shaftments – which equated to roughly six inches – such as candles, hazel rods, tree grafts, tool handles and so on. Other units of measurement constituted parts or multiples of the shaftment: a *digit*, the width of the top of the middle finger (one-eighth of a shaftment); a *finger*, the width of the knuckle of the middle finger (roughly a seventh of a shaftment); or a *palm*, half a shaftment. A *hand* or *handfull* was two-thirds of a shaftment or the breadth of the human hand with fingers and thumb held parallel. The hand as a measurement, and its use for measuring a horse, was standardised in the sixteenth century by Henry VIII but had been employed for centuries. For an accurate height, horse traders had to measure the 'lowest parte of the hove of the forefoote unto the highest parte of the wither'.

From the mighty horse to the very wee, it seems everything could be measured by the art of comparison. In the thirteenth century, the 'Composition of Yards and Perches' attempted to bring some stand-ardisation to the process. One of the most endearing measurements mentioned is the *barleycorn*, the equivalent to a third of an inch. The statute explained: 'It is ordained that 3 grains of barley dry and round do make an inch, 12 inches make 1 foot, 3 feet make 1 yard, 5 yards and a half make a perch, and 40 perches in length and 4 in breadth make an acre.'

Measurements of all kinds mattered in the ever-expanding world of markets and trade. This object, called a steelyard weight, was used as a counterweight when attached to a balance. Traders and merchants would use these weights to measure goods when they were offloaded from ships – this one was found in Suffolk but bears the chevrons of the Earl of Cornwall, a stamp of authority and reliability. Those caught short-changing their customers were swiftly punished. The *Judicium Pillorie* (Judgement of the Pillory), written in 1266 but used as a legal guideline well into the fourteenth century, advised that brewers and bakers should be castigated for serving short measures – 'a baker to the pillory, and a brewer to the tumbrel'. It's thought that a 'baker's dozen' comes from this time, with overcautious bakers throwing in an extra loaf or bun to avoid punishment.

Another obsolete measurement is the *ell*. It literally translates to 'arm' and initially measured the same as a *cubit*, the distance from the 'ell-bow' to the tip of the middle finger. The ell became the tailor and clothmaker's measurement, the *cloth-ell* or *double-ell*, a unit that could vary from region to region. England's measured 45 inches, while the Scottish ell was 37 inches and the Flemish ell just 27 inches. Importers and exporters of woollen cloth had dizzying formulas to help with their calculations, and, as we'll see from our next object, were not helped by the fact that fabric and fleece were starting to exchange hands in mindboggling quantities.

50.

STAINED GLASS ROUNDEL

C. 1340–45

We owe sheep a huge debt of gratitude. Many of the villages, market towns and churches of medieval Britain were built on the back of sheep wool, a commodity enthusiastically traded for hundreds of years. During the Iron Age, farmers kept sheep for meat, manure and milk. They were also skilled spinners and weavers, able to transform the rough fleeces of their native sheep (small, goat-like breeds) into cloth. Indeed, one item of Celtic clothing – the duffle-coat-like *birrus* – was in such demand that it was exported across the continent in vast numbers.

When the Romans arrived in Britain, they are thought to have imported their fine, white-woolled sheep – a breed developed in the Mediterranean – and by the early medieval period, mentions of sheep and wool cloth in charters and diplomatic documents suggest a countryside farming sheep on a significant scale. In 796, Charlemagne, the king of the Franks, wrote to Offa, then King of Mercia, asking whether he could once again buy the Anglo-Saxon woollen cloaks 'as they used to come to us in old times'. Viking settlers also brought their own flocks, including the ancestors of the Lake District's famous Herdwick sheep.

By the time of the Domesday Book, sheep were ubiquitous. The few regions that did return specific livestock numbers in the survey recorded over three hundred thousand sheep alone, a figure that represented just a fraction of the countryside's entire flock. Their purpose is revealed in Henry of Huntingdon's *Historia Anglorum* (History of the English), an ambitious chronicle written less than fifty years after Domesday. The country, it seems, was exporting far greater quantities of goods than it was importing, generating huge amounts of revenue. To Germany alone, it was sending different kinds of fish (including herrings and oysters), beef cattle and, most notably, its 'most precious wool'.

Many of the most successful and profitable sheep farms were run by monasteries. These large religious houses owned vast tracts of pasture and had a capable and energetic workforce in the form of *conversi*, farming monks, and lay workers employed from the local area. Monasteries acted as large-scale producers, not only raising sheep but also shearing, processing the wool, and negotiating with continental wool merchants, who would purchase years' worth of wool in advance to secure a supply. Medieval Europe – especially France, Italy and the Low Countries – clamoured for the stuff, turning the country's prized, soft wool into fine cloth for resale. Such was the scale of monastic wool farming that it even paid a king's ransom. When Richard I was captured on his return from one of his many crusades to the Holy Land in the 1190s, it fell to the monasteries to secure his release with the proceeds from the sale of their entire year's wool crop, an estimated ten million sheep's fleeces.

For religious institutions, sheep and their wool weren't just an excellent money spinner. Shepherds, flocks and helpless lambs were also brilliant metaphors for teaching the Christian message to a largely illiterate population. From the parable of the Good Shepherd to the Lamb of God, the close relationship between herder and flock, and the roles each were expected to fulfil, wouldn't have been lost on the peasant congregation. Stained glass also helped convey the message, as this object so beautifully illuminates. It's a roundel, depicting the Annunciation to the Shepherds, the moment when the angels tell a group of sheep-herders about the birth of Jesus.

Made sometime in the 1340s, in England, and now in the Victoria and Albert Museum in London, the roundel also tells us something about sheep farming at the time. While the breed of sheep can't be discerned, they do have long wavy fleeces. English wool was highly prized partly because so much of it came from long-woolled breeds. Long fibres were needed to make worsted, a luxurious finely woven cloth that commanded high prices at European cloth fairs. The fleeces from short-wool breeds were also coveted, especially those of the Ryeland, which produced soft, extra-fine yarn for stockings. Fleeces and finished cloth were briskly traded across the English Channel and North Sea, bringing untold riches to merchants and monasteries alike. Few, however, could have predicted the horror lurking in the ships' holds.

51.

LEAD CROSS
C. 1348–49

We can only imagine what must have been going through the mind of the desperate priest who scratched the following graffiti into the walls of his rural church: 'There was a plague, pitiable, fierce, violent [...] a wretched people survived to witness.' These words were carved into the tower of St Mary's Church, Ashwell, in Hertfordshire just a few years after the Black Death had ravaged the countryside, leaving carnage in its wake.

The Black Death, or bubonic plague, most likely arrived in south-western England in June 1348 through the port of Melcombe Regis in Dorset. Ships had ferried the terrible pestilence, *Yersina pestis*, in their cargo, a bacterium carried by fleas but also spread, air-borne, through close contact. The disease was fabulously indiscriminate, scything down both rich and poor, and lethally efficient, sometimes killing its victims in a matter of a few hours.

According to the English chronicler, Geoffrey the Baker: 'It came to England and first began in the towns and ports joining on the seacoasts, in Dorsetshire, where, as in other counties, it made the country quite void of inhabitants so that there were almost none left alive. From there it passed into Devonshire and Somersetshire, even unto Bristol, and raged in such sort that the Gloucestershire men would not suffer the Bristol men to have access to them by any means.

But at length it came to Gloucester, yea even to Oxford and to London, and finally it spread over all England and so wasted the people that scarce the tenth person of any sort was left alive.'

The plague moved with alarming swiftness across the countryside; estimates put its speed of transmission at anywhere between a mile and four miles a day. It leapt from village to village, town to town, sometimes by road, sometimes by river. Busy trading ports were particular vulnerable entry points, ships helping the disease hop quickly around the coastline. Archaeologists recently discovered a mass grave at Thornton Abbey, for example, a medieval priory just a stone's throw from the Humber Estuary in Lincolnshire and an important shipping gateway to the continent. Nearly fifty individuals had succumbed to the plague, half of whom were children, and had been hastily buried within days of each other. Researchers suspect that stricken local people probably looked to the monks of the abbey for help in their final hours, hoping for last rites and a burial in consecrated ground when their own village and churches had been overwhelmed.

Geoffrey the Baker's calamitous mortality rate turned out to be only a slight overstatement. Modern historians put the death toll at between a third and half the entire population of England, Wales, Scotland and Ireland, a figure matched across most of Europe. No one was immune from its effects, including the faithful. Monasteries, which often doubled as rudimentary hospitals, were badly hit; in Gloucester, the plague finished off a quarter of the town's monks and two-thirds of its canons. Bury St Edmunds lost half its friars.

The object pictured here demonstrates the haste with which many religious institutions had to bury their own dead while trying to deal with the barely living. A crude cross, quickly fashioned from lead, it was found on the body of a Greyfriars monk who had died when the Black Death reached London. Lead crosses were often interred with religious figures, lead being a humble material that symbolised egalitarianism before God. Being buried with a cross also made sure the deceased could rest, protected from further ills, a sentiment no doubt heightened during the plague.

When the dust had settled, the country was badly bruised. In England alone, the population had plummeted from 4.8 to 2.6 million between 1348 and 1351, a figure exacerbated by widespread crop failures and food shortages in the preceding years. For all its devastation, however, the Black Death gave those who survived a stronger bargaining position and the courage to challenge authority, a situation best summed up by our graffiti in the tower of St Mary's Church. Next to the doom-laden scrawl about the horrors of the plague, our scribe had carefully scratched, in Latin, a daring and contentious extra thought: 'The Archdeacon is an ass.'

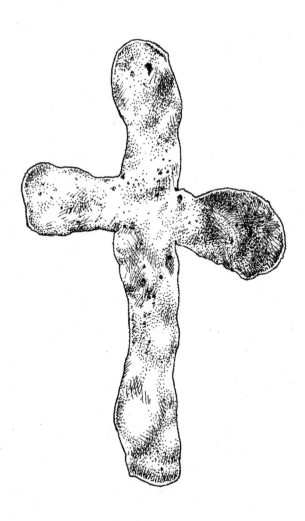

52.

OWL MISERICORD
14ᵀᴴ CENTURY

What do owls and the Black Death have in common? The word *bubo* described a swelling in the groin (hence the bubonic plague) but, in ancient Latin, it also translated as 'owl'. Each meaning came from a different etymological origin but, in the medieval mind, the similarity of the words only reinforced the deep suspicion with which owls were viewed.

Medieval bestiaries or 'books of beasts' are fascinating places to look for clues about how our predecessors viewed the natural world. They're not only zoological encyclopaedias, giving the reader vivid descriptions of a creature and its habits, but were also used for religious teaching. Animals and their behaviours became allegories; some beasts were worryingly lustful, like the wild boar. Others – such as bees – virtuous, chaste and hardworking. Mystical beasts were described as earnestly as those found in the forests and fields – the medieval country dweller believed no less in the rooster-serpent 'cockatrice' than the crane or the bat.

Bestiaries were also sumptuously illustrated. Their aim was to convey the wonder and mystery of the natural world, a reflection of God's work, but they were also beautiful objects to own and share. As proudly announced by the scribe in the *Aberdeen Bestiary*, created around 1200: 'In painting this picture I intend to improve the minds of ordinary people, in such a way that their soul will at least perceive physically things which it has difficulty in grasping mentally; that what they have difficulty comprehending with their ears, they will perceive with their eyes.'

Animals from bestiaries – both real and imagined – were everywhere. Not only did they grace the colour plates and margins of important manuscripts but they also found their way into religious carvings, tapestries and furniture. This glorious wooden model of an owl is from St Hugh's Choir at Lincoln Cathedral. It was carved into a misericord (a kind of standing seat for the clergy) in the late fourteenth century and would have conveyed a specific message. The medieval bestiary was particularly unkind about owls, a bird believed to be a harbinger of death and misfortune. It was also thought to be a lazy bird with dubious toilet habits, readily soiling its own nest, and was often blamed for outbreaks of pestilence. Its nocturnal habits, however, were its most worrying. The owl preferred darkness to light, a perfect metaphor for spiritual ignorance and lost souls yet to embrace the teachings of the gospel.

Other countryside creatures were also vilified. The hedgehog was condemned for stealing apples and grapes, which it did by allegedly impaling them on its quills and then hoarding the fruit in hollow trees. The badger was a hive robber and stealer of honeycombs. The fox was deceitful, tricking its prey by playing dead and incapable of walking in straight lines.

Perhaps the strangest description, however, was reserved for the beaver. When chased by a hunter, the beaver was said to bite off its own testicles and hurl them at its pursuer. While the beaver's gonads are actually located internally, both male and female beavers do produce a musky substance called *castoreum* from sacs near their anal glands, which is used to mark their territory. Castoreum was highly prized in medieval times and added to medicines, perfume and food to such an extent that the beaver was hunted to extinction in Britain by the sixteenth century. Castor oil, which is instead extracted from plant seeds, was so called because it was thought to replicate the benefits of beaver secretions.

Many of Britain's archaeological sites have revealed evidence of beaver exploitation. Beavers were useful not only for their musk glands but also for their fur, meat, bones and teeth. Large beaver lodges were even repurposed as platforms in wetland areas. At Stonehenge, for example, archaeologists have discovered beavers were being butchered and eaten as early as the fourth millennium BCE. Even further back in time, at the Mesolithic site of Star Carr, the dig revealed a beaver jaw with teeth that had, in all likelihood, been used as a woodworking tool. By the sixteenth century, along with the lynx, bear and wolf, the beaver had become yet another native species to disappear from the landscape. As we'll see later in this book, however, it might not be quite goodbye.

53.

WHARRAM PERCY MERRILLS BOARD
13TH CENTURY

It's hard to choose an object that represents a void. And yet this game-board etched into stone is a poignant symbol of a lost village, just one of hundreds abandoned after the Black Death.

Wharram Percy is perhaps the most famous of them all. Tucked into one of the Yorkshire Wolds' many hidden valleys, the village bustled for more than six hundred years before being deserted. Grassy fields now cover the landscape but traces of the original homes can still be seen, along with the painterly remains of the village church and silent millpond.

The Black Death didn't affect the countryside in a uniform way. Some villages were barely touched, others almost totally emptied. For villages that held the dubious honour of losing just an 'average' number of its inhabitants – around half of its men, women and children – the fate of the community could go either way. In many instances, as was the case with Wharram Percy, the plague didn't extinguish the settlement overnight. Instead, it exacerbated existing problems and brought new struggles that rural villages simply couldn't overcome.

Wharram Percy represents a microcosm of national events leading up to and after the plague. Sporadically occupied since the Iron Age, a recognisable village emerged sometime in the ninth century, with a wooden church, green and parish boundaries. Before the Norman Conquest, the land seems to have been owned by people with Viking ancestry but, as with much of the countryside after 1066, William the Conqueror confiscated the land and gave it to a Norman baron. By the end of the thirteenth century, the village was a thriving community with a new stone church, watermill, and about forty houses.

At the beginning of the fourteenth century, things started to go wrong. Repeated raids by the Scots, and a failure by the landholding family to provide an heir, left the village vulnerable. By 1323, two-thirds of Wharram Percy's fields were fallow and the mill had stopped turning. A brief resurgence in the 1330s pushed the village's occupants up to eighteen or so households, including a manor house, but then disaster struck. In 1349, the plague killed the lord of the manor and left only forty-five residents alive.

Across the country, with the agricultural population decimated, those few left standing began to demand higher wages. In 1351, a panicked parliament pushed through the Statute of Labourers, a set of laws designed to fix wages at their pre-plague levels and compel all the able-bodied to work. Those who didn't abide by the new rules would be severely punished; for good measure, the statute insisted that new stocks be erected in every village as a deterrent.

With the population in tatters, wages under dispute, but the countryside's wool still in great demand, many landlords decided to shift from arable to sheep farming. One shepherd, and his large flock, could now bring in the income of multiple peasant tenants. The change from plough to pasture, however, didn't always happen quickly. After the Black Death, although peasants didn't own the land they farmed, they did have some tenure rights. These were varied and often fluid – some peasants held land for one generation, others for three. Some had their fields seized on a scigncurial whim, others fought to retain their claim to long-standing holdings. Nonetheless, many villages didn't survive the transition. Wharram Percy's population steadily declined throughout the fifteenth century and the eviction of the last four families around 1500 sealed the village's fate.

By 1543, the land that once provided sustenance for around two hundred people comprised just two shepherds and over twelve hundred sheep.

This thirteenth-century board game, carved into stone, comes from a moment when the village was at its height. Merrills or Nine-Men's-Morris was a noughts-and-crosses-like game, popular with medieval rural communities. Children and adults alike would create a game-board by scraping a grid into a surface and using pebbles for counters. The game even gets a mention in Shakespeare's *A Midsummer Night's Dream*: 'The nine men's morris is filled up with mud', a reference to an unseasonably rainy summer in 1594. As we'll see from our next object, however, people found plenty of other ways to amuse themselves.

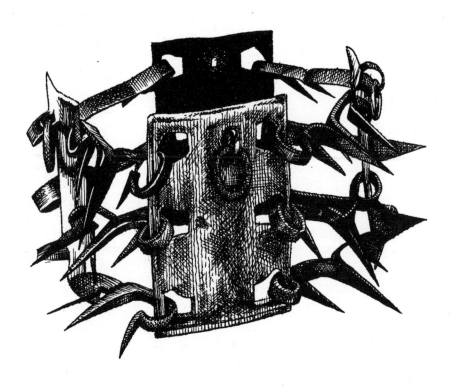

54.

SPIKED DOG COLLAR
15TH CENTURY

When you own a dog these days, few people ask what it's *for*. Canines, for the main part, are simply companions, agreeable members of the family who keep us company in return for food and regular walks. For most of history, however, dogs needed to earn their keep. And while the occasional pooch lived a pampered, petted life, most countryside dogs were expected to put in a hard day's work.

This object, an iron spiked collar, tells us plenty about the risks of being a working canine. In the 1570s, the English clergyman, William Harrison, penned *Of Our English Dogs and Their Qualities*. Clearly a canine lover, he enthused that 'There is no country that may (as I take it) compare with ours in number, excellency, and diversity of dogs.' He also categorised canines into their uses rather than breeds, a system that reveals the preoccupations of their owners.

The most common dogs were 'shepherd's curs or mastiffs', used to keep herds or flocks together. Livestock guardian dogs often wore 'wolf collars', fitted with spikes to prevent predators attacking the dog around the neck. In use since the time of Ancient Greece, by the sixteenth century these ferocious-looking collars would have been largely redundant in England and Wales, where wolves had been hunted to near-extinction. They were still useful, however, as protection against other large dogs; Harrison noted that mastiff-like canines were often so aggressive that they were called 'band dogs' or 'tie dogs', because they had to be chained up to prevent the creature 'doing hurt abroad'. Far from seeing this as a problem, owners actually encouraged their dogs to be combative. As Harrison explained: 'although this kind of dog be capable of courage, violent, valiant, stout, and bold: yet will they increase these their stomachs by teaching them to bait the bear, the bull, the lion, and other such like cruel and bloody beasts'.

Other types of dogs were kept for hunting. Used for either chasing or flushing out game, spaniels, harriers (large beagle-like dogs), and sagaces (scent hounds) were sent on the trail to pursue all manner of creatures, including 'the fox, the hare, the wolf (if we had any), hart, buck, badger, otter, polecat, lopstart [stoat], weasel' and so on. Such was the close bond between handler and hunting dog, claimed Harrison, that they 'delight more in their dogs [...] than they do in children', a charge still aimed at many an indulgent owner.

Of the other uses of dogs, a few are particularly worthy of note. 'Warners' and 'snap dogs' were the ultimate yappers, small pooches kept for their ability to bark incessantly and give warning. 'Turnspits' could include a whole range of breeds all with one shared purpose: to turn a wheel like a hamster in a cage. Mastiffs were made to 'draw water in great wheels out of deep wells' but most turnspit dogs seem to have had short legs and long bodies, and were distant relatives of the corgi, perhaps, or the terrier. Turnspits did exactly that, propelling a wheel that rotated a spit in front of a kitchen fire, so the meat would cook evenly. And finally, there were 'dancers', dogs trained to perform to music or drum beats – a skill that could earn a busker a few much-needed pennies.

Harrison is also keen to describe some dangerous hybrids. A cross between a wolf and a dog bitch, he warned, produced a 'wolfdog', an animal with high levels of aggression and territoriality. His other hybrids, however, are the stuff of Tudor fantasy: 'there is none more ugly and odious in sight, cruel and fierce in deed, nor untractable in hand,' wrote Harrison, 'than that which is begotten between the bear and the band dog'. While a dangerous 'bear-hound' might have been a genetic impossibility, there were, nevertheless, plenty of other rural dangers to be wary of ...

55.

BOLLOCK DAGGER
15TH CENTURY

Country life is not without its risks. Farming, forestry and fishing have always been dangerous jobs and still are, with some of the worst fatal injury rates of any occupation. Of the varied and painful ways to die in these careers, the most common are being hit by a vehicle, falling from a height, being injured by an animal, accidents with machinery and tools, and drowning. And, looking at the everyday hazards of country life in the sixteenth century, it seems it was ever thus.

Two Oxford academics, Steven Gunn and Tomasz Gromelski, dug into Tudor coroners' reports and found that everyday fatal hazards in the 1500s were both familiar and fascinating. Cart accidents were particularly common, especially when fully laden. Axles snapped, wheels fell off, carters ran over themselves or their colleagues, and entire vehicles overturned. Nervous horses often reared or bolted, killing both driver and passers-by, while the parlous state of country roads, churned up with wheel tracks, was also lethal. In March 1550, for example, John Rusey, a labourer, stumbled on a 'carte rote' and stabbed himself in the stomach with his own knife, which was hanging off his belt. Accidental knife injuries weren't uncommon, especially with the popularity of cheap, wooden-handled 'bollock daggers' like this one, worn by all classes for self-defence. So named because of its distinctive shaft, the bollock first appeared around the fourteenth century and remained popular for three hundred years. Carried on the hip, it was employed by soldiers and civilians for close combat and, depending on the blade, was also used as a utensil or tool.

Watery mishaps were also frequent. Indeed, drowning accounts for around half of all accidental deaths during this time. Overloaded or badly maintained fishing boats and ferries were disasters waiting to happen, while others got into difficulty dredging for shellfish. Rivers could be treacherous places, and not just those that flowed at speed. Swamps and mudbanks too claimed the unwary. In May 1530, for instance, Hugh Jones was catching 'craves' or crayfish on the Thames but died falling into a 'myre'. In another bizarre incident, farm-hand William Hall decided to ride a ram across a stream after finishing washing his flock. Almost as soon as the ram entered the water, Hall fell off and drowned. Fetching water and washing clothes were similarly perilous – ponds and streams often seemed to claim the young, drunk or careless, especially as a large percentage of the population never learned to swim.

The weather, too, could be capricious. Lightning strikes claimed a number of victims, especially those working out in the sultry heat of summer harvests. July was a particularly risky month. In 1570, Norfolk child labourer Agnes Daye was out in the open, picking peapods, when she was struck and killed instantly by lightning. Just a few years later, another young female servant in York was walking through a field when an electrical strike lethally set her hair, 'hatt and lynen clothing' on fire. Indeed, as we'll find out later in this book, children died doing many different country jobs such as handling horses or carrying heavy weights. Around a third of all deaths for those aged seven to thirteen were work-related.

Waterwheels and windmills could be deadly, partly because of the sheer might of their mechanical workings but also due to the unpredictably of the forces that powered them. Floods and sudden gales made both very dangerous places; in one notable incident in 1599, an aptly named Essex miller, Thomas Folly, attempted to remove the sail-cloths from his windmill. Mid-task, a strong gust of wind turned the sails, taking Folly round with them. Needless to say, as the sails reached their zenith, Folly plummeted to his death.

Working dogs were often indiscriminate in their aggression, attacking other dogs and people. In one report, a Suffolk tanner, Simon Reve, was killed by his own canines. When Reve's two mastiffs had attacked another man's greyhound, Reve attempted to intervene. Both Reve and the unlucky greyhound died from their bites. Tree falls were also calamitous. Tudor coroners' reports include accidents while collecting holly and ivy, scrumping for apples and plums, shaking acorns for pig pannage, and stealing eggs and chicks from nests. Given that tree climbing was so risky, our next object explains why anyone bothered at all.

56.

BOXWOOD NUTCRACKER

16TH CENTURY

In 1581, English writer George Pettie published his translation of an Italian work called *Civile Conversation* by Stefano Guazzo. The book had some interesting advice for its readers: 'A woman, an asse, and a walnut tree, Bring the more fruit, the more beaten they bee.'

Blatant misogyny and animal cruelty aside, this advice drew on earlier wisdom: that whipping or whacking a walnut tree in spring would help it to produce more nuts in early autumn and the finest timber for woodworking. Quite why this technique worked isn't known. Walnuts are wind pollinated, so thrashing a tree while in blossom may, albeit clumsily, help disperse the pollen. Others have suggested that breaking the branches encourages new side shoots to appear.

The walnut was a popular tree in the Tudor countryside. Not only is its timber beautifully dense and tightly grained but its nuts are tremendously nutritious. The Tudors valued walnuts so much they even recommended them as a preventative against both the plague and, curiously, impotence. Walnut shells or '*walsh-note shales*' also made excellent brown dyes and inks. The tree's timber was so highly prized that carpenters tried to pass off cheaper woods by disguising them with walnut stain. In John Evelyn's 1664 *Sylva: Or A Discourse of Forest Trees*, a love-letter to all things tree-related, he wrote of walnut: 'were this timber in greater plenty among us, we should have far better utensils of all sorts for our houses, as chairs, stools, bedsteads, tables, wainscot, cabinets, &c. instead of the more vulgar beech, subject to the worm, weak, and unsightly; but which to counterfeit, and deceive the unwary, they wash over with a decoction made of the green-husks of walnuts.'

The walnut and other edible nuts were used as potent metaphors in Christian teaching. The nut represented Jesus Christ: the outer hull his flesh; the tough wooden shell the cross; and the sweet, wholesome kernel Christ's divine nature and the fruitfulness of his ministry. One sixteenth-century calligrapher, Peter Bales, took his faith one step further and produced a Bible so tiny he could fit it inside a walnut shell. Now a lost treasure, the only clue to its existence is a note from 1586 that read: 'A most strange and rare piece of worke [...] the Whole Bible to be written by hym everie word at length within an English Wallnut no bigger then a hennes egg.'

During the sixteenth century, elaborately carved nutcrackers – like this one – became all the rage in the wealthy households. Designed to be showy talking points at a feast, these expensive box- or yew-wood nutcrackers used a lever-action to open the figure's mouth to insert the nut. Most were expertly carved in France and England, and the imagery is often rich with heraldry, classical motifs and mythical beasts. Many also featured a whistle in their handle, to summon servants quickly to the table. These kinds of nutcrackers probably worked best, not on walnuts, but on smaller hazelnuts. The hazelnut was also called the 'filbert', reputedly named after St Philibert. Philibert's feast day is 20 August and traditionally coincided with the beginning of the hazelnut harvest.

Wild hazel trees and bushes grew across the countryside but cultivated varieties – cobnuts – have also been grown since at least the sixteenth century. Also called cobill nuts (from cob, meaning rounded), they were not only used for food and oil. 'Cobnuts' was also a children's game. Randle Cotgrave's 1611 *A French & English*

Dictionary explained the contest, which was also called *chastelet* or *castelletto* (little castle): 'the throwing of a Ball at a heape of Nuts, which done, the thrower takes as many as he hath hit, or scattered'. Hazel trees, coppiced to produce lots of thin, long rods, were endlessly useful for the countryside dweller. John Evelyn cheerfully jotted down just a few; 'poles, spars, hoops, forks, angling-rods, faggots, cudgels, coals, and springs to catch birds'. Many uses of hazel are now lost in time; hazel chips to purify wine, charcoal for artists, riding switches and divining rods. The last of these, however, 'was used for detecting not just 'mines, and subterraneous treasure, and springs of water, but [also] criminals, guilty of murder'. Nuts.

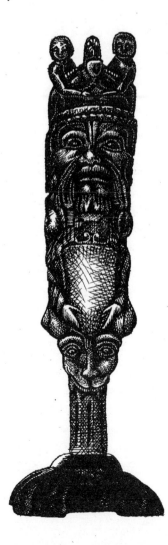

57.

WOODCUT FROM
DE ARTE NATANDI
1587

Everard Digby was an eccentric man at the best of times. A fellow of St John's College, Cambridge, he lived a life of self-inflicted penury. He also seemed to make a habit of bad-mouthing the college's master, fishing when he should have been in chapel, and annoying students by blasting his horn and 'halloing' around the grounds. In 1587, however, the same year he was ignominiously booted out of college, he published a rather remarkable and ground-breaking book.

De Arte Natandi (The Art of Swimming) was the first of its kind. A book of two halves, the first section explained the theory of swimming while the second detailed the various strokes and methods for staying afloat. Digby was also careful to include beautiful woodcuts of swimmers in different positions, as well as advice about how to enter water safely and the importance of not swimming alone.

It seems an obvious topic to write about and yet, by all accounts, most of Tudor society had forgotten how to swim. Indeed, in some professions it was actively discouraged. Sailors weren't required to be swimmers until the nineteenth century; why seamen chose not to learn isn't clear, but in heavy seas, or with no rescue equipment on board, it was probably seen as a mercy to drown quickly. Digby's book, however, spoke to a more general audience: the men, women and children at risk from the very real threat of drowning in the countryside's watery places.

Why the art of swimming was lost isn't fully understood. The Romans were famously enthusiastic dippers and learned, like children today, by lying on rush or cork floats and thrashing about with their arms. Stories of Caesar's swimming prowess were legendary; one tale tells of him escaping a battle by thundering through the waves with his cloak clenched between his teeth, 'lest the enemy get it as a trophy'. And the Romans weren't the only ones confident in water. At least two Iron Age tribes were recorded as good swimmers: the Batavi, who were said to swim across waterways with their horses, and the Germani, who apparently bathed in rivers in reindeer-skin swimming trunks and cloaks.

Anglo-Saxon culture also revered the strong swimmer in its epic poetry. *Beowulf* celebrates diving and underwater swimming with great pride. Heroes in Early Welsh tales dive into dangerous seas and swim 'as well as the best fish', while Viking sagas feature kings and ordinary folk swimming, including slaves and farm-hands. By the sixteenth century, however, this can-do attitude to swimming seems to have changed. In some places it was even banned. In 1571, while Digby was still at Cambridge, the university forbade its students from swimming in 'any river, pool or water' or face a public whipping.

After the Norman Conquest, attitudes towards what constituted physical prowess and military strength may have changed. A new kind of hero emerged – the armoured knight on horseback – and swimming as both a military and a courtly skill seemed to lose its status. The Church's teachings also unintentionally sullied the image of swimming, which it used as a metaphor for the ungodly man, one at the mercy of dangerous elements.

Those few that could swim were mostly men. As swimming had to be performed naked, or scantily dressed, it was deemed unseemly for women to indulge in it. There was also a general view that people just weren't designed to swim. As one author noted a century later, it is: 'generally believed by most people; and I account it none of the smallest reasons that so many are unfortunately drowned […] That all Creatures naturally can Swim, Mankind only excepted; which opinion, with the fear of death working upon the *Imagination*, possesses the *patient* with such a senseless fear, that he endeavours not to *Swim* to help himself, but yields up his life to […] the *most merciless Element.*'

Digby, however, had no such fear. He was so proficient he even invented a version of synchronised swimming and loved 'to caper with both his legges at once above the water' or 'swimme with one legge right up'. As we'll read next, however, it wasn't always favourable to float.

58.

DRIED CAT
17TH CENTURY

While Digby was larking around in the River Cam, another kind of splashing about was to be avoided altogether. By the sixteenth century, the practice of 'swimming a witch' was already common. Of the various bizarre methods used to determine whether someone was a witch, tying them up and flinging them into deep water was particularly popular. The logic was impeccably mad. If someone was innocent, they would sink to the bottom and probably drown. If guilty, they'd float, only to be dragged out and executed. King James I of England obsessed over the problem of witchcraft and even penned his own book, *Daemonologie*, in 1597. In his view, swimming a witch was like a holy baptism – while the water would eagerly engulf the innocent, it would 'refuse' a witch, forcing her to stay on the surface.

Belief in witches was ancient. Indeed, the Bible had called its readers to arms with the unequivocal 'Thou shalt not suffer a witch to live' (Exodus 22:18). Witch hunting in the sixteenth and seventeenth centuries, however, gathered pace thanks to legislation that made being a witch a specific crime and, in many cases, punishable by death. The growing influence of the Church stoked the fire. Witches weren't just accused of dabbling in supernatural forces, good or ill, but of the specific crime of *heresy*, having an opinion contrary to the orthodox religion. In many ways, the Church and witchcraft were in competition. The Church offered believers rituals of its own, ones that promised healing, protection and justice in a way that traditional magic had done for centuries.

In many witchcraft trials, the accused were charged with making a pact with the devil in return for dangerous powers. These maleficent talents could then be used for everything from murder to spoiling milk. Deaths among livestock, failed harvests, poor weather and pestilence were all blamed on witchcraft, as were minor niggles such as bad dreams or butter not churning properly.

While witchcraft trials sought to expose and punish witches in the public realm, ordinary folk sought their own protection. From the sixteenth century well into the nineteenth, people relied on a bewildering array of charms and amulets to keep witches at bay in their homes. Exit and entry points, such as chimneys and doorways, were thought particularly vulnerable. To scare away witches or confuse them, therefore, it became common practice to conceal 'apotropaic' or evil-averting objects in canny places. This dried cat, carefully bound in wrappings like an Egyptian mummy, was found secreted in the chimney of a seventeenth-century Devon cottage.

Dozens of similar examples have come to light in recent years, often when a period building is renovated. Other desiccated animals have also been found – mice, birds, even chickens – but cats are the most common and were almost always dead when stuffed into their final resting places. The choice of a cat is curious, nevertheless, as people often accused felines of being witches' familiars, animals that carried out malevolent requests. The cat's mystical ambiguity, however, may have given it extra potency for the suspicious country dweller. Perhaps they hoped, in death, the cat would attract a witch, and then somehow trap her, or scare away other witches' feline familiars.

Cats were not the only objects people hid in their cottages. Shoes were also a favourite, especially those that belonged to a child. Three thousand concealed shoes have come to light from the Scilly Isles to the Shetlands, and they are almost always single and worn out. Witches were thought to be attracted to the human scent of a shoe, but would then inadvertently find themselves trapped inside. This belief dated to at least the fourteenth century and the legend of John Schorn, a Buckinghamshire rector who famously 'caught' the devil in a boot after an exorcism. And if you didn't have a moggy or old shoe to hand, a witch bottle would do. Take a vessel and fill it with pins or nails, strands of human hair or nail clippings, and some blood or urine. Place this cure against bewitchment under the floorboards, or in the hearth, and sleep soundly in the knowledge that a witch could do you no harm.

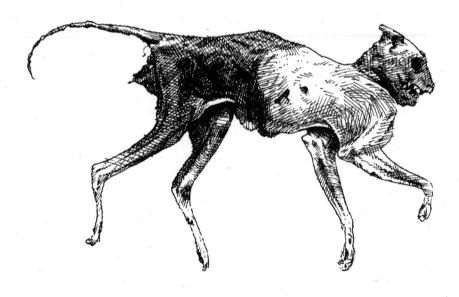

59.

DELFT TILE
1660

For most of Britain's history, a good chunk of the countryside was under water. Or, at least, incredibly soggy. Wetlands were everywhere, not just along the coastline, but from the Cambridgeshire Fens to the Somerset Levels. Often considered inhospitable by outsiders, the people who lived on or around wetlands capitalised on its unique, rich environment. Wetlands changed with the seasons; in the summer, when the water subsided, the rich pasture could support cattle, horses and sheep, allowing a pastoral economy to thrive. During the wetter, flooded months, fowling and fishing could flourish.

Wetlands, however, were prone to 'marsh ague' or malaria, a disease that diarist Samuel Pepys, and William Shakespeare, both wrote about with alarming frequency. For all their troublesome mosquitoes, the countryside's marshes and swamps nevertheless came with many benefits. Eels were plentiful, as were wild birds, while the saturated land could provide peat for fuel and reeds and grasses for thatching and candle-lights.

Despite its utility and biodiversity, for thousands of years people have attempted to reclaim watery land for agriculture and settlements. The most significant, however, was the 'Great Draining' of the seventeenth century thanks to King James I and, later, his son, Charles I. In 1620, James announced that 'the Honour of the Kingdom would not suffer the said Land to be absorbed to the Will of the Waters, not let it keep Waste and unprofitable'. The Crown invited Dutch engineer, Cornelius Vermuyden, to tackle the country's wetlands. Vermuyden had learned his craft at home, where land reclamation, financed by Dutch investors, had been underway since the fourteenth century. The Dutch were masters of their art, creating parcels of land called *polders* using dykes and drainage, and Vermuyden was set to work in Essex, Yorkshire, Lincolnshire and the Fens.

Tensions between engineers and locals frequently ran high, especially as reclaimed land was often given to the former as part of the deal. In the Fens, for example, residents and land reclaimers came to blows when locals were no longer able to collect the reeds, peat and other resources upon which their livelihoods depended. Anti-Dutch feeling ran high among Fen dwellers, who resented both the loss of common land and the planting of showy but ultimately useless 'foreign crops'; one 1646 leaflet asked, in despair: 'What is Cole-seed and Rape, they are but Dutch commodities, and but trash and trumpery.'

One of the features of land reclamation was the use of windmills. We often think of windmills as buildings solely for making flour. But, while corn-processing windmills had been known in England since the twelfth century, wind power could be put to other uses. The Dutch had developed windmills that could pump water out of their sodden land – most windmills in the Netherlands are still used for this purpose, not for crushing grain.

A good deal of the historic windmills that still dot the Fens and other areas of reclaimed land were, in fact, 'windpumps', strategically placed to keep land from flooding. Windmills could also change their core function over time. One of the most striking is the mill at St Benet's Abbey in East Norfolk, built sometime in the early 1700s. Unceremoniously plonked inside the ruins of a medieval gatehouse, the mill seems to have been both a windpump and a wind-powered rape-oil mill in its early years, depending on the whims of the economy.

During the seventeenth century, along with windmills, England also developed a passion for Dutch 'Delft'. Tin-glazed tiles, such as this one made around 1660, dazzled the English and were made to resemble

Chinese blue and white pottery. Tiles often incorporated scenes from Dutch life – ships, farmers, flowers and, of course, windmills. Paper windmills, or pinwheels, were a popular toy, as this object shows, but the Anglo-Dutch tile trade was no child's play. These bucolic ceramics were exported in such great quantities that eventually England decided to go into production for itself. In 1676 a Dutch potter, Jan Ariens van Hamme, was granted a warrant to make tiles in London. By the early 1700s, England was pumping out its own version, 'Delftware', at a fraction of the price, and by the end of the century, many other parts of the country had followed suit. Liverpool, Staffordshire, the West Country, Scotland and Ireland were all crafting their own cheap Delftware, sending Dutch windmills and countryside scenes back across the water.

60.

PLAYING CARD
C. 1670–85

From seventeenth-century literature and drawings, we can glean that people from all walks of life were keen to have fun. Some pastimes – like cards or board games – involved concentration and memory, while others embraced a gloriously reckless attitude to health and safety.

Playing cards arrived in Europe, probably from the Middle East or India, in the fourteenth century. Early decks were hand-painted and expensive but, thanks to advances in printing techniques, by the 1600s playing cards were affordable for most people. Their success lay in their portability – cards can be played almost anywhere, from sheep field to ship's galley. But, more importantly, they could also be used for gambling. Card games became so popular, and no doubt quar-relled over, that in 1674 the first games compendium – *The Compleat Gamester* – was published. It set out the rules and regulations for all kinds of pastimes – from bowls to billiards, 'together with all manner of usual and gentile games either on cards or dice'.

The book also covered the finer points of less salubrious country-side 'sports'. The practice of sparring cockerels in Britain goes back as far as the Iron Age, and by the seventeenth century cock-fighting was wildly popular among gentry and rural folk alike. Taverns and market squares set aside rings for cock-fighting, but events were also commonly held at fairs, public schools, horse races and even church-yards. Some games were tied to seasonal celebrations. Cock-throwing, for example, provided plenty of cruel japes on Shrove Tuesdays and didn't need any prized birds or arenas. Contestants simply had to find an unfortunate rooster, tie it by one leg to a post in the ground, and pelt it with sticks. If it was knocked over or killed, the winner got to keep the bird.

Our object, a three-of-spades playing card from the last quarter of the seventeenth century, is just one of a complete pack. Made in England, this sumptuous deck of cards is decorated with all manner of birds and beasts. Tellingly, many of the creatures are the subject of 'sport', including fighting bulls and tormented bears. Other cards in the pack include stags, hares, boars, rabbits, squirrels, ducks. The four of clubs even depicts a fight between a lion and bull, a horrible contest that would have only been possible backed by serious money.

Bear-baiting was a particularly popular diversion. One or more dogs – usually mastiffs – would be set loose on a bear chained to the centre of an arena. Large towns would have their own purpose-built bear pits, but country dwellers didn't miss out. Commercial bear bait-ers, who were known as 'bearwards', travelled the length and breadth of the nation to bring their violent trade to a rural audience. Regions also had their own bearwards, who often named their animals after a particular place. When fights were arranged between local bears and out-of-town rivals, residents could cheer on 'Judith of Cambridge' or 'Chester the Bear' in the same way modern sports fans support their local team.

Being a bearward wasn't without its dangers, however. One Lancashire bearward in 1638 explained his missing a court hearing because he had been 'most daungerly wounded [by] one of his Beares & is in greate feare to be lamed by that acsident & misfortune'. Bears were prized assets and, despite their mistreatment, would often survive a number of baitings before finally succumbing to their injuries and poor living conditions.

Even after death, bears were still valuable. Owners sold their corpses for fur, meat and, surprisingly, bear grease. In his 1653 herbal, *The*

Physician's Library, Nicholas Culpepper assured readers that 'Bears Grease [stops] the falling off of the hair.' Because bears were so furry, it was believed that rubbing their fat onto the scalp would somehow encourage it to sprout. During the eighteenth century, the popularity of this grease rocketed thanks to a tax on hair powder. William Pitt the Younger, raising money for war with France, introduced a series of taxes, including one guinea for the right to use hair powder. Many disgruntled wig-wearers abandoned their hairpieces in favour of the natural look. Those keen to boost their thinning tresses reached, in desperation, for a dollop of bears' grease.

61.

JOHN WORLIDGE'S *TREATISE OF CIDER*

1678

If a handful of learned men had got their way in the seventeenth century, the countryside would now be covered in apples. Men of science – such as the Royal Society's John Evelyn and Christopher Merret – had become convinced that the nation needed to invest in its orchards. Supplies of wine from the continent were being constantly hindered by trade wars and tariffs, a solution that could be solved in a stroke with the planting of acre upon acre of apple trees. This earthly 'Garden of Eden' wouldn't just cover the country with perfumed blossom but would provide men and women from all walks of life with what was considered one of the most wholesome and delightful everyday beverages: cider.

High society was particularly taken with the idea thanks to a number of key developments. A particularly fine cider apple – the Scudamore Crab – had recently been introduced to the country from France, transforming the potential for fermented apple juice to become more than a simple, labourer's beverage. The Scudamore apple made a cider refined enough to rival a good-quality foreign wine and, if stored properly, aged into a rich, fortifying drink. The invention of a wine bottle strong enough to withstand high pressure and the perfection of 'second-fermentation' – the process of adding fizz to alcohol – also allowed cider to be transformed from a rustic beverage into highly desirable 'apple champagne'.

Such was the excitement surrounding cider, apple champagne and fruit orchards, a number of influential treatises were published on the subject. This one, by noted agriculturalist and cider-enthusiast John Worlidge, was printed in 1676 and again in 1678, becoming one of the go-to guides on the propagation of fruit trees and cider production. For the expanded second edition, Worlidge also took the enlightened step of including a section on beekeeping and the value of these 'small, profitable, laborious, loyal, nimble, cunning, industrious and resolute' insects to the orchard grower.

While England's brief love affair with apple champagne fizzled out following a resumption of the continental wine trade, apple cider did help English colonists start a new life in North America. Of all the crops the Pilgrim Fathers and subsequent settlers took with them across the Atlantic, few were as wildly successful as apples. Thanks to the peculiarities of apple tree reproduction, growing apples from pips often creates trees that produce sour fruit, called 'spitters'. While these are poor eating apples, they make fantastic cider, a quality not lost on farming communities desperate to make anything familiar grow on unfamiliar terrain. The strains of barley brought across by colonists, for instance, had proved ill-suited to the new climate, but apple pips took with ease. Cider not only offered a safe alternative to water, but was also invaluable as a disinfectant, medicine, food preservative and much more besides. Apple cider could also be concentrated into a fiery, stronger spirit called 'apple jack' by freezing it in barrels, a technique perfectly suited to icy, East Coast winters.

In the same way that Worlidge had linked orchards and honeybees, so too had the settlers. America didn't have its own native honeybee; in 1621, London sent the Governor of Virginia a ship's worth of smallholding goodies, including seeds, fruit trees, pigeons, rabbits, mastiff dogs and, crucially, beehives, in the hope that honeybees could pollinate the colonies' new orchards. By the middle of the century, a small number of apiaries had been established but honeybees had also escaped and gone feral, swarming to create their own wild colonies and slowly spreading from state to state.

Back in Britain, while the fashion for 'apple champagne' had popped its cork among the elite, cider continued to be a popular drink among ordinary rural folk. In counties such as Kent, Herefordshire, Somerset and Worcestershire – which grew apples with the high tannin levels required for good cider – people from all walks of life relished apple alcohol. Seventeenth-century Herefordshire historian John Beale claimed many people imbibed from morning to eventide; 'Very few of our cottagers, yea, very few of our wealthiest yeomen, drink anything else.' And, as we'll find out next, the mood for a drink could even strike in the middle of the night.

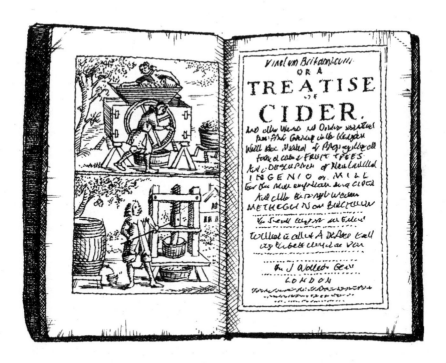

62.

RUSH NIPS
17TH CENTURY

When William the Conqueror ascended to the throne, he formalised a custom that had been in place since the ninth century. He demanded that a 'curfew' bell must be rung at eight o'clock in the evening, signalling for all villagers and townspeople to smother any open flames or face harsh penalties. The word 'curfew' comes from the Old French, *couvre feu*, meaning 'fire cover' and required householders to refrain from lighting fires until morning. Rather than kill a fire completely, however, it was possible to blanket it with ash and let it rumble on until dawn, when it could be fuffed back to life with bellows.

While William's draconian punishments for failing to obey a curfew were extinguished only a few decades later, the practice of ringing a curfew bell smouldered on for centuries. St Peter's Church in Sandwich, Kent, still peals its curfew bell at 8pm. Known locally as the 'pigbell', it not only told residents that it was time to dampen any naked flames but allowed anyone who owned pigs to release them into the streets so that the hungry porkers could gobble up all the rubbish that had piled up during the day.

Eight o'clock in the evening sounds like an early bedtime but, for most country dwellers, there wasn't a compelling reason to stay up beyond this time, especially in autumn and winter. From documentary evidence, it seems that well into the seventeenth century, many people slept in two shifts. The 'first sleep' started after the curfew and finished around midnight. A period of wakefulness, known as the 'watch', would last about one or two hours, followed by a 'second sleep' that was broken at dawn. The time during the watch, depending on the moonlight or availability of candles, could be one for intimacy, a drink, checking the fire, feeding babies, or household chores. An Early English ballad, 'Old Robin of Portingale', trilled: 'at the wakening of your first sleepe, You shall have a hott drinke made, And at the wakening of your next sleepe, Your sorrowes will have a slake.'

After sunset, how much lighting you had depended on your budget. Wealthy manors and churches could afford beeswax candles, which burnt bright, long and with a pleasant smell, unlike their cheaper cousin, the tallow candle. Tallow is a hard wax rendered from cows and sheep fat (although inferior candles were sometimes cut with softer, fast-burning pigs' lard). Tallow candles tended to smoke, and smell acrid, but were still considered superior to the humble rushlight.

Well into the nineteenth century, most poor rural households relied solely on the light from their hearths and rushlights. In the late summer months, women and children would collect armfuls of common rushes from areas of wetland or river banks. These were then soaked, peeled and their strong pithy centres hung up to dry. When stiff, the peeled rush was then repeatedly drawn through a pan of melted animal fat to create a waxy taper and left to set. Families could produce hundreds of pencil-thin rushlights at a time, each rush giving around half an hour's light per foot in length. A rushlight also needed a holder of some kind – usually a set of clamp 'nips' like this one – although some rushlights were mounted on a wall or hung from a rafter.

Seventeenth-century sources suggest that even a frugal family needed around two thousand rushlights a year, enough to illuminate evenings, dark mornings and indoor work such as weaving or spinning. The British poet Edwin Waugh recorded one Lake District family who were still using rushlights well into the nineteenth century: 'They made as many in two days as lasted the whole year. These rush dips are not much thicker than a strong knitting needle and gave a dreary light to people accustomed to gas. But they seemed to think the light was very good; beside, they went to bed soon o'nights.'

Not everyone was able to go to bed early, however. For some, lights out and nightfall marked a whole new shift of work …

63.

KNITTING SHEATH

LATE 17TH CENTURY

Author and devout Quaker, William Howitt, was a keen people watcher. In 1838, he published *The Rural Life of England*, based on his observations of countryside folk and their customs. In one evocative scene, Howitt described 'lights out' in the Yorkshire Dales: 'As soon as it becomes dark, and the usual business of the day is over, and the young children are put to bed, they rake or put out the fire; take their cloaks and lanterns, and set out with their knitting to the house of the neighbour [...] The whole troop of neighbours being collected, they sit and knit, singing knitting-songs, and tell knitting-stories [...] They burn no candle, but knit by the light of the peat fire [and] with crooked pins called pricks; and use a knitting-sheath consisting commonly of a hollow piece of wood.'

By the fifteenth century, knitting had arrived in Europe from the Middle East and was a craft the rural poor quickly took to their hearts. It was simple to learn and allowed country folk to make their own clothes but also earn money by knitting woollen stockings, gloves and hats to sell. The beauty of knitting was that it could be done almost anywhere and worked on in stages. This gave men, women and children the opportunity to clack away between other tasks. Fisherwomen knitted on the harbourside. Shepherds knitted in their huts or alongside their flocks. Women even knitted carrying baskets of peat or fish on their backs or walking to market. And, after dark, families could knit by the fireside.

Children were taught to knit as soon as their hands could hold the needles, and experienced knitters worked faster than the eye could see. To reach such dizzying speeds as two hundred stitches per minute, knitters often used a 'sheath' holder like this one. The knitter pushed one needle into a hole at the end of the sheath, which was then anchored to the knitter's waist by a belt or apron springs. The needle was thus held steady, freeing up both hands to work quickly and smoothly with the yarn and one, two or three more needles. Working multiple needles at once allowed crafters to create seamless tubes of knitting, perfect for stockings, gloves and hats.

Knitting sheaths were invaluable tools but also treasured, personal items. Family members would painstakingly carve sheaths for each other, adding affectionate messages, names and initials. Lovers also whittled knitting sheaths for their partners, knowing they would be kept close to the body. This carved boxwood example bears the initials A.T. and the date 1679. It reads: 'I am box and brass within, my place is on your apron string.' Intimate gifts such as these were often given as tokens of love and more than just an affectionate gesture. Such personal presents were designed to tempt someone to agree to marriage or publicly seal a promise.

Until the Marriage Act of 1653, the age of consent for marriage was twelve for girls and fourteen for boys. Most people in the countryside waited, however, until their twenties before tying the knot. And, then, only married after a period of service or apprenticeship that allowed both parties to gain the skills and savings necessary to set up home together. Before the change in law, couples also didn't have to get married in a church – records show people getting hitched at the tavern, in bed or even standing in a field – the ceremony little more than some informal 'words of present consent' between the two lovers.

The 1653 Marriage Act, however, formalised the process and set in stone many of the traditions that still accompany a wedding. Parishes had to employ a registrar to keep a record of all marriages and every wedding required the reading of the banns on three consecutive Holy Days at the church or three market-days in a row. The vows were also standardised, including the couple's promise to be 'loving and faithful', and the wife's pledge of obedience. The age of consent for marriage was also raised – to fourteen for girls and sixteen for boys: a limit that was only increased to sixteen for both sexes in 1929, and then to eighteen in 2022.

64.

THE PITCHFORD HALL CUP
1684

Warm stockings and knitted woolly hats would have been needed when this object was made. This is the Pitchford Hall Cup, a tiny 6-centimetre-high glass mug, and a souvenir from one of the country's most famous frost fairs. A replica of a life-size mug used for strong ale, it has the words 'Bought on ye Thames ice Janu: ye 1683/4' engraved on its silver rim.

Between the fifteenth and nineteenth centuries there were at least two dozen winters when the River Thames completely froze over. During this period – which was later dubbed the 'Little Ice Age' – parts of the world experienced unseasonably cool temperatures. Scientists still disagree over the extent and causes of this geological climate change, citing volcanic eruptions, solar activity and other possible natural processes. The effects of hard winters, however, were catastrophic in some years, with rural communities suffering cycles of crop failures, famine and livestock deaths. People were quick to blame certain groups for the deterioration of the climate. Historians attribute both the fury and the extent of the witchcraft trials and numerous waves of anti-Semitic violence across Europe to the uncertainty created by this long period of global cooling.

When rivers froze, however, some people took the opportunity to celebrate. The London frost fairs are well documented. Stalls sprang up overnight on the ice, selling mementoes and personalised souvenir tickets, as did pop-up coffee shops, taverns and roasting spits. Ice-skating, football, sleigh rides, skittles, bear-baiting, and even organised fights drew huge crowds, keen to make the most of an open space in a crowded city. Less is known, however, about regional frost fairs and the effects of frozen winters on those living in the countryside. There are, however, some fascinating snippets.

North Yorkshire, for example, held at least two frost fairs when the River Ouse froze in 1607 and again in 1614, which even included a fantastically ill-advised horse race across the ice. Newcastle had one too, in 1814, on the River Tyne. One local journalist wrote with glee: 'The desire of recreation shone forth in every face. Horse shoes, football, "toss or buy," rolly polly, fiddlers, pipers, razor grinders, recruiting parties, and racers with and without skates, were all alive to the moment. Hats, breeches, shifts, stockings, ribbons, and even legs of mutton, were the rewards of the racers, who turned night into day; the brilliancy of the full moon contributing to their diversions until late beyond midnight.'

In 1684, the Tees completely froze for fifty days, allowing a tent to be erected and a sheep roasted on the ice. The same year, Nottinghamshire's Trent river also clogged to an arctic standstill. When sub-zero temperatures descended on Shrewsbury on Christmas Eve 1739, and continued for three months, residents held a frost fair on the River Severn, famously erecting a printing press on the ice to mark the occasion.

For many country dwellers, however, brutally harsh winters were bewildering and deadly. The same year as the 1683 London frost fair, residents in Somerset recorded snow on the ground for thirteen weeks. Farmers lost cattle in head-high drifts, while hungry villagers who attempted to walk to nearby towns perished in the snow: 'the sharpness of the season tooke off the most parte of them that was aged and of them that was under infermities, the people did die so fast, that it was the greatest parte of their work to burie the dead [...] the ice was a yard and fower foot thick.'

Down in Southampton, ten miles of tidal estuary froze so thickly that people who usually relied on a ferry walked freely from one side to the other.

Perhaps the most vivid recollection of a 'great frost', however, came from a small boy in 1809, who was employed to scare birds near Malling, Kent. On approaching a field full of rooks, he was surprised when they didn't fly away. Even after throwing a snowball at them, they refused to budge. As he got closer, the boy realised the poor birds – which totalled twenty-seven rooks, a pheasant, ninety larks and a buzzard – were frozen to the spot. Only the buzzard, 'struggled hard for his liberty, broke his icy fetters and effected his escape'.

65.

SET OF STADDLE STONES

EARLY 18ᵀᴴ CENTURY

Until the beginning of the eighteenth century, the most troublesome pests a farmer faced were the house mouse and the black rat. The mouse, which originated in Central Asia, and the black rat, a native to south-west Asia, were both sneaky stowaways, piggybacking on human trade and migration across Europe until they reached British shores with Roman contact.

Both the mouse and the black rat could be a serious nuisance, nibbling away at valuable grain stores, but they rarely threatened a farmer's entire yield. When a new, greedier species of rat landed in the British countryside in the early 1700s, however, all that was to change. The brown rat, also known as the sewer rat or, erroneously, the Norwegian rat, was native to northern China and Mongolia. It arrived in Europe sometime in the 1500s, reaching Britain and Ireland in the early eighteenth century. It was no ordinary rat; double the size of a black rat and more aggressive, the brown rat was also a first-rate swimmer, burrower and, unfortunately, voracious eater.

Writing in 1782, vermin expert Daniel Holland recalled the recent arrival of the brown rat and its effect on the countryside. 'It is more strongly made than the common black rat [...] swims very well, and lives on grain and fruits, but will destroy poultry and game [...] they are very bold and fierce [...] These rats not only frequent barns, but migrate in great numbers into rocks, sewers, hen-houses, hog-sties, under floor in houses [...] and do much mischief.'

The brown rat was also fast displacing the black rat to virtual extinction. 'The common rat, which is the old genuine English house rat, is of a dusky brownish colour,' Holland explained, almost misty eyed. 'Their propagation has been considerably diminished by the Norway rats, as the latter devour and banish them whenever they meet.'

By the middle of the eighteenth century, farmers were increasingly alarmed about the amount of grain being lost to the brown rat. Agricultural author William Marshall, in his 1788 book, *The Rural Economy of Yorkshire*, declared the new species 'a growing evil' and warned: 'should their numbers continue to increase, with the same rapidity they have done since the present breed got a footing in the island', the countryside will have a 'serious calamity' on its hands. Such was the anxiety surrounding rodents there was even talk of a terrifying, fantastical breed of 'killer rat'. After his learned description of the brown rat, Holland added a note of warning: 'there is [...] the bloody rat, which has two claws on the feet instead of one. These rats frequent churchyards, and prey upon corpses; they have been also known when in dwelling houses to seize people in their beds, and to murder children.'

When it came to the brown rat, farmers were particular concerned about their granaries. While black rats and mice could be a pest, farmers often managed to keep their threshed grains safe thanks to the assiduous efforts of farm cats, ratting dogs such as terriers, and barn owls. Many grain barns even had access holes in their gable ends to encourage barn owls to hunt inside. The catastrophic threat presented by brown rats, however, had to be tackled differently.

Stone and brick barns from this time were often adapted to include a mezzanine level or were purpose-built to include a first-floor grain store. More creative, however, was the use of staddle stones such as these, which raised an entire wooden barn two or three feet off the ground. The word 'staddle' comes from the Old English *statho*, meaning stand or base. Farmers realised that although brown rats excelled at most things, climbing upside down wasn't their forte. The staddle's mushroom shape was a particularly effective deterrent; a brown rat might be able to climb up the 'stalk' of the staddle but it struggled to get around the cap.

While some barns with staddle stones predate the eighteenth century, the appearance of many of these extraordinary and historic countryside buildings coincide with the arrival of the brown rat. It's surprising to think that such a small creature had such a profound effect on one of the countryside's most iconic buildings.

66.

LUMBRIC ALUM
18TH CENTURY

The humble earthworm is not only the farmer's friend, but a subterranean superhero. Without these engineers of the earth, our soil would be lifeless and fields barren. Worms recycle decaying organic material, returning nutrients to the tilth. And, with their tireless burrowing, earthworms also keep the soil structure light and perfectly plumped.

It's fascinating, however, to see how our attitudes to earthworms have changed over time. Throughout the eighteenth century, they were considered vermin, a pest that destroyed seeds and damaged crops. Many a horticultural or farmers' gazetteer offered helpful tips on how to rid the soil of its most 'noisome creature'. Remedies included throwing quicklime or salt onto the soil, luring earthworms to the surface during the night with a lantern, or repeatedly rolling soil until it was too compacted to support any kind of life. In 1792 William Marshall, our agricultural author who wrote so alarmingly about the arrival of the brown rat, also made note of a technique for killing earthworms. Developed by Dorsetshire flower growers, it involved making an infusion of walnut leaves to water the flowerbeds. 'The worms presently rise to the surface', concluded Marshall cheerfully, 'and die in apparent agony.'

It wasn't until the early nineteenth century that the burgeoning field of plant science began to recognise the good work done by the earthworm, often coming to blows with established horticultural and medical views. In the 1840s, while one treatise on soil cultivation was radically praising the earthworm for its role in aeration and drainage, gardeners' manuals were still recommending scalding earthworms with quicklime. Meanwhile, the newly emerging world of veterinary science continued to insist that earthworms were 'one of the three sorts of worms that infest the bodies of horses' while simultaneously endorsing earthworm poultices for lameness and sores.

There was, however, one area of life in which earthworms were highly regarded. Or, at least, in brisk demand. This eighteenth-century apothecary bottle contained a potent solution. The label reads 'Lumbric Alum UST', shorthand for *lumbricor* (powdered earthworm), *alum* (potassium aluminium sulphate) and *ustum*, the Latin for 'burnt'. Earthworms had a long and illustrious career as an ingredient in folk healing and 'medical' remedies. Pliny the Elder, writing in the first century, noted that they were employed for a number of ailments. The creature's remarkable ability to survive being chopped in half was deeply unusual and its self-healing abilities were thought to be transferable to the human body. The ashes of burnt earthworms, blended with oil, tar or honey, were believed to fix a whole range of ulcers and open cuts, and even knit broken bones.

Over the centuries, faith in earthworm cures only strengthened. One treatment for jaundice included in an Oxford professor's 1701 book, *Dr. Willis's Receipts for the Cure of all Distempers*, included powdered earthworm, goose dung, ground ivory and saffron. A decade later, Dr Johnson prescribed a poultice for gout made from breadcrumbs, milk, saffron, linseed oil and oil of earthworms (a blend of olive oil, wine and earthworms boiled and strained). A frankly bewildering treatment for deep wounds, offered by German physician Michael Ettmüller, applied a 'Mixture of the Oil of Earthworms, Oil of foxes, Man's Fat and juice of earthworms'.

The second to last of these ingredients was as hideous as it sounds. Between the sixteenth and the end of the nineteenth century, human fat was believed to have remarkable healing qualities. Traded under the respectable-sounding Latin title *Axungia hominis*, (*axungia* being the word for soft fat), human fat was boiled and rendered from the bodies gathered from executions and dissecting theatres, earning it the folk name 'poor sinner's fat'. Thankfully perhaps, *Axungia hominis* would have been too expensive for most country dwellers. Instead, home-made remedies and magical 'cures' were often the only recourse for ailments and wounds, frequently brought on by the sheer hard graft of rural life. The owner of our next object, however, would need a miracle to come back from his injuries.

67.

COAT FROM QUINTFALL HILL

C. 1700

In 1920, two peat cutters were working at Quintfall Hill in Caithness, the most north-easterly county on the Scottish mainland. To their horror, as they dug, they discovered human remains. Lying before them was the skeleton of a man, with arms flat against the side of his body. His skull had clearly received a heavy blow, killing him outright, before he was placed in the waterlogged ground.

To the peat cutters' amazement, the body was dressed in a complete set of clothing from the turn of the eighteenth century, much of it in a remarkable state of preservation. The unfortunate fellow was wearing a flat bonnet, low-heeled leather shoes and knitted stockings. To keep himself warm, he also wore two pairs of breeches and two coats, one on top of the other. This object, the wonderfully intact outer coat, fitted tightly around his waist and buttoned over an inner coat of a similar shape and fabric.

The Quintfall Hill find is extraordinary. Textile historians rarely unearth historic clothes in such good condition, especially those that belonged to ordinary rural folk. The discovery suggests that people who worked outdoors often had to layer their clothes, perhaps even wearing everything they owned. Wool, as a fabric, reigned supreme;

apart from the man's shoes, everything at Quintfall Hill – from the bonnet to the breeches – was made from it. Even the buttons were woollen, fashioned from scraps of cloth stretched over a small wad of fleece. The clothes had also been repeatedly mended. On the breeches, for example, holes at the knees had been patched up. When these reinforcements had worn thin again, through wear and tear, Quintfall Hill man had decided to turn his breeches back to front. The pattern of wear on the breeches also indicated that he was constantly crouching, or working with something rubbing on his knees.

Quintfall Hill man's death and burial in a peat bog remains an unsolved murder mystery. A leather purse was found in his only pocket containing nineteen 'bawbees' or Scottish sixpences, so researchers suspect that robbery wasn't the motive. What's less of a mystery, however, is that he was found in a peat bog. Now known as 'Flow Country', the vast, rolling expanse of peatland that stretches across Caithness and neighbouring Sutherland covers an impressive 1,500 square miles. Many parts of the British countryside are covered with peat bogs, with some stark regional and national differences. While Wales has only 4 per cent of its land covered in peat bogs, England has around a tenth. By comparison, both Scotland and Northern Ireland are blessed with nearer 25 per cent.

Peat bogs are unique and pivotal to the story of the countryside. Peat – a spongy material formed by the partial rotting of organic matter – has been exploited by rural communities for thousands of years. From the Somerset Levels to the Peak District, the East Anglian Fens to the Norfolk Broads, Britain's regions have undergone peat extraction since the Neolithic period. During the Iron Age, peat cutting seems to have been considered so important that it may even be one of the reasons bog bodies were sacrificed to the wetlands. By 1700, when Quintfall Hill man met his demise, many rural folk were taking blocks of peat from the landscape, a right in medieval times known as *turbary*.

In late spring through summer, peat would be cut into rectangular slabs – called turves – and stacked to dry. The most common use of peat was for fuel. It burnt slowly and consistently, making it easy to smother at night and reignite in the morning. A modest household might spend a week every year cutting turves, and burning a thousand a year at home, but peat was also useful as a building material, cattle bedding, fertiliser and fuel for industry, especially smelting and burning lime. Whether Quintfall Hill man was out cutting turves when he died isn't known but his clothes may be a giveaway. Techniques and tools vary between regions but many people cut peat horizontally, pushing a turf spade with their knees, or thighs, in a crouching position to give maximum force. No wonder people got holes in their breeches.

68.

LANCASHIRE LAMBING CHAIR

C. 1750

Peat was a lifeline for shepherds working out in the field. Hill farmers who raised sheep often relied on moving their flocks to higher ground, during the summer, where they could make use of marginal grazing in good weather. Shepherds could spend weeks, if not months, away with their flocks, sheltering in mobile huts or summer bothies, and keeping warm by burning peat turves that had been cut and stacked the previous year.

The role of shepherd is perhaps one of the oldest occupations in the countryside. Sheep need plenty of pasture. Since the domestication of sheep, shepherds have been entrusted with the important task of moving flocks between grazing areas, protecting them from theft and wild predators and orchestrating the major events in the ovine year, such as shearing and 'tupping': putting the ewes to a ram.

Of all the key events in the shepherd's yearly cycle, however, none carried such significance as lambing time. Tupping traditionally took place around Bonfire Night, on 5 November, which meant that ewes gave birth around April Fool's Day, on the first day of the month. The shepherds' rule of 'in with a bang and out like fools' meant that lambs were delivered just as the fresh spring grass sprang into life, ready to feed lactating ewes, and their weaned lambs, a month later.

Traditional 'primitive' breeds such as Soays or Hebridean sheep remain relatively unchanged from their wild mouflon ancestor and give birth easily by themselves, producing just one lamb. Thanks to centuries of sheep breeding for both wool and meat, however, many domesticated ewes have twins or even triplets. This increase in births, both in number and weight, has its downsides and has, for hundreds of years, forced shepherds to intervene in difficult deliveries or in reviving sickly lambs.

This beautiful, eighteenth-century 'lambing chair' speaks of the vigilance needed to be a shepherd. It allowed the shepherd to sit up all night, resting by an open fire, protected from the night's chill by the chair's wings and high back. The lack of any soft upholstery is typical country pragmatism, but the box sides kept draughts away and trapped the heat of the hearth. Lambing chairs display some delightful regional variations – some have hoods, for extra cosiness, while many had storage underneath, like this one from the Fylde coast in Lancashire. Large pull-out drawers were said to be used for keeping sickly lambs warm, in front of the fire, while smaller compartments might hold a reviving bottle of alcohol, the Bible or the shepherd's knitting.

Necessity affected the design of each lambing chair, and, indeed, that of another of the countryside's most iconic pieces of vernacular furniture. 'Welsh stick chairs' are a fine example of design dictated by a judicious use of materials. Essentially a stool, with whittled or turned spokes for the back and arms, stick chairs were often made using foraged timber found in hedgerows, such as oak or ash. Irish stick chairs are frequently called 'hedge chairs' for that reason. The people who made stick chairs weren't necessarily trained woodworkers. Many rural folk would have had the rudimentary skills needed to fashion a basic stick chair, but some were made by those bearing the now-long-lost job title of 'hedge carpenter' – a low-paid craftsman who also made the village's fence rails, posts and gates.

Perhaps the most beautiful of vernacular seats was the 'Orkney chair'. In the islands off the northern tip of Scotland, the lack of woodlands and scarcity of timber encouraged residents to come up with ingenious solutions. Crofters (people who subsisted on tenanted smallholdings) scoured the shoreline collecting driftwood to make the bare bones of the chair frame. The back, sides and seat were woven with straw left over from growing oats for food and animal fodder. Similar in design to a lambing chair, with a high, often hooded back and winged arms, the Orkney chair was, however, peculiarly low to the ground. By the seventeenth century most houses, including modest cottages, had a chimney or smoke-hood to take away the fumes. Orkney crofters stuck though to their rural traditions, however, and continued to burn their fires in the middle of the floor. The Orkney chair ingeniously kept its sitter close to the fire but low enough to the ground to dodge the smoke that curled upwards towards the roof.

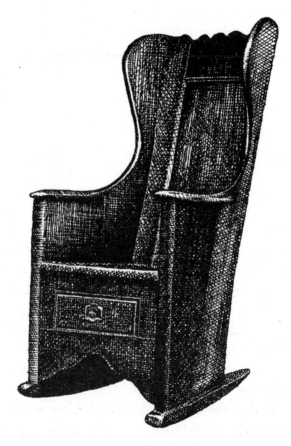

69.

PORTABLE STRONG BOX

C.17TH–18TH CENTURY

Throughout the history of the countryside, the spectre of poverty hung over many of its inhabitants. Having a large, loving family or a highly skilled trade provided no insurance against those events in life that could spell ruin. From failed harvests to nasty accidents, the death of a spouse to unemployment, it wasn't until the twentieth century that ordinary people could rely on a humane, well-funded welfare state. The most vulnerable in society – the elderly, widowed, orphaned and infirm – received little formal support until then.

The 'problem of the poor' had been tackled in different ways over the centuries. In medieval times, church law required that every person in a parish donate a tenth, a 'tithe', of their income or produce. Out of this financial pot, churches were expected to set aside a certain amount each year for poor relief. Monastic hospitals gave alms to the poor and sick, while people with infectious diseases, such as the plague or leprosy, also sought sanctuary in religious houses. Poverty was, in general, viewed as bad luck, not an inherent moral failing.

From the middle of the fourteenth century, attitudes to the poor began to change. *The Statute of Labourers*, enacted after the Black Death, made it clear that the state wouldn't tolerate begging from the able-bodied poor, and divided people into the 'deserving' and the 'undeserving' – an idea that still informs welfare policy today. Further legislation over the centuries only cemented this belief, with laws such as the *Vagabonds and Beggars Act* of 1494 requiring the homeless poor, 'the idle and suspected persons', to be put in village stocks for three days and nights and then sent back to the parish of their birth.

The Elizabethan Poor Law of 1601 made further distinctions between people in poverty and, more importantly, what society should do with them, a codification that went on to influence policy for the next three hundred years. The Poor Law established two principles: that every parish was responsible for dealing with its own poor using money raised through local poor rates, and that parishes should only support their own residents.

While some poor families were helped through 'outdoor relief', which allowed them to stay in their own homes, many had to fall on the mercy of institutions or 'indoor relief'. The distinction between the deserving and undeserving poor manifested itself over the decades in the architecture of rural villages and market towns. While poor-houses, which later became known as workhouses, were designed to set the 'idle poor' to work and create harsh conditions to act as a deterrent, almshouses represented a different mode of thought. They were built and funded by charities, and their residents were often hand-picked from the community as people regarded as having 'good character'. These would include the elderly, disabled and infirm, including members of trade guilds who could no longer manage in their own homes. Some were designed specifically for widows, or married couples, but the rules often required people to attend church or pray, practise teetotalism and wear certain clothes in return for board and a small living allowance.

Funding came from different places. Trade guilds levied their members for donations, and local landowners often bequeathed alms-houses to their own communities as part of their legacy. Churches would also collect money for the poor.

The urge to pilfer donations must have been tempting for members of the community who often lived close to the breadline themselves.

PORTABLE STRONG BOX

This strongbox, which was used to collect donations during services, has three padlocks, each with its own key. Each lock was the responsibility of a different keyholder, to prevent alms being stolen, and the box could only be opened when the priest and both churchwardens were present. With a national rural police force more than a century away from being established, solving crimes such as theft was often left to local initiative. As is clear from the next item, however, villagers were frequently more likely to consult a 'cunning person' than a local constable.

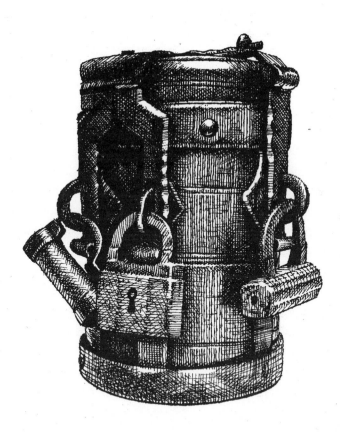

70.

SHEEP'S HEART STUCK WITH PINS AND NAILS
DATE UNKNOWN

At the end of the nineteenth century, a farmer in Chipstable, Somerset, was cleaning out his chimney. To his amazement, amid the soot he discovered more than thirty very old, desiccated animal hearts pushed up the flue. As one newspaper noted at the time: 'Some of the hearts were thickly covered with prickles. How they came in the chimney is not yet known.'

The farming life has always been one of triumphs and disasters. For centuries, sudden illness among livestock was attributed to witchcraft. The only way to tackle the problem, believed many rural folk, was to create a counter-spell. One of the more bizarre rituals for sickly sheep or cows was to stick pins into a dead animal's heart and then either burn it, bury it or thrust it up the farmhouse chimney, a place believed to be a vulnerable entry point for evil spirits. The act of piercing the heart with spikes was designed to cause excruciating pain for the witch, who would only gain relief if she lifted her spell.

People who looked after livestock were particularly superstitious, perhaps because the stakes were so high. The death of an animal was potentially ruinous; 'cattle plague', for example, an infectious disease now known as rinderpest, could decimate a herd. Outbreaks in the eighteenth century commonly led to mortality rates of 90 per cent or more. This period was a particularly interesting time for veterinary medicine, one in which the discipline emerged as distinct from human medicine with the establishment of veterinary schools in London in 1791, and Edinburgh in 1823. In its infancy, however, the profession was often no better equipped to treat illness than were farriers or herbalists. It also had to compete with traditional cures from 'cunning folk'.

Superstition and religion existed side by side in rural communities. Many people believed in the potency of spirits, both good and ill, and ideas about magic were often contradictory. Witches were thought to practise spiteful magic and were often blamed for sudden and catastrophic events, especially the loss of a child, a bad harvest or the unexpected death of livestock. 'Cunning' or 'wise folk', however, were different. These women and men, who dabbled in healing, spells and fortune-telling, were a valued part of a countryside community. Villagers would consult them on many different matters, including common ailments, relationship problems or finding lost or stolen items.

While veterinary medicine slowly gained public recognition over the nineteenth century, many farmers and animal owners continued to rely on folk magic and superstition well into the 1950s. On farms, it was common practice to hang 'hagstones' (stones with a naturally occurring hole) above the stable door or tied around a horse's neck to prevent them being ridden to exhaustion by witches overnight. Salt, stale urine and soot were also routinely added to animal 'cures' as ingredients with special powers. These potions were then often applied in three ways: sprinkled across the body, thrust down the throat or dribbled in the ear. In 1830, for example, one Yorkshire wiseman advocated a potent charm that combined the symbolism of hearts and pins, with the potency of sodium chloride: 'Bleed the sick animall and dip in among the Blood of som hair Cut of the animals mane tail and 4 Quarters then put in 3 Spoonfuls of Salt then have a Sheep's heart stuck with 9 new pins 9 new needles 9 small nails then roll the heart well in the blood and at 12 at night put the heart on a Good fire.'

Fire and smoke were thought to be particularly cleansing, a notion as old as time itself. Farmers often drove their cattle through bonfire fumes, to banish disease. In 1850, just two years after the first veterinary legislation was passed to control sheep pox, Scottish farmers were tackling an outbreak of livestock disease in their own time-honoured fashion. In Banffshire, one farmer was recorded burning a pig and sprinkling its ashes over his farm buildings, while in Orkney a cattle keeper was advised by the local 'cow doctor' to pick his finest beast and burn it over a roaring bonfire to save the rest of the herd.

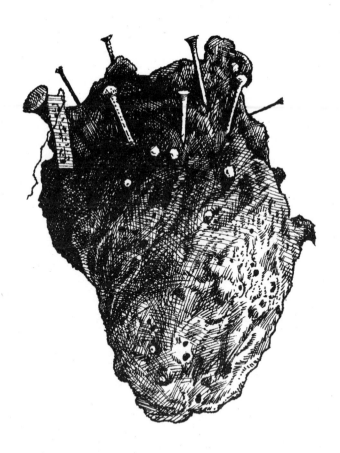

71.

TOBACCO CANISTER
1793

While farmers were busy driving their livestock through the fumes of 'cleansing' bonfires, British physicians were turning their attention to a different kind of smoke. Tobacco had first arrived in Europe from the New World in the sixteenth century. The leaves of the *Nicotiana* plant – a member of the nightshade family – had been used for centuries across the Americas, where smoking was central to many ceremonies and healing rituals. Many Western doctors were also convinced of its efficacy.

In 1618, the Royal College of Physicians first recommended smoking tobacco to counteract the symptoms of a cold. Half a century later, when Britain was in the grips of yet another outbreak of the plague, physicians advised all and sundry to start puffing away. The plague, it was believed, was spread by sickly air or 'miasmas'. Anyone who could stomach it was instructed to smoke indoors and to fumigate their house and clothes, while those who were charged with disposing of the dead also kept a clay pipe firmly clamped in their mouth to ward off infection. Even schoolchildren at Eton College were forced to smoke during the outbreak; those who refused were flogged.

Smoking or snorting weren't the only ways to administer tobacco's therapeutic benefits. Physicians were also fond of blowing smoke into patients' rectums, a treatment known as *insufflation*. It was commonly used for stomach pain and, inexplicably, to resuscitate victims of drowning and check whether the dead were truly deceased. Indeed, for a brief period, tobacco enema boxes were stationed at handy intervals along many of the rivers in capital cities in Europe, rather like lifebuoys today.

Most people, however, used *Nicotiana* for the sheer pleasure of it. During the seventeenth and eighteenth centuries, the fashion for smoking was often contingent on class and gender. For men of all stations, smoking in taverns and coffee houses was a perfectly respectable activity, while women from middling and wealthier backgrounds were expected to refrain. Objects such as this tobacco canister, however, show that the norms weren't always adhered to. Women from all walks of life did smoke, but often in the privacy of the domestic sphere. Jane Gibbs from East Sussex, the owner of this 'canester', was clearly wealthy enough to commission her own container in 1793, a treasured object that would have stored her personal supply of loose tobacco.

Working-class women and children in the countryside, however, smoked freely. While travelling through the West Country in 1688, Dutch statesman Constantijn Huygens was surprised to find rural 'women smoking without shame, even young girls of thirteen or fourteen'. Just a few years later, Celia Fiennes, writing in her diary about the customs of Cornwall, noted 'universall smoaking, both men women and children have all their pipes of tobacco in their mouths and soe sit round the fire smoaking'. No age, it seems, was too young to start. In 1702, Leeds writer Ralph Thoresby recorded his brother's 'sickly child of three years old fill its pipe of tobacco and smoke it as audfarandly [old-fashionedly] as a man of three score'.

Indeed, during the seventeenth century, smoking was so popular that many British farmers and retired seamen tried their hand at *Nicotiana*-growing on home soil. Pamphlets such as *An Advice how to Plant Tobacco in England*, published in 1615, helped the crop to flourish, and by the middle of the century, around forty English counties and many parts of Scotland were growing enough tobacco to sell to

Holland and Belgium. Thriving domestic production, however, soon attracted the attention of British owners of slave plantations. Home-grown tobacco was in direct competition with New World exports, a conflict that the government attempted to resolve with a 1652 law banning its cultivation on British soil.

Many counties initially ignored the ban, largely because tobacco was so profitable, but increasingly punitive punishments had all but stubbed out domestically grown tobacco by the end of the century. Yorkshire attempted a brief revival in the 1700s, an experiment that ended in crippling fines and imprisonment for its growers, and it wasn't until the beginning of the twentieth century that the ban on tobacco growing was finally lifted. By then, though, the idea of *Nicotiana* as a viable, profitable British crop had dissipated. Another member of the nightshade family, however, was to make an altogether more lasting impression on the countryside.

JANE GIBBS HER CANESTER SEPTEMBER 6

72.

POTATO RAKE
LATE 18TH CENTURY

John Evelyn, who penned *Sylva: Or A Discourse of Forest Trees* in 1664, also had a thing or two to say about vegetables. In his 1699 gourmet, *Acetaria, A Discourse of Sallets*, he drew the readers' attention to a new, exciting ingredient and possible ways to cook it. The novel potato, he wrote, when pickled, is an 'aggreable Sallet'. But, he continued teasingly, there was a better way to enjoy the humble tuber: 'roasted under the Embers, or otherwise, open'd with a Knife, the Pulp is butter'd in the Skin, of which it will take up a good Quantity, and is seasoned with a little Salt and Pepper'. He also added, with a final and rather surprising flourish: you could eat 'them with Sugar together in the Skin, which has a pleasant Crimpness. They are also stew'd and bak'd in Pyes.'

Despite this delicious description, the potato took a while to catch on. Writing a hundred years later in 1799, agriculturalist John Tuke – on his travels around the British countryside – noted that potatoes had only really started to become a feature of the farming landscape in the 1760s, 'before which time they were little known beyond the garden of the gentleman'. In the forty years between then and now, he added, the potato had proliferated 'from the table of the rich to the daily board of every cottage', a triumph of cheap and nutritious sustenance. The simplest way to roast them was in the embers of a dying hearth, crisped to perfection before being scooped out with the help of this object. It's a potato rake, a utensil now unseen in all but the most nostalgic of kitchens but once ubiquitous across rural households.

Potatoes were just one of a number of new experiments being trialled by British farmers from the eighteenth century onwards. Many different fields of learning were expanding their knowledge – astronomy, chemistry and medicine to name but a few. Ambitious, enthusiastic farmers such as Arthur Young began publishing their own ideas about 'scientific agriculture', the application of selective breeding, new machinery, produce such as potatoes, and radical ways of rotating crops for maximum productivity.

Since medieval times, farmers had left a third of their fields unplanted or 'fallow' at any one time, to recover the soil's nutrients. Over the course of three years, a field might have a cereal such as wheat in the first year, legumes such as peas or beans in the second, and lay fallow for the third. Rotating crops and leaving a field to rest helped restore the soil's fertility and stop the build-up of pests that can happen when one crop is grown on the same land year after year. Farmers in the Low Countries, however, had developed a system of inter-planting turnips and clover to replace three-field rotation. Adopted by British farmers in the eighteenth century, the new four-field rotation had, for example, wheat in the first year, barley in the second, turnips in the third, and finally clover. The turnips and clover fixed nitrogen into the soil, helping it to recover, but also provided fodder for animals over winter, which in turn yielded more milk, wool, meat and manure. Regions of the countryside where cereal crops didn't thrive could make use of new introductions such as the potato, rotating on a different system with legumes, brassicas and other crops.

The four-field rotation system – along with other developments in agriculture including mechanisation and land drainage – transformed the amount of food the countryside could produce, more than doubling agricultural output per farm labourer between 1650 and 1850. This 'Agricultural Revolution' and its intensification of farming allowed the country's population to double from around 5 million people in 1700 (not much more than it had been in Roman times) to 9 million just a century later. The look of the countryside also changed, with fallow fields all but disappearing from the landscape by the end of the nineteenth century. And while farm productivity increased, the plants, invertebrates and birds that had thrived on fallow land – such as lapwings and curlews – were left with nowhere to go. Furthermore, as we'll see in our next two objects, many people who once relied on traditional systems of farming also began to feel displaced.

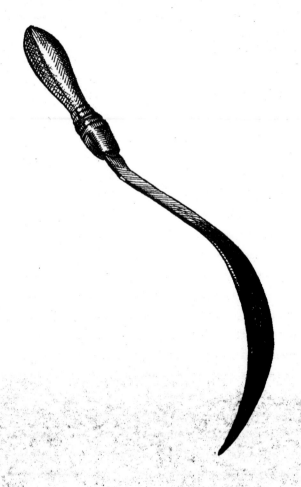

73.

PORTRAIT OF ROBERT BAKEWELL'S 'TWO-POUNDER'

LATE 18TH CENTURY

At the end of the eighteenth century, a new style of portrait became wildly popular among the countryside gentry. For decades, wealthy landowners had commissioned paintings of hunting and horse racing, passions that consumed inordinate amounts of time and money. With the emergence of scientific agriculture, however, many 'gentlemen farmers' had begun to dabble in livestock breeding, competing to produce prize-winning beasts.

One of the most notable was Robert Bakewell, born in 1725 to a successful tenant farming family in Dishley, Leicestershire. As a young man, Bakewell had travelled across England, Ireland and Holland, picking up new agricultural ideas and learning about livestock anatomy. In the 1760s, he took over the reins of the family farm from his able and ambitious father and quickly set to work 'improving' the livestock. By choosing and mating animals based on certain traits, he only allowed the most productive or largest to breed. Bakewell also perfected the controversial practice of 'in-and-in' breeding, the mating of very closely related animals, even parent and offspring, to exaggerate desirable traits such as carcass quality or milk yield.

Bakewell was one of the first to intensively breed cattle and sheep for meat, rather than traction or wool respectively. Overweight and oversize animals presented a solution to the problem of how to feed the country's ever-expanding urban population. Of the livestock he improved, two became particularly well known – the Longhorn cattle and the New Leicester sheep. Bakewell also developed a system of hiring his animals out for stud, a business model that earned him huge sums of money and kept improved breeds out of the financial reach of many small-scale farmers.

One of Bakewell's celebrated rams was known as 'Two-Pounder' and is pictured here in a painting by little-known Nottinghamshire artist Joseph Digby-Curtis. The fecund ram reputedly earned Bakewell 800 guineas in a single season – a staggering amount of money that would have taken a skilled labourer over twenty years to earn. Aware of the large sums of cash exchanging hands for improved stock, others soon followed suit. The biggest, most corpulent prize-winning animals were often celebrated in portraits commissioned by their owners. Pictures of monstrously overfed pigs, cows and sheep were painted side-on, to exaggerate the beasts' corpulence, while heads, tails and legs were often dwarfed in comparison, making them look comically unbalanced to the modern eye.

Bakewell and other livestock improvers focused on the capacity of an animal to mature quickly and 'acquire a state of fatness'. While improved breeding certainly met market demands in terms of the quantity of meat or milk an animal could produce, rampant inbreeding came with its own issues. New Leicester sheep, for example, had notoriously low fertility rates and were branded by some farmers as 'delicate and unhealthy', unable to cope with poor weather. Their enormous body weight also caused mobility problems, with one farmer describing them as 'waddling toads'. New Leicester meat was also described as insipid and fatty but the urban poor couldn't afford to be picky. Bakewell himself conceded, 'I do not breed mutton for gentlemen, but for the public', and found that his fatty sheep also

222

provided plenty of tallow, an ingredient increasingly used for lighting, soap and lubrication for early steam engines.

While prices for improved sheep continued to climb towards the end of the eighteenth century, many rural areas were struggling for survival. Two decades of poor harvests, high food prices and falling agricultural wages forced some impoverished country dwellers to turn to the theft of livestock – then a capital crime. A century earlier, only fifty offences were punishable by death. By 1800 it had soared to over two hundred, including many crimes against landowners' property such as stealing sheep, robbing a rabbit warren and cutting down trees. Age was no barrier to conviction or the noose, it seems. Records during this time show death sentences applied to perpetrators in their eighties and children as young as seven. Up against such challenges, it is perhaps no surprise that some people looked for other ways to escape ...

74.

ASTLEY CIRCUS POSTER

1784

Few people described the thrill of the circus better than Charles Dickens. In 1841, in *Master Humphrey's Clock*, his words captured the delicious tension of a show about to begin; 'with all the paint, gilding, and looking-glass, the vague smell of horses suggestive of coming wonders, the curtain that hid such gorgeous mysteries, the clean white sawdust down in the circus'. With glamorous, exotic entertainments few and far between in the countryside, the arrival of the travelling circus was perhaps one of the most electrifying events in the rural year. While fairs and market-days had, for centuries, attracted jugglers, bear baiters and other performers, it wasn't until the end of the eighteenth century that the circus fully arrived.

Philip Astley was born in Newcastle-under-Lyme, in the Midlands, in 1742. His father was a cabinetmaker but had a tempestuous relationship with his son, prompting Philip at the age of seventeen to leave home and enlist in the Light Dragoons, a formidable cavalry regiment. He turned out to be rather good with horses, both an expert rider and a gifted trainer. After leaving the army in 1768, Astley secured a plot of land in Lambeth, which was then open fields, and started a riding school where he gave lessons in the mornings and performed feats of horsemanship after lunch. He marked out a circular arena for his display. Not only did it give every audience member a good view but the act of galloping in circles generated the perfect amount of centrifugal force to help him stand on his horse.

His performances were an immediate success and Astley began to add other exciting or comedic acts, a technique already employed by theatres to fill gaps in their running order. By 1770, he was offering a show that dazzled audiences with an intoxicating blend of equestrian tricks and stunt riding, acrobatic feats, pantomime, and clowns – the modern circus was born. When he wasn't entertaining audiences in the London, Astley toured across Britain, Ireland and mainland Europe. Our object, a poster for his Parisian 'Amphitheatre Anglais', performed with his son John, shows the breadth and ambition of their show. It boasts of 'two hundred feats of strength, flexibility and balance', all on horseback, with musical delights, parades, sword shows, staged fights, tomfoolery and trumpet fanfares all thrown in for good measure.

Competitors soon followed Astley's example. Circus performances, including Astley's, were originally performed in wooden amphitheatres. In 1825, an American called Joshuah Purdy Brown became the first person to use a canvas tent, the forerunner of the 'big top'. The circus had come to America in the 1790s with British equestrian John Bill Ricketts. Ricketts, with an entourage of tumblers, rope-dancers and clowns, made his debut to an eager audience in Philadelphia. The show was a knock-out success but America at the time didn't have enough large cities that could host a permanent circus. To make any money, circus troupes had to take their show on the road, performing to rural audiences and frontier settlements. Travelling shows needed portable venues and Purdy Brown's canvas big top provided the ideal solution.

During the nineteenth century, circuses became wildly popular among British audiences. Travelling shows moved from county to county, helped in no small part by the arrival of the railways from the 1840s onwards. One particularly successful show, George Sanger's Circus, boasted that there was not a place in England with a population of more than a hundred people that had not been visited by the show. The whiff of danger, bright lights and sparkling costumes wowed rural audiences, but it was the menageries of animals that many came to gawp at. Sanger had started his act modestly, training finches, mice and hares to walk tiny tightropes and fire miniature cannons, but by the 1870s he had a travelling show that visited over two hundred towns every nine-month season. On the move, Sanger's Circus dragged two miles' worth of carriages, living wagons and wild animals along for the ride, including more than a hundred and fifty horses. As we'll find out next, whether circus horses lived better lives than their country cousins remained to be seen.

Puc Terailler du Mufrjaane le Harbert - Gezzel de Alu

LES TROIS DERNIERS JOURS DE REPRESENTATION A PARIS.

75.

STAFFORDSHIRE HORSE

C. 1780–90

When the Domesday Book was compiled, over 90 per cent of the draught power in the countryside was provided by oxen. By the end of the nineteenth century, to see an ox pulling a plough or cart would have seemed a quaint anachronism.

A hundred years earlier, at the end of eighteenth century, many of the issues that had prevented horses from galloping ahead as the most useful animal on the farm had been resolved. Traditionally, oxen were the weightlifters of the countryside and excelled at sheer pulling power. This made them the ideal beast to drag heavy ploughs through difficult soil. The invention of niftier, lighter ploughs in the 1700s – ones that could be pulled along by a lively two-horse duo instead of four to eight oxen with a team of men – appealed to many landowners and farmers keen to cut costs and speed up cultivation.

The virtue of oxen compared to horses had always been that they were cheap to feed as long as you had plenty of pasture, often in the form of common or waste land. Oxen thrived where grass was plentiful but horses needed plenty of extra food, especially oats, to keep pace with their bovine cousins. As farming methods changed, large areas of grassland were enclosed. The countryside also began to produce more grain for food and fodder, allowing the horse to steal the lead.

People who used oxen around the farm traditionally put them to work around the age of two and sold them off to specialist grazers for fattening up around the age of six. Retired oxen produced delicious roasting joints, which were quickly snapped up by wealthy households and caterers, or taken to one of the many large Christmas markets around the country. Thanks to the legacy of Robert Bakewell and other livestock improvers, however, cattle could reach slaughter weight in just two or three years. Demand for cheaper, lower-quality meat, from younger animals, acted as a disincentive to keeping older bovines, especially draught oxen, which were three times the age of most beef cattle.

Horses were also more useful than oxen on roads. Trade between the countryside and urban centres had gained traction in the eighteenth century. Rural hinterlands provided growing towns and cities not only with fruit, grain, milk and many other foodstuffs, but also with timber, building materials, coal, minerals and many other necessities. Poor roads had long hampered long-distance travel but the Turnpike Act in 1706, which was followed by a flurry of road construction, meant that by the end of the century around fifteen thousand miles of toll roads had been created. Shoed horses could cope with hard, stony surfaces but oxen struggled. It wasn't impossible to shoe an ox, just ruddy difficult, thanks to the peculiarity of cattle's split toes. And, even if you managed it, the ox isn't a speedy beast. Averaging two miles an hour, with a limit of ten miles a day, the ponderous, gentle ox couldn't compete with the brisk, staminous horse and cart.

Horses were also used to transport goods across rural areas, even places that wheeled vehicles couldn't reach. The Potteries in Staffordshire, for example, had been a centre of the ceramic industry since the seventeenth century. The region was already rich in potter's clay and coal, essential for making and firing ceramics, but in the early 1700s, Staffordshire potters had begun to import different clays and flints from the south-west to expand their repertoire. The Potteries, however, lay miles from any navigable rivers and much of their raw material, and the finished ceramics, had to be carried, laboriously, to and from the kilns by packhorses.

Many of the statuettes crafted by the Staffordshire artisans were sentimental renderings of countryside creatures and bucolic scenes, destined for a new urban market wanting to be reminded of their rural roots. Spirited, charming horses, such as this object, were particularly popular but a far cry from the tough, short-legged ponies that were forced to lug 100 kilograms of pots and figurines over twenty miles a day. As we'll see from our next object, however, all this was about to change.

76.

PONTCYSYLLTE AQUEDUCT

1805

Ceramics made Staffordshire entrepreneur, Josiah Wedgwood, fabulously wealthy. One of his less well-known accomplishments, however, was his role in the Trent and Mersey Canal. Wedgwood was frustrated by the costs of bringing raw materials, especially coal, to and from his furnaces. He was also horrified by the constant breakages of finished goods in transit, an expensive problem when fragile ceramics were transported by packhorse.

The Trent and Mersey Canal was designed by engineer James Brindley, who had cut his teeth on one of Britain's first canal projects – the Bridgewater Canal. Opened in 1761, the Bridgewater Canal had been commissioned by the young Duke of Bridgewater in a shrewd move to cut the cost of transporting coal from his mines west of Manchester into the heart of the city. The canal soon proved the concept worked, connecting heavy industry with waterways, an idea that could potentially benefit the Potteries. Wedgwood duly raised the investment to pay for the Trent and Mersey Canal and, in 1777, it opened.

Canals are one of the most picturesque features of the modern countryside, a by-word for slow living and connection to nature. And yet their purpose was always to facilitate the sweat and grind of heavy industry. When the Trent and Mersey Canal opened, it was the biggest civil engineering project of its day and, at ninety-four miles long, it went on to form one of the major arteries of Britain's canal network. By 1790, the country had a web of canals that, for the first time in history, created a national transport system that linked the Rivers Mersey, Trent, Severn and Thames. By the 1830s, the countryside had nearly four thousand miles of canals.

The relatively short six-mile stretch of the Bridgewater route had alone cost the Duke the equivalent of £24 million. The expense of building canals was eye-watering, largely because engineers had to overcome Britain's gloriously undulating countryside. Remarkable feats of tunnelling and lock construction overcame many obstacles but the most impressive features from this extraordinary period are the country's aqueducts. The first was Barton Aqueduct, opened in 1761 by James Brindley, who immediately 'retired to his bed for several days' when the engineer's new structure almost instantly began to sag. More successful and notable, however, is this object – unarguably the largest in this book – the Pontcysyllte Aqueduct in north-east Wales. Dubbed the 'stream in the sky', this extraordinary structure measures over 300 metres in length and straddles the River Dee. A testament both to British engineering and the giddy sums of money thrown at canals, it is not only the longest aqueduct in the country but, at 38 metres off the valley floor, the highest anywhere in the world.

The fillip for such huge investments of money, however, was the promise of a good return. Britain's most important canals were built, not by government money, but private investment. Merchants, mine owners, and textile and pottery giants hoped their canals would soon pay for themselves with drastically reduced transport costs. Speculators invested their cash hoping for healthy dividends from canal tolls. Many agricultural producers also benefited. Grain could now be floated to flour mills, beer to bottling factories, fruit to jam factories and marmalade makers. Even cheese was carried along Britain's new canals. In return, farmers also found that the costs of raw materials for use around the farm – such a chalk fertiliser or coal – also dropped.

The benefit of canals wasn't only their connectivity. While one packhorse could manage around 100 kg in its panniers, or a horse and cart between 500 and 2000 kg depending on the state of the road, a canal boat pulled by a single horse along a tow path could drag between 30 and 50 tonnes, or 30,000 and 50,000 kg. The staggering volume of material that could be conveyed by canal, compared to road transport, drastically cut the cost of moving materials and finished goods across the countryside. Within a year of opening, the Bridgewater Canal had cut the price of coal in Manchester by half. The Trent and Mersey Canal had a similar effect for the Potteries and, to Wedgwood's delight, all but ended the problem of smashed pots and headless figurines.

77.

BIRD SCARER
EARLY 19ᵀᴴ CENTURY

By the age of seven, George Edwards, who went on to become a British Member of Parliament, had been employed in eight different jobs. Born in Norfolk in 1850, into a poor agricultural family, Edwards had been put to work at the tender age of six. In a later biography, one of the few detailed first-hand accounts of life as a rural child labourer, he vividly described his punishing routine.

His first job, which he secured after the entire family had endured a winter in the workhouse, was bird scaring. When farmers sowed their cereal crops – in either spring or autumn – they paid young children to act as human scarecrows. Edwards was given a shilling for a seven-day week (about 40 pence a day) to stand in the field and constantly rattle a bird scarer similar to this one. A wooden tongue flicked over the cog as it revolved, creating a loud clacking to frighten away crows and pigeons. The work was lonely, boring and, if it was spring, wet and cold.

Edwards worked through March until early summer, when the farmer no longer needed the seeds protecting. He then quickly found a job managing an entire herd of cows, taking them from field to milking parlour twice a day. When harvest time came in August, he earned thruppence making ties for sheathes and leading the horse and cart, laden with wheat, back to the farm. After harvest, Edwards and his mother went gleaning in the stubble, an ancient practice of scavenging for leftover cereal grains, before he returned to cow-keeping until autumn. Towards the back end of the year, he worked again as a bird scarer and, with frozen hands, cleaned muddy turnips in the snow. And he did all this, he wrote, with a small piece of bread in his stomach from breakfast, no lunch, and just two slices of bread, a meagre piece of cheese and an onion for supper.

Edwards was by no means unique. During the late eighteenth and nineteenth centuries, around a tenth of the countryside workforce was children. While the average age of a rural child labourer was ten years old, many were younger. Wages for children were just a fraction of the going rate for an adult, often as little as one-fifth, and many even worked for free as an extra pair of hands for a busy parent. Other rural industries, such as brickmaking, chimney sweeping and mining, also employed children in their droves.

Decades before Edwards had even been born, social commentators had expressed concerns about the country's growing reliance on child labour. In 1840 Parliament had established its Royal Commission of Inquiry into Children's Employment, after talking to many of the country's working children, some as young as five years old, to find out about their daily lives and diet. The Commission covered mining and colliery regions, but also places that employed children for metalwork, pottery making, hosiery, tobacco and many other trades.

The results of the Commission's report, published in 1842, shocked the nation. It contained countless stories of brutality, ill health and the avaricious exploitation of the country's youth by many of its most successful industries. Legislation such as the Mines Act of 1842 and the Factory Act of 1844 attempted to curb the worst excesses, but children in the countryside were almost entirely ignored despite constituting the lion's share of under-age labour. In the 1851 Census, excluding London, of the 560,000 working children aged between ten and fourteen, 60 per cent were employed in farming and fisheries, compared to just 25 per cent in factory work. It wasn't until the 1870 Education Act, which made school compulsory for children aged five to thirteen (or ten if you were very bright), that rural children slowly filtered from crop field to classroom.

Until that point, however, countryside children like Edwards were expected to fulfil an onerous roll-call of duties, from leading horses and driving carts to threshing, looking after livestock, picking hops and haymaking. There was also another lucrative side-line for rural children, but only if they had the stomach for it.

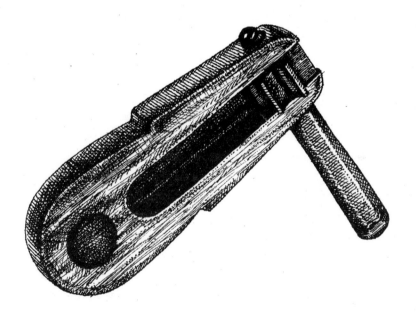

78.

KINGFISHER TRAP

MID 19TH CENTURY

During the eighteenth and nineteenth centuries, few people in the countryside had anything nice to say about sparrows. The French naturalist, Georges-Louis Leclerc, had described the bird with feverish hostility: 'It is extremely destructive. Its plumage is entirely useless, its flesh indifferent food, its notes grating to the ear, and its familiarity and petulance disgusting.' While few other writers could match Leclerc's hysteria, all agreed that it was a menace to farming. Even the English natural historian and engraver Thomas Bewick, in his immensely amiable and avian-friendly *A History of British Birds*, concluded that the sparrow 'follows society, and lives at its expense: granaries, barns, courtyards, pigeon-houses, and in short all places where grain is scattered, are its favourite resorts'.

Almost every stage of growing and using cereal crops, it was reported, was hampered by the bird. From sowing seeds to threshing wheat, storing grain to feeding poultry, showers of sparrows followed in their wake. The problem was particularly bad thanks to decades of what one Victorian ornithologist called 'the silly destruction of hawks and owls'. People had found plenty of reasons to trap and kill raptors. Many assumed they ate grain or other crops, or stole small livestock such as lambs, ducks, pigeons and chickens. Others hunted raptors for taxidermy or feathers, while collectors snatched eggs in greedy handfuls.

During the 1800s, the countryside's raptor population crashed, with a third of Britain's birds of prey persecuted to extinction by the century's close. Meanwhile, numbers of sparrows – with so few prey species around – exploded. One journalist, writing in the *Essex Country Standard* in 1842, calculated that 'the country is robbed by these monsters in the passerine form to the amount of £27,000,000, more than sufficient to pay the annual interest of the National Debt'. While our irate writer's suggestion was to encourage everyone to make 'sparrow puddings', serving up the 'little villains in the very dough that would have been snatched out of our mouths', most farmers and parishes took a more pragmatic approach and paid children a half-penny for every sparrow caught and killed. Village 'sparrow clubs' were also established, funded by donations from farmers and land-owners. Groups of men and children would go out to catch sparrows with nets, or plunder nests for eggs and chicks. Whatever was caught or collected would be brought back to the sparrow club for payment of 'sparrer-money'.

While sparrows were considered a nuisance among cereal farmers, it was kingfishers that especially irked river keepers. This fiendish object is a kingfisher trap, the smallest kind of 'pole trap' made in Britain designed to catch an animal by its leg. At just two inches wide, it was used, with pitiless effectiveness, to maim kingfishers that were perceived as a threat to managed fish stocks, especially young salmon and trout. The trap capitalised on the kingfishers' habit of patrolling a favourite stretch of river and having easily identifiable perches where they sit and hunt.

While Victorian river keepers raged against the kingfisher, not everyone felt such antipathy. Indeed, the often blasé cruelty displayed to the countryside's creatures was beginning to create a backlash among early conservationists. In his remarkably compas-sionate book, *The River-side Naturalist*, Victorian writer Edward Hamilton – who was also a keen fisherman – argued passionately against the destruction of the kingfisher and other birds that were thought to threaten commercial fish stocks and game. Moreover, he was one of the first authors to ask his readers to wonder at the beauty of nature and, with startling prescience, revel in its therapeutic benefits.

The British countryside would go on to inspire generations of lyrical nature writers from John Lewis-Stempel to Richard Mabey, with authors such as Hamilton blazing the trail. 'Go where you will', he mused, 'on the placid waters of the meres and lakes, by the rushing rivers or babbling brooks—animated nature is above and around you. Birds are singing in the air, resting in the bushes, creeping or hiding in the reeds. Listen to the warning *Churr-churr* of the sedge-warbler— hark to the carol of the lark, a speck in the blue ether—watch the rapid flight of the swift, now skimming the surface of the water in front of us, and now far away over the distant meadows.'

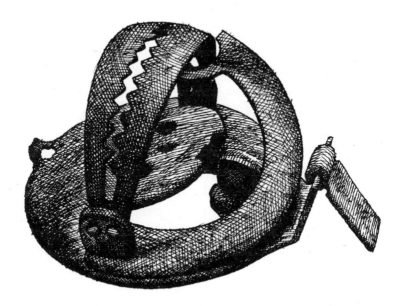

79.

JAR FROM THE WRECK OF THE *KATHERINE SHEARER*
19ᵀᴴ CENTURY

The wealth created during the Agricultural Revolution didn't filter through to everyone. While farming output was higher than it had ever been, many people who worked the land found their lives irrevocably changed. For centuries, ordinary rural folk didn't own the land they farmed but they were entitled to use it in certain ways. These ancient privileges allowed villagers not only to farm strips of land for crops but also to graze their animals, collect firewood and mast, and utilise other important resources.

In a process known as 'enclosure', however, this communal land was taken back in hand by local landholders and ring-fenced, both metaphorically and physically, for their own exclusive use. Enclosure began in a piecemeal fashion after the Black Death in the fourteenth century, with manorial lords keen to embrace wool farming, but the process gathered pace during the eighteenth century in the name of agricultural efficiency and commercial farming.

While productivity no doubt increased, the effects on the poorest sections of rural society were devastating. Most rural dwellers became casual, waged labourers, a system of employment that often left them at the mercy of a volatile agricultural sector. Weather, disease, wars, trade disputes and other problems often dramatically affected the value of rural work. While under the medieval system, villagers might spread their liabilities over a few crops, a handful of animals, a craft, perhaps, and foraged resources, the waged rural labourer found him or herself particularly vulnerable to the whims of the market.

Advances in technology also reduced the need for labour, with developments such as threshing and winnowing machines slashing the man-hours required to bring in a harvest and removing one of the key sources of employment over autumn and winter. Between the 1750s and 1850s, rural wages fell in real terms. Smaller tenant farmers also found themselves squeezed by higher rents charged by landlords keen to recoup their investment in new buildings, crops and machinery.

Many countryside dwellers decided they'd had enough. Some headed to the growing urban centres, places where newly opened factories and mills promised regular work and higher wages. Others, however, decided to take the unimaginably plucky decision to sail for the colonies. During the late eighteenth and nineteenth centuries, Britain's villages lost huge swathes of their residents – around four million are believed to have upped sticks and headed for the country's towns and cities, while at least ten million sailed to America, Canada, Australia and New Zealand hoping for a better life. Many colonies actively encouraged rural people to come, desperate to fill skill shortages in their newly established communities. Free passage and plots of land sweetened the deal, an offer that tempted shepherds, farm labourers, domestics, wagoners, miners and many other skilled trades, and their families, to head for the horizon.

It's almost impossible to overstate how courageous, or desperate, emigrants were. The vagaries of the weather, the ship, the time of year, even the skill of the captain could have a dramatic effect on the duration and safety of the long journey. While most made it across, it wasn't unusual for things to go wrong. This seemingly unrelated object, a jar of anchovy paste, speaks poignantly of one such disaster. Almost daily, London's *Telegraph & Courier* newspaper covered stories of British shipping disasters, involving many of the vessels that were taking emigrants to the colonies.

On 31 August 1855, the newspaper printed a list of dozens of vessels variously described as wrecked, lost, stranded, and 'very leaky'. Included in this tragic roll-call was the *Katherine Shearer*, a barque or three-mast sailing ship that had set off from London to Tasmania only to flounder at the final hour. On arriving in the port of Hobart Town, she caught fire, igniting a cargo of gunpowder and exploded into smithereens. While the crew and its passengers were rescued, albeit in 'a destitute and most deplorable' state, all their worldly goods – including precious, comforting reminders of home such as this humble jar of fish paste – were lost to the sea. It must have seemed to many emigrants from the British countryside as if they'd jumped from the frying pan into the fire.

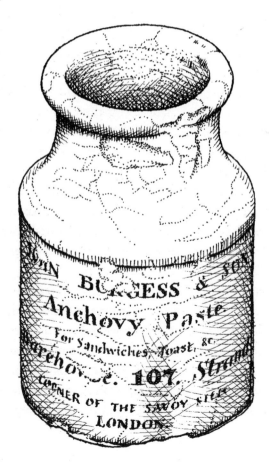

80.

DR MERRYWEATHER'S TEMPEST PROGNOSTICATOR

1850

During his long career, Vice-Admiral Robert Fitzroy was no stranger to shipwrecks. A talented but troubled officer in the Royal Navy, he had spent an illustrious life on the waves, navigating the oceans and even captaining Charles Darwin's famous HMS *Beagle* voyage. For all the pleasure and privileges that life at sea had afforded him, however, Fitzroy was pained by the endless marine disasters that dogged his industry. In just one month alone, in January 1855, over a hundred British ships were sunk, wrecked or grounded. Loss of life was massive. Not only were passengers consigned to the waves; so too were seamen, a fact no doubt exacerbated by the fact that the Royal Navy didn't require its sailors to learn to swim until 1879.

Fitzroy had long been interested in the weather and was a great friend of Francis Beaufort, inventor of the titular wind scale and a fellow naval officer who had himself been shipwrecked as a child. On HMS *Beagle*, while Darwin was absorbed in exotic flora and fauna, Fitzroy was taking careful readings of the ship's barometers and humidity gauges, using them to predict atmospheric changes. In 1851, back on dry land, he was elected to the Royal Society, an honour that helped him secure a new job, three years later, as chief statistician to the newly formed Meteorological Office. His job was to collect weather data from ships' logbooks, but he soon began sending out barometers to ports and fishing harbours so that local crews could check the readings before venturing out.

In 1859, an appalling storm shipwrecked the *Royal Charter*, a steam clipper carrying men, women and children between Liverpool and Australia. More than four hundred and fifty lives were lost, a tragedy that spurred Fitzroy to develop the world's first 'forecasts', using readings taken from around the country to create predictive weather charts, details of which could be telegraphed to coastal stations if a storm approached. The modern forecast was born, a gift not only to fishermen and sailors but also to farming communities, whose lives were intimately connected to the weather.

Until Fitzroy's ground-breaking development, predicting the weather relied on a haphazard marriage of superstition and keen observation. People living in the countryside looked for clues wherever they could find them. Many omens were taken as signs of imminent bad weather; from cows sitting down to geese flying low, the smell of pipe tobacco getting stronger to frogs croaking more loudly. Sayings and rhymes helped rural dwellers remember useful nuggets of weather lore, but one particular poem, the 'Signs of Rain' by physician Edward Jenner (incidentally the same man who pioneered vaccines), inspired an eccentric Yorkshire doctor to build his own weather predictor in 1850.

Jenner, who kept leeches in glass jars for medical treatments, noted that when a storm approached '*The leech, disturb'd, is newly risen. Quite to the summit of his prison.*' A Whitby doctor, George Merryweather, decided to capitalise on this strange phenomenon. He built this remarkable object – the *Tempest Prognosticator* – a device consisting of a dozen leeches trapped inside a dozen jars. When his 'jury of leeches' were agitated by electrical conditions in the atmosphere, they'd try to climb out of their bottles, which in turn triggered a small hammer to ring a bell. The more 'tings', the greater the likelihood of a storm. Remarkably, Merryweather's leech barometer had some success in predicting storms but, perhaps not unsurprisingly, it failed to become a commercial success.

Fitzroy's weather forecasts, however, stood the test of time. First published in 1861 in *The Times* newspaper, accurate weather predictions proved enormously valuable to the countryside, and continue to influence many of the year's major decisions surrounding crops and livestock. As with modern meteorology, however, Fitzroy's forecasting was an expression of probability, not precise fortune-telling. When his storm warnings failed to materialise or, even worse, when he missed a major weather event, he was pilloried by the press. Sadly, Fitzroy's wealth and mental health proved as turbulent as the weather he attempted to predict. Having used up much of his fortune perfecting his work, he spent his last few years broke and increasingly depressed. In April 1865, just four years after his first forecast for *The Times*, the man who saved countless lives at sea and gave farmers a fighting chance against the elements, decided he could weather his own storm no longer and took his own life.

81.

KEILLER'S MARMALADE JAR
19TH CENTURY

If weather forecasts had been invented in the eighteenth century, Britain might never have experienced the Paddington Bear delights of marmalade. Legend has it that Dundee confectioner Janet Keiller invented marmalade in 1797 after her husband James snapped up a job-lot of Seville oranges from a storm-damaged cargo ship. Her son, also called James, went on to expand the businesses, turning a local delicacy into the first commercial marmalade brand. While the tale is more likely sticky myth than culinary truth (although Janet Keiller was probably the first to add shreds of orange peel to marmalade), this object tells us plenty about the development of another staple of countryside living: the village shop.

By the middle of the nineteenth century, most decent-sized villages had their own general store. Before then, countryside folk had tended to grow, make or barter many of the things they needed. Itinerant sellers, called cheapjacks or pedlars, would also travel around the countryside selling hardware, while many people attended weekly or fortnightly local markets to pick up fresh seasonal produce. William Howitt, in his 1838 *Rural Life of England* , described the buzz of 'men and women, with their baskets on their arms containing their butter, eggs, apples, mushrooms, walnuts, nuts, elderberries, blackberries, bundles of herbs, young pigeons, fowls or whatever happened to be in season'. Craftspeople such as shoemakers and ironmongers also had premises within a village, offering both services and items for sale.

With the expansion of turnpike roads and the canal network in the eighteenth century, goods that were previously difficult to obtain in the countryside – such as spices, inks, dried fruit and exotic fabrics – were starting to become more available. Descriptions of some village shops from this time often make them sound more like bazaars than basic food stores. The inventories of Thomas Turner's 1760s village shop in East Hoathy, Sussex, for example, reads like an Aladdin's cave. Turner's shelves were stocked with everything from clogs to coats, tobacco to beehives, and chocolate to fine china, although most of these products would have been beyond the financial reach of rural labourers. Grocers like Turner acted as middlemen, buying bulk goods at wholesale or direct from importers, to split up and sell in smaller quantities. Even the job title 'grocer' comes from the act of buying in gross quantities.

The changes in rural life that came with the Agricultural Revolution, especially the introduction of the waged labourer and the removal of common land where people could procure their own food, created a situation in which country folk now needed to buy most necessities. Village shops excelled at selling loose goods such as tea, coffee, flour, sweets, salt and sugar, items that country folk could buy in modest but frequent quantities or on credit, but this was a system that only worked in small, tight-knit communities.

By the early nineteenth century, news of food-adulteration scandals began to rock consumer confidence. Unscrupulous shopkeepers were often accused of cutting bread flour with chalk, for example, or tea leaves with sheep's manure. Customers were increasingly drawn to the reassurance that a sealed, commercial jar, packet or tin of food could offer. Many products also promised pre-prepared ingredients, cutting down on cooking time, or cheap ways to boost the flavour of an otherwise bland diet. A number of now well-known brands emerged during this period and many touted their products' health benefits alongside their hygienic packaging. Keiller's marmalade was said to aid digestion, for example, while early Guinness advertisements boldly promised 'Health, peace and prosperity'. Other household names also began to fill the shelves of village stores, including Colman's Mustard, Hartley's Jam and Lea & Perrins Worcestershire Sauce.

The importance of the village shop was boosted by the improvement of the postal system. Although a limited postal service had been available to the public since the 1600s, it wasn't until the introduction of the Penny Post in 1840 – the first pre-paid, flat-rate postage stamp – that mail was brought to the masses. While towns and cities often had purpose-built post offices, villages often relied on their own general stores to act as sub-post offices, offering postal services alongside their stone bottles of ginger beer, cheap cures for gout and our next object.

82.

SPRATT'S DOG FOOD ADVERT

19ᵀᴴ CENTURY

Alongside the shepherd, one of the oldest jobs in the countryside is the knacker. Now viewed as a rather unpleasant and unusual job, the task of the knacker was once a hugely important cog in the rural machine. If an animal was dead or irretrievably ill, the knacker would take it away and, back at the knacker's yard, turn the carcass into useful by-products. Bones could be transformed into soil fertilisers, animal food, cutlery handles and combs. Boiled down, they yielded gelatine, glue and neatsfoot oil, a crucial balm for softening leather. Animal fats and tallow could be converted into lubricants, soaps, candles and used in printmaking. Even horse hair was useful, puffing up upholstery, binding lime plaster, and creating brushes and theatrical wigs.

Hides and sheepskins were often passed on to fellmongers, who would remove and sell the 'pulled wool' and make the skins into leather. Despite their utility, both knacker and fellmonger were viewed as tough, unforgiving professions, even in a world used to chimney sweeps and well diggers. A book of suitable jobs for children, from 1761, called *The Parent's and Guardian's Directory, and the Youth's Guide, in the Choice of a Profession Or Trade*, described fellmongering as 'a very nasty stinking trade, much exposed to wet and cold, therefore not fit for weakly lads'.

One of the growing markets for knackers' yards, during the nineteenth century, was dog and cat food. Writing in the late 1840s, Henry Mayhew painted a solemn picture of the fate of many of London's worn-out horses and ponies, 38,000 of whom were sent to knackers every year. The countryside had a similar problem of what to do with all its drays and cart horses after they'd ploughed their last furrow – there were only so many that could be fed to the kennels of the local hunt. The rise of the horse as a means of transport and power had left the entire country with a pressing problem of what to do when old, exhausted or injured horses no longer served their purpose. While working oxen had been welcomed by butchers and gourmands, tough horsemeat had no culinary, if not nutritional, value. The Society for the Propagation of Horseflesh even organised a London dinner in 1868 to promote the idea of *hippophagy* as a way of feeding the country's poor. Unsurprisingly, its esteemed diners remained unconvinced. From one account, all the dishes had the odour of a 'well galloped' beast. Thanks to the work of livestock improvers, beef and mutton had also become more affordable.

The solution presented itself in the form of James Spratt, a Devon-born man who had emigrated to America and set himself up as an entrepreneur selling lightning rods. On a business trip back to England, he spotted sailors feeding ships' biscuits to stray dogs and wondered whether he might be able to make a mass-market version. In 1860, Spratt's Meat Fibrine Dog Cakes were ready for sale. While Spratt kept his recipe secret, many other British copycat pet food companies, such as Hildyard's and Walker & Harrison chased his tail, producing dog biscuits and 'hound meal' from cheap cereal and knackers' meat. Spratt proved masterly, however, at dog food marketing, directing his products at a growing breed of middle class and well-to-do dog owners who took an interest in the burgeoning field of dog shows and pure breeds, even creating pet foods for different stages of dogs' lives.

One of the most remarkable countryside coincidences to come out of this rather unpalatable story is the creation of Crufts, the world-famous dog show. Charles Alfred Cruft, who founded the eponymous competition, first became involved with the canine world when he worked at Spratt's dog biscuits. At the age of fourteen, he started as an office boy but quickly worked his way up to travelling salesman, visiting large country estates and sporting kennels around the British countryside. While working for Spratt's in France in 1878, Cruft was asked by dog breeders for his help with the forthcoming Paris Exhibition. In 1891, he ran his very first dog show in London and the rest, as they say, is history.

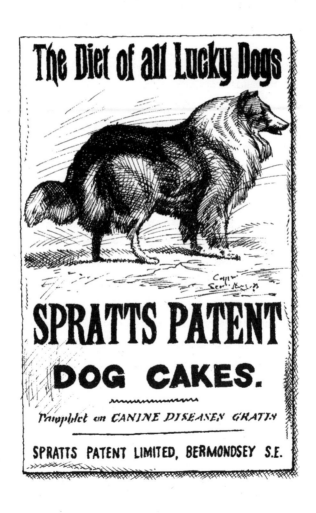

83.

HEN BASKET
19TH CENTURY

Rural life has never just been about growing food or keeping livestock. Throughout its history, the countryside has been inextricably linked with craft. For thousands of years, people made the things they needed. Craft is inherently functional. And is often constrained by the materials it relies on. But the familiarity and pleasure that comes with working with a natural resource, such as hazel or willow, often morphs into something else. Rural crafts regularly display virtuosity, design flourishes and unique regional traditions that mass-manufactured copies could never replicate.

Basket making is a perfect example. Archaeological discoveries have pushed back the earliest evidence of the craft to around twenty-seven thousand years ago, a huge stretch of time for weavers to perfect their techniques to pass on to the next generation. These early baskets fell into one of two techniques: open twining, which created net-like baskets for catching fish or sieving; and closed twining – tightly woven baskets that could hold pretty much anything. Some baskets were so tightly woven they were watertight.

The method for making baskets has changed little since but the range of different forms is extraordinary. Until the early twentieth century, for example, fishing communities relied on a dazzling array of woven baskets for retrieving, measuring and carrying their catch.

From cob maunds (for gutted fish) to eel pots, quarter cran measuring baskets (for landed herring) to cockle pads for shellfish, each basket had a distinctive purpose and shape.

Regions also came up with slightly different versions of baskets for the same task. Or created their own forms for jobs entirely specific to a place. Scotland, for example, has an incredibly textured history of basket making. Creels were woven so that people, often women, could carry heavy loads on their backs. East coast fishwives would lug huge quantities of fish landed locally to sell door to door locally or take inland. Another smaller bowl-shaped basket – called a *murlin* – would be balanced on top of the fishwife's creel for displaying a sample of the fish and to hold a chopping board and fish knife for gutting any fish she sold. Creels were also used in the Highlands and Western Isles to lug turves of peat and seaweed, and had a slightly different design to accommodate a carrying strap. Remarkably, women walking with creels on their backs often knitted at the same time.

Both east and west coast creels were often made from willow, but the 'treeless' landscapes of the Shetlands and Orkneys forced islanders to create a different version, called a *kishie* or *caisie*, made from softer materials such as oat straw or rushes. A smaller version for carrying bait or small fish was also made from heather or dockens (dock weed stalks), and was called a *cuddy* in Shetland and *cubbie* in Orkney. The regions' Norse origins are revealed in these ancient words – in Norway *kupa* still means a fish basket. Grasses and rushes could be woven so tightly they could hold the smallest grains of cereal or salt, or be woven into domed bee skeps.

One of the most charming of all the countryside's baskets, however, has to be this object: a hen basket. Its origins are also thought to be Scottish and it's known as an *Ose basket*, after a small coastal settlement on the Isle of Skye. The hen basket is traditionally made from willow – one of the few straggly species of tree that grows on the Scottish island, particularly along the shoreline – and is purported to have been used to carry broody hens from one croft to another. If a batch of fertilised eggs needed a mother hen, so the story goes, it was easier to bring the bird to the nest rather than risk cooling the eggs by moving them. A broody hen would nestle in the basket – its wings restricted by the narrow sides – to be safely brought to its new location. While its origin story might be a weave of fact and fiction, the design of the hen basket stood the test of time. In the 1950s, Brigitte Bardot turned the rustic poultry carrier into a must-have fashion accessory, using the basket as a handbag. Or, perhaps, should that be 'clutch' bag?

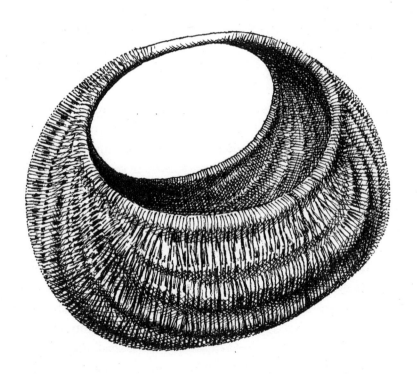

84.

CANAL BOAT 'CASTLES & ROSES' PANEL

LATE 19TH CENTURY

The arrival of the canal network created numerous jobs. It offered plenty of employment opportunities, from canal inspectors and bridge-keepers to rough, nomadic navvies, who heroically shifted tonnes of rock and mud by shovel. Canal men, with their horse-drawn boats, were paid by the weight of cargo they carried, not the hours they worked. This meant boats were often staffed by just two men: one to steer and one to chivvy the horse along. The more goods a small team could carry, the more they got paid.

By the middle of the nineteenth century, railways were beginning to threaten the canal network's monopoly. In 1840, Britain had just a handful of disparate and often unconnected railway lines; within a decade, entrepreneurs had laid down an almost complete network of tracks connecting towns and cities with virtually every corner of the countryside. The economics of train freight soon started to hurt Britain's waterways. Investment in canals slowed and wages stagnated. To stay competitive, boatmen cut costs by bringing their families along for the ride. This not only saved the expense of a house, but wives and children could also work, removing the need for a boat mate.

To make ends meet, people living on the canals often worked seven days a week, including Sunday, a transgression that a pious Victorian society struggled to accept. Canal life was an isolated, itinerant world and, as often happens with travelling communities, attracted mistrust from those who didn't understand the way of life. Social commentators sermonised about the tens of thousands of 'men, women and children, living and floating on our rivers and canals, in a state of wretchedness, misery, immorality, cruelty and evil training', blaming it on the unique peculiarities of canal living, rather than the meagre wages and decreasing status of boat work.

While many boat families did live in squalor, with high rates of overcrowding and illiteracy, there was also a strong sense of identity and proud separateness, a 'canal culture' that sought expression in the decoration of its boats. Families often transformed their cabins into highly ornate, neatly organised living spaces. A distinctive style of folk art also emerged – known as 'castles and roses' – and was used to cover almost every surface and utensil within the cabin. This object – a wooden panel from a boat interior – shows the bold motifs and confident, quick brushstrokes typical of this traditional, waterway craft.

For all its proud distinctiveness, however, nineteenth-century canal life was undoubtedly dangerous. According to George Smith, author of *Our Canal Population* – a description of canal life from the 1870s – fatalities among boat workers were twice as high as agricultural labourers. While drowning and boating accidents were commonplace, especially around locks and dockyards, a surprising number of incidents resulted from one of the canal networks' regular cargoes: explosives. The Victorian Age relied heavily on explosives for its mining and civil engineering projects, a volatile cargo that suited steady conveyance by boat. It also had the unfortunate tendency to blow its carriers sky-high. The final straw came when two barges, loaded with petroleum and gunpowder destined for a Nottinghamshire mine, detonated under a bridge on the Regent's Canal in London.

Three men and a boy were killed but it was the explosion's proximity to the capital that no doubt provoked Parliament's passing of the Explosives Act of 1875, which finally regulated their sale and transportation.

As for canal life, that went out with more of a whimper than a bang. By the end of the nineteenth century, railways were carrying a far greater volume of goods than canals. A third of Britain's canals were taken over by railway companies, and while a few were kept productive, many more were deliberately closed. Others fell into disrepair or silted up, while both world wars added to their neglect and shortage of labour.

Thanks to organisations such as the Inland Waterways Association, however, the future of the countryside's canals looks bright. Formed in 1946, the IWA has helped ensure that the waterways are now awash with people rediscovering canals for pleasure. In fact, there are now thought to be more boats floating up and down the country's canals than at any time in their commercial history.

85.

LEATHER FARM BOOT
C. 1880

A yomp through the countryside is one of life's great pleasures. Wellington boots embody the can-do, practical spirit of rural life, but it's interesting to think about how our ancestors navigated all that mud and muck before the invention of the rubber gumboot.

The world's oldest footwear ever found is the Areni-1 shoe and was discovered in an Armenian cave. At 5,500 years old, its design is remarkable familiar and timeless – a one-piece, slip-on leather moccasin laced together with leather cords. The shoe's form is similar to many historical and ethnographic examples, including the Irish *pampootie*, worn by Aran Islanders well into the middle of the twentieth century. Although flimsy to look at, the shoe was immensely practical. Pampooties were made from raw, untanned leather, often with the hair left on the outside for extra grip, and were regularly replaced when worn through.

Leather had always been the go-to material for outdoor shoes. Its flexibility and robustness are its greatest assets, but it can also repel water if treated with oil, wax or fat. When leather is saturated with water and then dries, it shrinks; on traditional footwear, this had the effect of closing the gaps between the stitched seams, adding to a shoe or boot's ability to resist moisture. The shrinkage also moulded the footwear to the foot, as beautifully demonstrated by this women's leather boot from the 1880s. It was found deliberately hidden under the bedroom floor of a farmhouse in Somerset and was almost certainly put there as house protection against witchcraft, in the same manner as dried cats and lucky horseshoes were often used. Not only do these 'concealed shoes' offer a fascinating glimpse into superstitious beliefs but the sheer numbers that have been found give textile historians a sense of the different footwear available to rural folk over the years.

For muddy conditions, people often strapped on a pair of pattens. These wooden or iron 'platforms' were fixed onto the bottom of existing shoes with straps, and the thickness of the patten's sole elevated its wearer above the grime and filth. As roads and pavements in Britain's towns and cities gradually improved, patten wearing fell out of fashion, but country folk continued to use them well into the nineteenth century.

A new type of footwear, however, was to revolutionise the experience of walking and working in the countryside. Soldiers had been wearing something called a Hessian boot since the eighteenth century. Made from soft, polished leather, these smart, tasselled riding boots came up to the knee. In the early 1800s, the Duke of Wellington asked his shoemaker to remodel the Hessian boot, creating a pair that stopped midcalf. The new fashion for trousers, rather than breeches, required a lower-cut boot, but one that was still dandy enough for evening wear. The 'Wellington' boot had arrived.

The transition from leather to rubber came slightly later. In 1844, American chemist Charles Goodyear had developed and patented vulcanised rubber. Within a decade, businessman Hiram Hutchinson had purchased the rights to use Goodyear's new material to make rubber footwear. He opened a factory in France in 1853 and named the new rubber shoe company Aigle (Eagle), a brand that's still going strong today.

Back in Britain, in 1856, two ambitious American entrepreneurs, Henry Lee Norris and Spencer Thomas Parmelee, arrived in Scotland with rubber boots on their mind. They purchased a large piece of land in Edinburgh and established the North British Rubber Company. By the end of the century, the company was making an impressive array of rubber goods – from hot water bottles to rubber flooring – but it was the First World War that finally put their rubber footwear on the map. British soldiers' feet were suffering terribly in the waterlogged trenches. The War Office asked the North British Rubber Company to design a boot sturdy enough to cope. By the end of the war, the firm – which later went on to become Hunter Boot Ltd – had sent over a million pairs of wellies to the Front. The company was called upon again during the Second World War and by the end of the conflict the wellington had established itself as *the* footwear for rugged outdoor use. Farmers and festival-goers never looked back.

86.

SERVANT BELLS AT DUNHAM MASSEY

19TH CENTURY

Country houses are bold exclamation marks on the landscape. They're some of the most awe-inspiring examples of British architecture, connoisseurship and craft, and one of the countryside's greatest tourist attractions. Few visitors, however, ever wonder where the money came from to build and run such impressive buildings.

The story of the British country estate starts with William the Conqueror, who, as we already know, declared that all land belonged to the Crown and portioned off significant swathes to his tenants-in-chief and the Church. Some of the country's most famous noble families – such as the House of Percy – can trace their ancestry to this time. With the dissolution of the monasteries in the sixteenth century, large tracts of church land were taken back in hand by Henry VIII. These were handed over to the king's supporters, who had backed his break from the Catholic Church and were handsomely rewarded for their loyalty. Many monastic sites were reworked into grand homes. The ecclesiastical remnants of religious buildings are tucked away in Britain's country houses, their undercrofts turned into cellars or abbot's quarters transformed into private lodgings.

With the succession of Henry's daughter, Elizabeth I, the nobility also began to commission 'prodigy houses' – large showy country homes designed to display a family's wealth and entice the new queen to visit on one of her annual royal tours. Between then and the nineteenth century, country houses were often the hub of an extensive landed estate that brought in a healthy income. Farm rents, shooting licences, milling rights, fishing, mining and other sources of revenue all paid for the lavish upkeep of the house and its family.

Between the seventeenth and nineteenth century, money also came from the expansion of British colonialism and slavery. The connections between country houses and colonialism aren't always obvious. While some wealthy families made money directly from slave trading and plantations, others benefited from more silent involvement in colonial bureaucracy, insurance or shareholding. Colonial money also brought wealth to those traditionally outside the nobility. During this time, more than a thousand country estates were bought or remodelled by merchants and military officers – 'commoners' who had made their fortunes in colonial trade.

Money begets money and colonial profits also allowed landowners to diversify into profitable schemes back in Britain, such as canal building. The canals, in turn, helped the slavery business boom, transporting goods across the countryside – such as cotton and tobacco – produced by enslaved people. Take Liverpool slave trader Moses Benson, for example, who owned an estate in Shropshire, but also invested heavily in the Lancaster Canal. Or plantation owner George Hyde Clarke, occupier of Hyde Hall in Cheshire, who was also a shareholder in the Peak Forest Canal, a waterway that made money transporting limestone from quarries in the Peak District to Manchester.

Country estates often employed large numbers of staff. As houses grew grander in scale, servants were increasingly removed to separate quarters and would service the house using a system of tunnels and staircases to avoid the two worlds coming into contact. This object – a section of the servant bells from Dunham Massey in Cheshire – demonstrates this new arrangement, with multiple rooms each requiring its own pull that would ring a bell inside the servants' quarters.

The staffing costs and expense of Britain's country-house lifestyle were, however, to prove its undoing. By the end the nineteenth century, the fortunes of many estates were beginning to falter. Countries such as North America and Australia had become significant producers of grain, meat and wool, economies of scale that could undercut Britain's agricultural prices. Between 1870 and 1914, agricultural land values plummeted by two-thirds.

Both world wars cost the economy and country estates dearly. Large houses were often requisitioned for the war effort and many left in a poor state. Both conflicts also maimed and killed not only a generation of heirs to country houses, but their household staff, groundsmen, and farm estate workers. Those employees that did survive the wars were often no longer willing to work as servants and found better-paid opportunities elsewhere. Rising taxes – especially death duties – dealt the final blow. From the late nineteenth century onwards, over fifteen hundred British country houses fell into ruin or were demolished. As we'll find out, however, a handful of people were starting to worry that the rest of Britain's countryside was destined for the same fate.

87.

PETER RABBIT'S 'OTHER TALE'

1901

The National Trust has been a custodian of Britain's countryside and many of its buildings for more than a hundred and twenty-five years. While many associate the charity with grand country houses, its origins began with the core belief that natural and historic places should be preserved for everyone.

By the late nineteenth century, many of the countryside's historic buildings, and rural estates, were in peril. Rapid industrialisation was also threatening to engulf the country's remaining green spaces, coastlines and sites of archaeological importance. Three social reformers – Octavia Hill, Sir Robert Hunter and Hardwicke Rawnsley – decided to do something about it.

For most of her life, Octavia Hill had worked tirelessly to improve the lives of the urban poor and she also believed strongly in the importance of nature for all. Sir Robert Hunter was a solicitor who used his legal expertise to help Hill with her campaigns to protect public access to green spaces. He also took a keen interest in the historic built environment, helping to pass the Ancient Monuments Protection Act in 1882 and, in the same year, he supported the artist William Morris in his creation of the Society for the Protection of Ancient Buildings

(SPAB). Hardwicke Rawnsley, an Anglican priest, lived in the Lake District and had been fighting to protect the region from the ravages of heavy industry and to preserve ancient rights of way. Together, in 1895, these three trailblazers joined forces and founded the National Trust for Places of Historic Interest or Natural Beauty.

Within just a few weeks, the charity had been given its first piece of land: five acres of Welsh clifftop at Dinas Oleu, donated by a philanthropist and friend of Rawnsley's, Fanny Talbot. Just a year later, the Trust purchased its first property – Alfriston Clergy House in East Sussex. A fourteenth-century timber-framed hall in a dire state, the Trust and SPAB worked closely together to sensitively conserve the building – a partnership that maintains a fruitful working relationship even today. In 1899, the Trust acquired its first nature reserve, Wicken Fen – two acres of wetland near Cambridge – and a year later it was gifted its first castle, Kanturk Castle in County Cork, Ireland.

The Trust went from strength to strength. In 1936, it set up the Country Houses Committee, which aimed to save countryside estates that owners could no longer afford to keep. Subsequent legislation allowed the Trust to accept gifts of large properties and their grounds, often in return for a family being allowed to lease the property long term. Perhaps the most famous partnership, however, was between the National Trust and one of the country's most beloved children's authors: Beatrix Potter. Potter and Rawnsley had been firm friends since meeting in the Lake District when Beatrix was on a family holiday. Rawnsley was not only a clergyman but an author and poet. Dazzled by her charming sketches of animals, he had encouraged Potter to write and illustrate her own books. She struggled, however, to get a book deal. Rawnsley – as a published writer – thought it might help if he rewrote *Peter Rabbit* as a light-hearted poem.

Our object, Rawnsley's version of *Peter Rabbit* 'done into rhyme', failed to impress the publisher Frederick Warne. Warne did, however, agree to publish Potter's own words and illustrations. By 1905, she had released six books, all runaway successes. With the proceeds, she bought her first farm – Hill Top – in the Lake District. Two and a half decades later, she used her substantial earnings to support the National

Trust's work in the region and, on her death, left nearly her entire estate to the charity.

Thanks to Peter Rabbit, Mrs Tiggy-Winkle and Potter's other creations, the Trust was gifted over four thousand acres of Lake District farmland, more than a dozen farms, cottages, numerous heads of cattle, and flocks of her favourite breed of sheep, the Herdwick. Potter had been a keen advocate of the Herdwick breed, promoting its importance to the history and sustainability of the fells. Her legacy, and the work of the National Trust, continue to preserve the Lakes landscape for many generations to come.

88.

WOMEN'S INSTITUTE 'GUILD OF LEARNERS' BADGE

EARLY 20TH CENTURY

The Women's Institute is often described as all 'jam and Jerusalem', an organisation that doughtily defends countryside traditions, fired up on patriotic anthems and sponge cake. And yet, as with many clichés, it's a lazy stereotype. Peel back the greaseproof paper of the WI and you'll find an organisation that has been championing rural education and women's issues for over a hundred years.

The Women's Institute began in Canada in 1897. Madge Watt, one of its founding members, was invited to Britain to organise the country's first WI meeting, which took place on 16 September 1915 in Anglesey, Wales. With First World War food shortages starting to bite, one of the WI's primary goals was to encourage rural women to grow and preserve food to boost supplies on the Home Front.

The WI, however, also had a more radical purpose: to give women, who had yet to win equal franchise, a collective voice. A 1921 edition of the WI magazine, *Home and Country*, explained: 'if one person alone cannot make her wants heard it becomes much easier when there are numbers wanting the same kind of things'. The organisation's all-female membership and convivial gatherings, fuelled by tea and cake, were easy for a male-dominated press and political system to mock. And yet, only two years after their inaugural meeting in a Welsh garden shed, the WI had over five thousand members. By 1925, it had swelled to forty times the number.

With such a vast and motivated membership came power to effect real change. The suffrage movement and the WI had plenty in common. Not only had some of the latter's founding members been involved in the campaign for women's votes, but the two shared an anthem. 'Jerusalem' had been composed in 1916 by Hubert Parry as a hymn to 'brace the spirit of the nation' and was subsequently adopted by the National Union of Suffrage Societies in 1918. Grace Hadow, who was both a lifelong suffragette and one of the founder members of the Women's Institute, suggested 'Jerusalem' as the perfect song for WI members to sing at their 1924 annual general meeting. Members gave such a rousing rendition it soon became the Women's Institute's official anthem.

The WI's approach to meetings was also far-reaching; members were taught how to chair, work as a committee and speak persuasively in public. These kinds of skills, which would have been unthinkable for many rural women, equipped them to campaign against injustices affecting women, children and the domestic sphere. In 1918, the WI resolved to campaign to improve rural housing, an area largely ignored as the country built its urban 'Homes Fit for Heroes' from the ashes of the war. With the bit between their teeth, the WI then focused its attention on securing women jurors and magistrates, increasing female police, and striving for equal pay and women's access to pensions and social security benefits.

The WI's association with craft is also well known and similarly had its heart in a desire to empower rural women. Through instruction in handicrafts, and other practical skills, the WI aimed to give women an opportunity to earn their own money and revive rural crafts such as basket making that were being lost in the onslaught of mass-production. Their 'Guild of Learners' was launched in 1920 to promote excellence and training in handicraft among rural women.

Members undertook courses and, if they passed a series of proficiency tests, could become craft leaders or demonstrators in their own right, earning the right to proudly sport a 'Guild of Learners' badge such as this.

Contrary to ideas about the Women's Institute and its perceived prudishness, the organisation also fought on issues such as sexual consent, securing financial support for unmarried mothers, and sex education free from gendered double-standards. Many of the WI's early campaigns were helped in no small part by Liberal MP and WI member Margaret Wintringham, only the second woman ever to take her seat in the House of Commons. And one of the WI's greatest achievements, as we'll see next, changed the health of the countryside forever.

89.

WATER FILTER
EARLY 20TH CENTURY

Life was tough for many women in the countryside. The daily grind of household chores and childcare was made doubly difficult by poor housing, with homes often having no access to running water or decent sanitation. The Women's Institute recognised this and, within just a few years of being formed, decided to put pressure on local councils to give rural families decent housing. In 1918, its members also pledged to persuade the government to bring piped water to every village dwelling.

Despite its formidable sway, the WI was still battling the same issue three decades later. Determined to see change, it conducted a survey into the state of the nation's water supply and sewerage. Thousands of villages responded to a detailed WI questionnaire, which asked about sanitary arrangements in local homes and schools. When the WI published its results in 1944, the country was stunned. As one MP remarked in a subsequent debate in the House of Commons: 'The Women's Institutes are not generally a revolutionary body, but they have produced a revolutionary document'. Its collected data showed that facilities in at least three and a half thousand parishes were woefully inadequate.

The survey revealed that a third of the nation's countryside didn't have access to clean, piped water. Sanitation was also deficient, with many rural villages relying on cesspits and earth closets little changed from medieval times.

Almost every county printed the results of the WI report in its local newspaper, revealing wide disparities between regions. In January 1945, for example, the *Leicester Evening Mail* published the findings for Leicestershire and Rutland. They surprised even its most hardened journalist, who lamented 'the primitive conditions under which country people have to live and work'. A quarter of all the region's village schools had no access to water *at all*. In one typical village, Great Dalby, the survey revealed that of its eighty homes, none were on mains supplies and at least half the women in the village had to carry their water from a pump more than 60 metres away. Nearly 85 per cent of the village's homes were also classed as having 'unsatisfactory' sanitary conditions. Of the few villages that were lucky enough to have piped water, the WI also found that most had their supplies cut off between 5pm and late morning, just the time when families needed it the most for bath-time and cooking.

The water and sewage industries were highly fragmented right up until the end of the Second World War. The arrival of mains water and drainage to an area was often driven by industry and urban expansion, rather than an inherent wish to improve public health. Each region across the nation organised its own services, often with wildly different geographical challenges and population numbers. At the time of the WI survey, there were more than a thousand private water companies and local authorities involved in the supply of water, and another fourteen hundred responsible for sewage. With little coordination at a national or even regional level, the countryside's plumbing lagged behind and was viewed as too difficult or unprofitable to update.

Even well-to-do rural dwellers and farmers couldn't magic piped water to their homes. Many had to rely on private wells and pumps to provide a personal supply of water, a situation that came with its own dangers. The 1930s had witnessed the last major outbreak of waterborne typhoid in the country but gastro-intestinal diseases caused by contaminated groundwater remained an ever-present threat. Those with the means bought rather grand charcoal water filters, such as this one by Cheavins. Started in the 1860s by Lincolnshire father-and-son team Squier and George Cheavin, the company went on to supply water filters to royalty, hospitals and governments across the British Empire well into the twentieth century.

The carbon in the charcoal filter absorbed some impurities but, unfortunately, did little about microbial contaminants such as bacteria. Something had to be done. Fortunately, the Women's Institute survey marked a watershed. Just a few months later, in June 1945, the government passed legislation that triggered the beginning of a reliable nationalised water supply. Thanks to the campaigning of countryside women, clean water now flowed regardless of whether you lived in London or a tiny Leicestershire village.

Cheavin's "SALUDOR" (SAFE WATER) FILTER

Drinking Water of Absolute Purity

51

90.

COMMUTER TRANSPORT POSTER

1910

Britain was the first country to experience rapid and widespread urbanisation. What began in the middle of the eighteenth century, and had nearly reached its completion by the First World War, saw not only a huge rise in population numbers but also a radical shift from rural to city living. In 1801, of the ten and a half million people who lived in Britain, only a quarter lived in towns or cities. By the outbreak of the First World War, the population had ballooned to over forty million. Four out of every five people now lived in urban areas. In just over a century, living in the countryside had gone from being the rule to the exception.

Towns and cities were also fundamentally different in character to rural areas. Not only were they more densely populated but the people who lived there were largely engaged in non-agricultural work. Cities such as Birmingham, Leeds, Glasgow, Manchester and many others flourished on the back of industry, drawing in people from the countryside with the promise of work that was better paid and, unlike seasonal rural jobs, available all year round. Unfortunately, large towns and cities were also overcrowded, polluted and riddled with disease.

With the increasing reliability and affordability of railway travel in the latter half of the nineteenth century came the new craze for commuting. Those who could afford to shunned busy urban centres and headed to the leafy suburbs and countryside beyond. Railway companies and developers often worked together to create semi-rural housing estates within travelling distances of major cities. Our object, a 1910 poster, tempted London dwellers to ditch the smog and head for Ruislip in 'Wooded Middlesex', then less than an hour's train ride for commuters. Cheaper fares induced frequent travellers or 'season ticket holders' to purchase months' worth of travel in advance, an idea that encouraged bulk buying and helped railway companies predict passenger numbers. The poster sweetly encouraged inner-city Londoners to 'Live like a Healthy Brown Mouse in Fresh Air and Freedom', avoiding the 'city's dust and din' but still enjoying its 'pleasures' thanks to the convenience of public transport.

After the Second World War, the motor car came to dominate all other forms of commuting. The post-war era also saw a surge in rural second-home ownership, especially in popular tourist destinations and coastal resorts. Whether this was a blessing or a curse for the countryside remains a moot point. While second-home ownership brought money to a rural region, in the form of local spend and regeneration, many full-time rural workers soon found themselves priced out of the market.

The situation remains unchanged. Wages in the countryside have failed to keep up with their urban counterparts. Relative to local salaries, rural housing is also more expensive and the stock more limited. For those on low incomes who live and work in the countryside, social housing is hard to come by: while a fifth of all urban homes are classed as such, the same can be said for only one in eight rural homes.

Rural life isn't just a landscape. The countryside is as much about the people who live and work there as its plants and animals. A shortage of rural affordable housing continues to affect traditional communities in many ways: young people and families are often forced to move away from their local areas, leaving the countryside with an ageing demographic. Rural employers struggle to find and retain staff and key workers, while some villages – especially those at the seaside – only truly come to life during tourist seasons. Homelessness in the countryside, a surprising and largely hidden problem, has also risen dramatically. Perhaps most surprisingly of all, however, is a new trend in commuting. Only this time in reverse. Some people now hop in their cars from less expensive urban areas and drive into the countryside for work.

91.

WALKER'S UNIVERSAL MIXTURE
LATE 19TH/EARLY 20TH CENTURY

When James Alfred Wight, better known as James Herriot, published his first book in 1970, he couldn't have dreamt of the success it, and subsequent books, would become. To date, Herriot's books have sold over sixty million copies. Fans of the series, and subsequent TV adaptations, still flock to the Yorkshire countryside in their multitudes, hoping to recapture something of his spirit and sense of place. For many, the farms and villages that were brought to life in his books – which straddle both the Dales and North York Moors – will forever be known as 'Herriot Country'.

Herriot's books were a winning combination of autobiography and lyrical invention, based on his experiences of working as a young vet. Born in 1916, in Sunderland, Herriot moved with his family to Glasgow where, at twenty-three, he qualified as a vet. After a brief stint back in Sunderland, he found a job in North Yorkshire at a rural practice in the market town of Thirsk, depicted in the books as Darrowby's 'Skeldale House'. Fiction and real life intertwined in Herriot's stories, with larger-than-life characters based on practice owner Donald Sinclair (Siegfried Farnon in the books), Sinclair's wayward younger brother Brian (fictionalised as Tristan) and Herriot's capable wife Joan (Helen).

Herriot's brilliance, however, was in his ability to communicate the often-complex relationship people have with their animals. From gruff farmers weeping over beloved cows to formidable dowagers and their pampered pets, Herriot never shied away from the contradictions of countryside life. His books highlighted the importance of humanity when treating animals and their owners, a skill that perhaps many veterinary courses at the time failed to convey.

Herriot's books also revealed how early twentieth-century veterinary science had one foot in the past and one in the future, a tension that wasn't always easy to negotiate. He recalled advice from Donald Sinclair that hinted that veterinarian work was as much about showmanship as medical science: 'give everything a name and never admit you don't know what's wrong,' Sinclair counselled, 'and never leave a farm without injecting something, even if it's just a shot of vitamins, just do something!'

In many ways, veterinary medicine had changed little from its late eighteenth-century beginnings. Animal medicines were often concocted for individual cases, by a chemist or apothecary, and relied heavily on ingredients that often did more harm than good. 'Cures' were often designed to either purge animals or bung them up. Castor oil, chalk, Epsom salts, linseed oil, paraffin and sulphur were regularly thrust down animals' throats, interspersed with bracing doses of highly toxic strychnine powder, liquid ammonia, and mercury chloride. In Herriot's first book – *If Only They Could Talk* – he described Siegfried's flamboyant approach to prescription. Gentian violet pessaries turned a cow's 'discharges a very pretty colour. Really looks like it's doing something' – while the reaction of iodine with turpentine, which smoked furiously and forced the chemicals deep into a wound, 'looks wonderful. Impresses the toughest client'.

From the late 1920s onwards, pre-made veterinary products began to appear, ones that were heavily marketed and sold directly to the practice by representatives from manufacturers. 'Universal medicines' were particular popular – a catch-all term for remedies that claimed to alleviate practically every ailment from coughs to chills, milk fever to mastitis. Almost all universal mixtures also purported to cure 'scour', a wonderfully ancient word for diarrhoea that probably originated from the Norse *skur*, meaning 'shower', or the Old French *escorre* – 'to run out'. Our object, Walker's Universal Mixture, was just one of many brands, but its label reveals the scattergun approach of early twentieth-century veterinary medicine. Not only does it advertise that it can be applied willy-nilly to both sheep and cows, but it recommends it should be administered by the gloriously vague 'wine-glassful' or tablespoon, depending on a rough guess at the poor creature's 'size and strength'.

Mercifully, the Second World War changed the face of veterinary science, fast-tracking developments in human medicine and applied chemistry that also improved animal care. From antibiotics and vaccines, to parasitic treatments, chemotherapy and surgery, almost every aspect of veterinary work was revolutionised in the decades after the conflict. As we'll see next, however, one particular breakthrough should have come with a health warning.

92.

'DDT IS GOOD FOR ME' ADVERT

1947

Wartime shortages fired up the nation's desire to grow more food. From the late 1940s this goal only strengthened, turning agriculture into agribusiness. Traditional mixed farming, where a farmer might produce a 'bit of everything', began to look outdated with the shiny promise of intensive agriculture. Efficient food production was now taking its inspiration from industry, especially its mechanisation, economies of scale and specialisation. The adoption of new monocrops – such as sugar beet and oil-seed rape – also offered profitable avenues for farmers.

Central to this radical shift, however, was the application of synthetic pesticides and weedkillers. The science of chemical warfare – that had been honed during both world wars – had found a new home in agriculture. The now infamous DDT, for example, which was used liberally post-war as an insecticide, started life as a way of combating malaria and other insect-borne diseases among Second World War military personnel and civilians. In a similar vein, the popular herbicide called 2,4-D was initially developed in secret by the British and Americans to ruin crops and starve Germany and Japan into submission.

Farmers, conservative by nature, weren't always quick to switch to new techniques. Experts from both government and the agrochemicals industry, who felt they were working together to reach a national goal, often visited farms offering advice about which miraculous chemicals were needed and how to apply them properly. Without being plagued by ticks and lice, dairy cows produced more milk and beef cattle grew bigger. Apples and other orchard fruit were no longer spoiled by moths and maggots. Cereal crop yields improved now they didn't have to compete with weeds or fungal infections. Even the most ancient adversaries of the farmer – the mouse and the brown rat – didn't stand a chance. Between the end of the Second World War and the 1970s, Britain's cereal production tripled. The countryside's output of sugar beet, milk, eggs, beef, pork, poultry and oil-seed rape also went through the roof.

This astonishing advert for DDT, from *Time* magazine in 1947, presents the child-like optimism of post-war agrochemicals. Pennsalt, which started life in the 1850s as a caustic soda manufacturer, had turned its hand to chemical products for 'industry, farm and home', including DDT. In the editorial that accompanied the cartoon, Pennsalt explained the benefits of this 'amazing insecticide': beef cattle gained 50 lb more meat, dairy cows produced a fifth more milk, potato fields grew an extra 25 barrels per acre, while orchards boasted bigger, juicier apples free from unsightly blemishes.

By 1960, the vast majority of the country's cereals, vegetables, orchards and soft fruit were being treated with synthetic pesticides. A growing and increasingly vocal body of scientists, farmers and campaigners, however, were concerned that the countryside was slowly drowning in toxins. Mammals, birds, fish, invertebrates and non-target plants were being routinely poisoned, while consumers were starting to worry about chemical residues on their fruit and vegetables. Some pesticides and herbicides also proved to be remarkably persistent, remaining in the soil and rivers for months, even years. Other chemicals unexpectedly killed or weakened animals through a slow process of low-dose accumulation.

During the late 1950s, conservation groups such as the RSPB, Game Research Association, and British Trust for Ornithology gathered evidence that the countryside's wildlife – from peregrine falcons to foxes – was being fatally poisoned by agricultural chemicals. News stories of pesticides accidentally killing farm animals and household pets also started to make headlines. It was, however, Rachel Carson's landmark book on the dangers of pesticide over-use, *Silent Spring*, that finally galvanised public concern in 1962. The period that followed proved momentous for the ecological movement. By the end of the 1960s most households owned a television set, and the rise of environmentally themed programmes brought countryside issues and the fragility of nature directly into people's living rooms. In 1970 the British government opened its first Department of the Environment, and *The Ecologist* magazine launched the same year. Friends of the Earth began its first UK campaign in 1971 and the political forerunner to the Green Party formed a year later. The politics of countryside pollution was here to stay.

93.

CHICKEN GOGGLES
C. 1930

One of the most striking developments of the twentieth century, and its effect on the countryside, was the introduction of factory farming. This system of intensive agriculture was developed to produce large quantities of meat, milk and eggs to feed a growing population while minimising costs and using as little land as possible. To achieve this, animals such as cows, pigs and poultry are kept closely packed together or, as it's known in farming, at 'high stocking densities'.

Under such unnatural conditions, producers are forced to use a wide range of techniques to keep their animals healthy, whether it's the routine use of medicines and antibiotics, climate-controlled facilities, or high-energy feed that's fortified with vitamins and mineral supplements. Developing breeds of animals that can tolerate the stress of confinement, lay more eggs, produce more milk, or grow to their slaughter weight more quickly, has also been part of this process.

While factory farming no doubt lowered the price of protein, many would argue that it came at too high a cost to both creature and countryside. And, perhaps, of all intensively reared animals, the chicken best represents this dilemma. For most of history, the chicken didn't make much of a culinary impact. Until the end of the nineteenth century, most hens weighed little more than a pheasant and few produced more than six dozen eggs a year. Chicken meat was a rare addition to the plate: while the wealthy might enjoy the odd fattened capon (a castrated cockerel), most made do with old egg-laying hens and unwanted cockerels, both tough birds that needed hours of slow cooking.

The early twentieth century saw a number of developments that revolutionised chicken farming. A scientific approach to cross-breeding created a new type of hen that could lay an egg almost every day and a different meat breed that rapidly bulked up around the breast and thighs. The discovery of vitamin D allowed farmers to keep chickens indoors away from sunlight without suffering from rickets, while Second World War improvements in vaccines, antibiotics and other medicines mitigated some of the health problems created by keeping animals in crowded conditions.

Some factory farming innovations didn't stand the test of time, however. Chicken goggles such as these briefly solved the problem of birds pecking each other when crammed into small spaces. They were tinted red, in the belief that it would deter a chicken from pecking at another bird's existing wounds. Although comical at first glance, these tiny glasses were often held onto the beak by a split-pin shoved through the bird's nostrils. Chicken spectacles enjoyed a brief stint of popularity but were superseded by debeaking, a contentious and widespread practice that physically removes the end of the chicken's beak.

Perhaps the most controversial technique used by factory farming is the battery cage. First developed in the 1930s, keeping hens in wire cages stacked on top of each other solved a number of pressing issues for the egg farmer. By limiting the movement and energy expended by a hen it needed less food to produce the same amount of eggs. Sloping floors and conveyor belts allowed for non-stop, automatic egg collection, while keeping hens on wire mesh made it easier to remove their manure, all of which reduced labour costs. For the hen, however, life in a battery cage – which prevented all of its natural behaviours such as perching, flapping, foraging and dust-bathing – was intolerable.

In 1964, animal rights campaigner Ruth Harrison published *Animal Machines*, the first book to throw open the barn doors of factory farming and reveal the suffering inflicted on animals in the name of mechanised, large-scale animal husbandry. Meticulously researched, it detailed how animals were raised, confined and slaughtered on factory farms. Moreover, it revealed the gaping chasm between the idyllic image of farming portrayed by those who marketed meat, dairy and eggs, and the often grim reality. Her descriptions of battery cages for hens, veal crates for calves and tether stalls for sows inspired Britain's first farm animal welfare legislation in 1968 and the creation of the Farm Animal Welfare Council a year later. During her lifetime, Harrison also saw the banning of veal crates and tether stalls for pregnant sows in Britain and the gradual phasing out of battery cages. Many, however, would argue there's still work to be done.

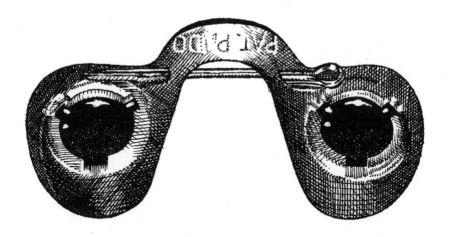

94.

PUBLIC FOOTPATH SIGN

20TH CENTURY

On 24 April 1932, hundreds of ramblers travelled from Manchester and Sheffield to take part in one of the countryside's most important acts of civil disobedience. They were headed for Kinder Scout, an area of moorland in the Peak District, with one goal in mind. Trespass. Writing about it later in his life, political activist and rally leader Benny Rothman remembered this peculiarly British of demonstrations: 'There were hundreds of young men and women, lads and girls, in their picturesque rambling gear: shorts of every length and colour, flannels and breeches, even overalls, vivid colours and drab khaki [...] multicoloured sweaters and pullovers, army packs and rucksacks of every size and shape.'

For all its Blyton-esque overtones, the protest meant business. It sought to highlight the frustrations of walkers who were being denied access to the open countryside. Since the late 1800s, there had been a swell in the numbers of ramblers and cycling groups, many of whom were factory workers from inner cities. They wanted to escape the pollution and overcrowding for a few hours at the weekend, often combining exercise and escape with overt political purpose. Their visits, however, were often unwelcome. Ramblers clashed with local landowners who had ring-fenced large areas of moorland for grouse shooting and employed gamekeepers to prevent public access. For some, the right to ramble was part of a wider political sentiment. Writing about people being chased from Kinder Scout by wardens and their dogs, the Communist Party of Great Britain branded the situation unjust and 'an object lesson in elementary politics'.

The Kinder Scout mass trespass ended in violent clashes and the arrest of six protestors, including rally leader Benny Rothman. Speaking at his trial, Rothman made an impassioned plea. It was not, he claimed, unreasonable for working-class people to be allowed access to all peaks and uncultivated moorland: 'We ramblers, after a hard week's work, in smoky towns and cities, go out rambling on weekends for relaxation, for a breath of fresh air, and for a little sunshine. And we find, when we go out, that the finest rambling country is closed to us. Because certain individuals wish to shoot for about ten days per annum, we are forced to walk on muddy crowded paths, and denied the pleasure of enjoying, to the utmost, the countryside.'

The harsh sentences handed out to the six protestors outraged the nation and only served to popularise the 'right to roam' cause. Just a few weeks later, ten thousand protestors gathered at a second location in the Peak District, Winnats Pass, for the largest gathering of walkers in rambling history.

Three years later, in 1935, the Ramblers Association (now simply known as the Ramblers) was formed and the right-to-roam movement quickly gathered momentum. In 1949, it was pivotal in securing the National Parks and Access to the Countryside Act, which led to the establishment of National Trails, long-distance public footpaths such as the well-trodden Cleveland Way and Coast to Coast route. It also brought about the countryside's first National Parks, of which there are now ten in England, three in Wales and two in Scotland. From the dramatic peaks of Snowdonia to the golden Pembrokeshire coast, the gently rolling South Downs to the vast, snow-topped Cairngorms, almost every type of countryside is represented and protected by the National Parks.

The Act also required that every county council must create and maintain a 'definitive map' of all public rights of way, including footpaths. Many of the countryside's walkways had been in use for hundreds if not thousands of years, created by the constant toing and froing of people travelling to church, fields, market, woodland and neighbouring villages. While the rights to use these footpaths were rooted in ancient common law, until 1949 it was often difficult to prevent landowners diverting them or blocking them up entirely. Anyone attempting to oppose the closure of a footpath had to go to court, an expense too great for most countryside folk. The creation of a 'definitive map' was a landmark moment in the history of access and legally recognised approximately a hundred and forty thousand miles of public rights of way in England and Wales. (There is no definitive map for Scotland but a record is maintained by the Scottish Rights of Way and Access Society.) Viewed by many as the public's 'title deeds' to its rural rights of way, the enshrinement of Britain's ancient paths meant they could never again be closed on a whim.

95.

LAND ROVER WITH HORSE TRAILER DINKY TOY

1960

Every child who opened a Dinky toy for Christmas would have known they were playing with models of the country's most recognisable and up-to-date vehicles. Made in England from 1934 to the late 1970s, Dinky toys charted the extraordinary and often dizzyingly fast development of transport during the twentieth century. This particularly lovely set of a Land Rover and Horse Trailer, released in September 1960, would have offered hours of contented play. But for anyone interested in the history of the countryside, these equestrian toys also represent a pivotal moment in time.

In 1920, despite the horrible losses of horses in the First World War, there remained well over a million working equines in Britain. Hauling everything from carts to ploughs, seed drills to wagons, the horse still powered a large percentage of British agriculture. Every farm relied on its drays and ponies for everything from land preparation to sowing, haulage to bringing in the harvest. Just four decades later, however, fewer than a hundred thousand working horses were still treading the landscape. By the 1960s, most people who owned horses now kept them for pleasure and sport, an expensive hobby that often necessitated a horse-box – a vehicle that itself had only become commonplace in the previous decade. Around the farm, the work of the horse had been replaced by two key heavyweights: the tractor and, as our Dinky car so perfectly captures, the newly arrived Land Rover.

Steam engines reigned supreme during the nineteenth century. For the first fifty years, these were static machines, providing power for other operations such as threshing. They could be moved around a farm, or between locations, but only with the help of a team of horses. After 1850, self-propelled steam engines or 'traction engines' started to appear, removing the need for horses altogether. Although undoubtedly mighty, traction engines were also slow and difficult to manoeuvre, and only truly excelled at pulling heavy loads or providing power to other machinery. They also needed plenty of coal to keep running.

In 1892, American inventor John Froelich developed the first internal combustion tractor, petrol driven with forward and reverse gears. Other US and British companies soon followed suit. The shortage of men in agricultural labour during the First World War only served to hasten the popularity of the tractor. At the beginning of the war, American car-giant Henry Ford – who had grown up in agriculture and understood 'the burden of farming' – developed his first mass-produced tractor, the Fordson. By 1917, Britain was importing them in their thousands.

While these early tractors simply replaced the action of horses, dragging along wheeled ploughs, drills and other implements, in 1926 Irish mechanic Harry Ferguson patented a new system called the 'three-point linkage' (also known as a three-point hitch). This simple but brilliant invention allowed ploughs and other farming implements to be fixed onto three 'arms' at the back of a tractor. The driver could then raise, lower and even tilt the arms using hydraulic pumps. The tractor also carried some or all of the weight of the attachment. This not only made farming tasks much easier and safer but extended the range of implements a farmer could attach to their vehicle. By the

1960s, the countryside thrummed to the sound of over half a million tractors.

While the 1914–18 conflict secured the future of the tractor, the Land Rover grew out of the Second World War. In 1948, the first Land Rover – known as the Series I – made its debut at a car show in Amsterdam. Maurice Wilks, the head engineer for the British car company Rover, had come up with a design for an agricultural vehicle. Inspired by his own Second World War American Willys Jeep, which he used around his own farm but struggled to get spare parts for, Wilks created his own version. It combined the manoeuvrability of a car with some of the brute strength of a tractor. Post-war Britain had no appetite for flashy, expensive cars and Wilks's no-nonsense, four-wheel drive 'workhorse' quickly ploughed ahead. Land Rovers proved popular not only with farmers and other rural workers, but also with military, police and rescue personnel, who had to contend with unmade rural roads. By 1976, the company had sold its one millionth Land Rover. The working horse, meanwhile, slowly trotted into obscurity.

96.

YORKSHIRE BILLHOOK

EARLY 20ᵀᴴ CENTURY

Few features of the rural landscape are as quintessentially British as the hedgerow. It's origins, however, are as tangled as the briars that weave their way through its branches. While many of us imagine that our nation's hedgerows sprang up as field boundaries, with enclosure in the eighteenth and nineteenth centuries, around half of the countryside's hedgerows reach back further in time. Indeed, some are truly ancient.

'Judith's Hedge' in Cambridgeshire, for example, is thought to be almost a thousand years old and a throwback to Norman Britain. It's believed to mark the boundary of a manor given to Judith, William the Conqueror's favourite niece, and is a type of woodland hedge called an 'assart', formed by shrubs and trees left behind after forest clearance for farmland. In Devon, which experienced widespread and early field enclosure between the thirteenth to fifteenth centuries, as many as three-quarters of its 30,000 miles of hedgerow are thought to be medieval in origin. Deeper still in history, archaeologists have excavated remnants of British hedgerows dating back four thousand years to the Bronze Age.

The word hedge comes from *haga* – 'enclosure' in Old English, the language of the Anglo-Saxons. It's etymology, however, is probably far older, from the root *kagh*, meaning to seize or trap. Research into the ancient uses of hedgerows suggests they were often so much more than simple boundaries. Many were created to corral cattle or sheep, protect crops from animals and wind, or to provide a formidable defensive barrier. Particularly prickly species, such as blackthorn, are virtually impenetrable if planted thickly; as many modern gardeners know, those unlucky enough to find themselves savaged by a black-thorn hedge often experience joint inflammation thanks to its poisonous thorns.

Hedgerows are living constructs, however; not wild features. Left to its own devices, a hedge will eventually become a row of tall trees and shrubs, before falling into senescence. The key to a hedgerow's signif-icant longevity is its management by humans. Constant trimming and coppicing encourages more branches to shoot, but it's the ancient skill of 'laying' that allows a hedge to fully renew itself from the ground up. Laying involves cutting the trunks of a hedgerow almost entirely through at ground level. These are then bent over near horizontally and pinned down. This forces the hedge to reshoot from the base upwards, rather than at the top, making it more stock-proof and giving it a new lease of life.

Hedge-laying was a valued rural trade and every layer had their preferred billhook, a chopping tool little altered since the Iron Age. Lots of woodland crafts needed billhooks for cutting, splitting and trimming green (freshly cut) wood, from thatchers to broom-makers, vine cutters to hedge-layers. Different regions also developed their own styles of billhooks, a name that came not from its curved blade but from the Anglo-Saxon words for sword, *bill*, and *hack*, to chop roughly. Blacksmiths created vernacular versions of the billhook, often reflective of local traditions and the tasks they were intended for.

Despite the mass-manufacturing of tools during the Industrial Revolution, this glorious variety remained. Pre-Second World War tool catalogues still listed dozens of differently tweaked versions, from the sickle-shaped 'Hampshire hurdling' to the meaty, cleaver-like 'Pontypool'. This object, a 'Yorkshire billhook', has a characteristically long handle and double-edged blade. Its curved tip allowed the hedge-layer to chop downwards towards the ground without any danger of the cutting edge hitting the ground. The curl also allowed you to cut around a branch as you pulled it towards you. The straight-edged blade and long handle, when held in both hands, could be used like a small axe for making notches and felling small trees.

After the Second World War, government food policy encouraged miles of hedgerows to be torn up to accommodate large farm machinery that couldn't be manoeuvred in small fields. In 1950, the country had over six hundred thousand miles of hedgerow. By the end of the century, this figure had dwindled to less than half. While new hedgerows are now being planted, and ancient ones protected by law, the continuation of the hedge-laying craft is central to their health and survival. We also now know that hedgerows are key to biodiversity, providing shelter and food for an astonishing variety of birds, invertebrates and mammals, including the next beloved icon of the countryside …

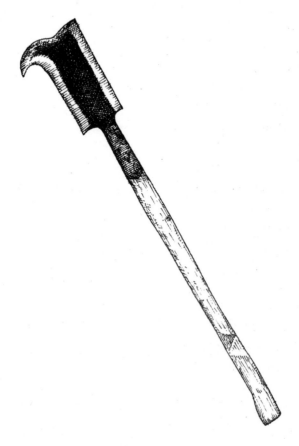

97.

HEDGEHOG ROAD SIGN

2019

In 2019, the government unveiled a new hedgehog traffic sign. It was designed to warn drivers of the potential hazard of small mammals ahead and, by doing so, hopefully reduce the number of people injured every year in road accidents involving wildlife.

The choice of mascot for the new road sign was a significant one. The hedgehog, with its bumbling charm and gentle independence, is one of the nation's most cherished wild creatures. It's also fast becoming the symbol of a countryside in crisis. In the 1950s, there were around 30 million hedgehogs in Britain. Recent studies suggest the current population is now less than a million. The drop is catastrophic but not fully understood. Loss of wild habitat, lack of food, over-use of insecticides, predation – all of these factors are putting our prickly friend under immense pressure. But, perhaps, one of the least advertised causes of the hedgehog's decline is the nation's ever-expanding road network.

Citizen science and the collection of roadkill data has been instrumental in assessing the scale of the problem. Initiatives such as Cardiff University's 'Project Splatter' and the People's Trust for Endangered Species (PTES) 'Mammals on Roads Survey' gathered information about wildlife mortality on the nation's highways. They found that an extraordinary number of creatures were perishing under the country's wheels. Hedgehog roadkills, for example, were estimated to be between 167,000 and 335,000 every year, an alarmingly sizeable percentage of the overall hedgehog population.

In a similar 'National Road Death Survey', completed by the Mammal Society in conjunction with the Hawk and Owl Trust, the hedgehog also won the dubious honour of being the wild mammal most likely to be injured or killed by traffic. Almost a third of all recorded wildlife road casualties were hedgehogs, closely followed by badgers and foxes. Birds of prey also featured heavily in the survey, especially tawny owls, kestrels and the barn owl.

The drive to create more roads has been at the heart of national policy for over a hundred years. Successive governments have held fast to the notion that building more, and bigger roads, reduces traffic congestion and boosts the economy. The damage to the landscape and environment has long been viewed as acceptable collateral for the greater good. More recent studies, however, have begun to challenge that narrative. Research commissioned by the Campaign to Protect Rural England (CPRE), for example, used the government's own data to assess the impact of road building on countryside communities and the environment. The results were fascinating. Building more roads actually increased the volume of traffic both in the short and long term, a phenomenon known as 'induced demand'. Creating more roads in rural and semi-rural areas also encouraged building developments that relied on cars, such as out-of-town shopping areas and housing estates.

The CPRE also found that new road schemes were, in the majority of cases, failing to bring the economic benefits promised. By drawing business away, some new roads even negatively affected existing villages and towns, where people could walk, cycle or use public transport more easily. Natural landscapes were also found to be damaged by the creation of road schemes in 80 per cent of cases, many of which were deemed to be locally or nationally significant in terms of wildlife or cultural heritage. With road use and car numbers forecasted to only increase in the next few decades, the need to invest in different ways to help people move around the countryside, and between urban and rural areas, has never been greater.

The fate of the hedgehog also says something about our attitudes to the countryside and its future. The hedgehog is an animal almost universally loved, one that is firmly embedded in the nation's affections. It was recently crowned, by a huge majority in the Royal Society of Biology's public vote, Britain's favourite mammal. If we can allow such a treasured icon to fall by the wayside, the rest of the countryside's creatures are surely heading for a similar crash.

98.

GRANNY SMITH FIRST CLASS STAMP

2003

The National Fruit Collection at Brogdale, Kent, has an extraordinary array of apple tree varieties. You could munch a different kind of apple every day and still not get through their entire collection in five years. And yet, visit any supermarket in Britain and you'd be lucky to see more than four or five apple varieties stacked on the shelves.

Until the Second World War, Britain was an enthusiastic nation of apple-growers. Apples flourish in its gentle climate. The country's chilly winters are central to the apple tree's ability to set blossom and fruit every year, while its warm, wet summers bring just the right balance of sweetness and acidity. Victorian orchardists and gardeners, with their new-found love of plant science, spent hours creating new varieties and improving old ones. From pulpy cookers and crisp eaters to syrupy juicers and mouth-puckering 'spitters' for cider, it seemed there was an apple for almost any culinary occasion.

Regional varieties blossomed, each with its own distinctive flavour and use: the clove-scented Cornish Gilliflower, for example, or strawberry-tinged Worcester Pearmain, tart Yorkshire Goosesauce or no-nonsense Galloway Pippin. Across the countryside, orchards were also an important means of self-sufficiency for both farms and villages. What wasn't consumed could be sold, often to newly established jam manufacturers and confectioners who turned apple pulp into delicious, sticky treats.

The second half of the twentieth century, however, spelled ruin for British apples. Between 1950 and the century's close, the nation's orchards largely vanished. A countryside that was once perfumed with over a quarter of a million acres of apple trees was left with a core of just sixty thousand. Over three-quarters of the landscape's apple trees had gone. Unlike cereals, meat and dairy, which had been given a huge impetus for growth after the Second World War, orchards were viewed as a national liability. Although apple-growers had been praised for keeping the country's fruit bowls filled during the Second World War, with peacetime the government changed tack. Orchards, along with hedgerows, were viewed as a hindrance to intensive agriculture; the land could be put to better purpose growing staple commodities such as wheat, potatoes or sugar beet.

Other apple-growing countries, according to expert opinion, were also doing it bigger and better. Since the mid-nineteenth century, Britain had imported apples from across the world but – thanks to Britain's insatiable appetite for the pome – there was enough demand to please everyone. After the war, Britain faced stiff competition not only from its old apple-growing rivals America, Canada and South Africa, but also from large commercial orchards in Japan, Australia, New Zealand and European countries such as France and Holland. High-yielding, sweet, cosmetically perfect, consistent performers such as the bland but blemish-free Golden Delicious or highly polished Fuji replaced once-popular traditional varieties. Three-quarters of the 500,000 tonnes of apples Britons eat a year are now imported. Half of these are just two varieties – the Gala and Braeburn – both of which started life in New Zealand.

When the Royal Mail issued its 'Fun Fruit and Veg' set of stamps in 2003, its choice of apple would have been the lunch-box staple of almost every schoolchild. As an iconic symbol of British fruit, however, it was a dud. The ubiquitous Granny Smith, which was developed in Australia, is an apple poorly suited to the British countryside and needs a long, hot season to ripen properly. Its popularity has also, along with a handful of other international varieties, replaced the extraordinary multiplicity that once characterised the British orchard. From Norfolk Beefings, which were slowly squashed and cooked to create sticky Dickensian treats called 'biffins', to the mouth-puckeringly sherbety Grenadier, perfect for fluffy apple sauce, many varieties are in danger of being lost. Far from being just a question of gastronomic snobbery, loss of apple diversity is fast becoming a problem for biodiversity and food security worldwide. Genetic strength, disease resistance and the ability to adapt to a changing climate are under threat if growers stick to a handful of specific and often trademarked varieties. Almost every other crop in the countryside, and commercial livestock, faces the same challenge.

99.

ACH VALLEY TUSK
C. 36000–30000 BCE

Since the dawn of time, humans have been mesmerised by the night sky. Early cultures took a passionate interest in the movements of the sun and moon, and the positions of the stars. Their iridescent, unknowable beauty inspired creation stories and heroic tales, mythical creatures and ideas about the afterlife. Many used the night sky to get their bearings both on land and at sea. Studies of ancient DNA, for example, suggest that the earliest farming communities from the Near East were also skilled sailors, leapfrogging around Europe via coastal routes over the Aegean and Mediterranean seas. We similarly know that the only way Neolithic farmers made it to Britain and Ireland, around 4000 BCE, was by sea. Whether they headed out at dawn, or relied on cues from the night sky, there's a good chance that many of our ancestors took a mental note of the positions of the stars before they pushed out into the waves.

Constellations throughout the year gradually shift thanks to the Earth's orbit around the sun. In summer, we see a different night sky than in winter. Searching for the positions of the stars would have given our ancient forebears a sense of the seasons, another way of marking time's endless cycles. The changing diorama of the dark would have also acted as a reminder of when to plant, harvest, breed, slaughter, celebrate or ask for divine providence.

For almost the entire twelve or so thousand years covered in this book, the night sky was pristine. In 1879, Mosley Street in Newcastle was the first to have electric streetlights and the country has remained illuminated ever since. While electric lighting has had immeasurably positive benefits, it has come with some unexpected downsides. The slow creep of artificial lighting – everything from streetlamps to outdoor advertising, garden lighting to twenty-four-hour factories – is turning the night into an extension of the day, even over large stretches of the countryside.

Our circadian rhythms, however, are still the same as those of the men, women and children who slept under the stars thousands of years ago. Lighting up the night-time has proven to have adverse impacts on our health and sleep patterns. Wildlife also relies on a clear distinction between night and day – blurring these lines is having a catastrophically confusing effect on many nocturnal creatures, from bats to migrating birds, amphibians to pollinating insects.

The darkness constitutes half of our experience of the countryside and yet, unlike many other rural issues, the night sky has no legal protection. There are, however, plenty of dark sky champions. From the National Parks to the Campaign for Dark Skies, constellations of like-minded groups are working hard to protect the night sky. Many areas around the countryside are now officially recognised as 'Dark Sky' sites, for their lack of light pollution.

These valuable places are often divided up into two levels of visibility. The first are *Milky Way* sites, the gold standard of dark skies and only now found in remote, pitch-black rural areas. There, astronomers can contemplate our very own galaxy, a hazy streak of spilt cream across the sky. A greater number, however, are *Orion* sites, places where the seven main stars in the winter constellation are visible to the naked eye. Betelgeuse, the huge star on Orion's shoulder, is one of the largest known to man. Its light takes over four hundred years to reach Earth. It's humbling to think that, as the starlight left Betelgeuse, our sixteenth-century swimmer, Everard Digby, was just putting pen to paper.

Orion's familiar human form has caught the eye of stargazers for thousands of years. Indeed, our object, a tiny sliver of mammoth tusk carved to represent the outstretched arms and legs of a man, is thought to be the oldest depiction of the Orion constellation. At around thirty-two to thirty-eight thousand years old, it was discovered in a German cave and was crafted by the Aurignacian people, about whom we know almost nothing. What it does, perhaps, reveal is the magnificent antiquity of our relationship with the night sky, one that should be protected and treasured for generations to come. Looking up at the billions of stars, it's tempting to picture our countryside ancestors doing the same, pondering their past, present and future.

100.

ROBO-BEE
21ST CENTURY

The history of the countryside is an extraordinary one. For those who imagine rural life to be unchanging, preserved in aspic, even a brief rattle through the last twelve thousand years reveals how dynamic and tumultuous the countryside has been. The landscape, and its plants and creatures, have been forever shifting. From field shapes to hedgerows, woodland to wild animals, there has been a long tussle between people and their rural surroundings. Beginning with Star Carr's hunter-gatherers, and their tentative attempts to clear the woodland, to the wholescale reorganisation of farming post-Second World War, we have always used the countryside for our own ends, good or ill.

The people who have made the countryside their home have also been incredibly diverse. The story of rural Britain is one of changing population and different ethnicities, an often-bewildering scuffle between conflict and subjugation, intermarriage and gentle integration. Anyone who attempts to squeeze a definition of British ethnicity into a narrow band of people blatantly ignores the remarkable journey we took to get here.

There has never been a period in history when the countryside was perfect; or, at least, perfect for the people who lived there. There have always been problems; every time one was 'solved', it threw up its own new challenges. Farming communities have long lived on a knife-edge.

Until the nineteenth century, one spoiled harvest or a decimated herd could be catastrophic. Under such circumstances, it's perhaps understandable why many of our native predators and wildlife were hunted to extinction, only to leave other crop-damaging species to thrive.

Equally, how exhilarating it must have been to live through the Agricultural Revolution if you were a gentleman farmer. With a headful of new scientific principles and a decent wadge of cash in your back pocket, the countryside and its livestock must have seemed like prizes waiting to be claimed. For those at the other end of the social scale, however, the consequences of the Agricultural Revolution were enough to prompt many country dwellers to leap on the next ship heading to the colonies.

Even post-war, in the twentieth century, it would be churlish to pass too harsh a judgement on agricultural policy that was designed to feed the nation. Bruised and battered from two horrific world wars, Britain wanted to ensure that she could never ever face food shortages again, whatever the cost to the countryside. Taking control of farming, and supercharging it with machinery, fertilisers and chemicals, seemed a smart move and produced miraculous results almost overnight. The countryside is, and always will be, a product of the generations of people who came before us and the decisions they made about the best use of the rural landscape.

Our final object, however, says something about where we are now. It's a Robo-Bee, a minuscule drone developed by Harvard University to try and solve the problem of how to pollinate crops in a countryside that is rapidly losing its bees. Created with the best of intentions, this tiny, insect-sized, solar-powered, miraculous piece of engineering is astonishing in its brilliance. It's also, however, a hopeless sticking-plaster to fix a haemorrhaging rural landscape.

The future of the countryside is both terrifying and terrifically exciting. Our understanding of the importance of nature, biodiversity and a healthy climate has never been greater. Empathy for both wildlife and domesticated animals is part of our national character. Our national sports are no longer bear-baiting and cock-fighting, but watching nature programmes and treating our pets like members of the family. A love of nature and appreciation of the countryside – both its historic buildings and diverse landscapes – abounds.

And yet we have a major problem. Conservation groups, government bodies and many people involve in caring for the countryside, including farmers, agree that we can't go on like we have been. The basic strategy for twentieth-century farming was to make the most of agrochemicals, machinery and fossil-fuel energy. Like an athlete on steroids, the agricultural performance of the countryside raced ahead, revolutionising farming, enabling population growth and economic prosperity. There are only so many years, however, that a pumped runner can compete before they collapse.

Scientific evidence shows, overwhelmingly, that if we carry on behaving as we have been we will end up destroying all the things we treasure about the countryside – polluting our rivers and air, degrading our soils, releasing more carbon and methane into the atmosphere, and driving many species to extinction, including those we rely on to support human life. It's already happening. Many of the countryside icons we treasure – from bumblebees to barn owls, the wildflowers of our childhood to venerable, ancient trees – are dwindling. Britain has the dubious honour of being one of the most nature-deprived countries in the world. The unavoidable truth is that, if we continue down this track, we will reach a dead end. Literally.

Fortunately, we already have the answers. Many people involved in food production, farming and conservation are working hard to bring about a new relationship with the countryside. One that encompasses not only how we farm, but also our consumption habits, how food is produced and sold. It brings in other radical ideas too – such as rewilding, rights to roam, new technology, transport and local housing initiatives.

There's no one-size-fits-all approach. Two interesting ideas have emerged, both of which attempt to help biodiversity and food production. One is called 'land sparing', in which Britain reduces the amount of land it dedicates to farming and increases areas for nature and wildlife. New, inventive ways are being used to produce food such as growing crops without soil, vertical farming and artificial photosynthesis, which allows crops to be grown underground.

Urban spaces are also being turned into places that can grow food and allow nature to thrive. This has the potential to produce fresh food in traditionally nature-deprived spaces and with a lower carbon-footprint than food that is transported long distances. Far from being a pipe-dream, urban farming already creates about a fifth of the world's food. Technology is also a huge part of the solution. Farming is adopting a wide range of innovations, including robots, GPS, drones, temperature and moisture sensors, and aerial images. This allows farmers to be much more precise with their water use and their application of fertilisers and chemicals, instead of adopting a blanket approach. Software can also help farmers monitor how their plants are faring.

The other idea is 'land sharing', the principle of working in harmony with nature to create productive farms that also host biodiversity. Regenerative farming, for example, is gaining widespread support, a common-sense approach that moves away from single crops, high chemical input and intensive livestock. Many of its key practices – growing different crops and beneficial plants simultaneously, agroforestry (where livestock pasture and crops are integrated with trees and hedgerows) and combining free-range grazing livestock and arable crop – have their roots in ancient farming methods.

Its detractors worry that if we de-intensify how we farm the countryside, we'll not be able to grow enough to feed ourselves or end up using more land to grow the same amount of food. Recent research suggests, however, that if Britain cut its food waste by half (supermarkets and consumers currently throw away *a third* of the food we grow, instead of us eating it) and consume less but higher-welfare meat (about 40 per cent of the countryside's arable land grows food for livestock), the goal is more than achievable. What and how we eat directly affects our rural landscape. People love wild swimming, for example, but don't see the connection between the cheap chicken they crave and the industrial poultry farms that pollute our waterways. Equally, we throw our hands in the air with dismay about the plight of British orchards but only ever buy a handful of super-sweet super-market varieties shipped from thousands of miles away.

Farmers get blamed for trashing the countryside but, with cheap imports to compete with, and supermarkets demanding ultra-low prices, switching to a less intensive way of growing crops or raising animals leaves them vulnerable. British farming can't be expected to change its own food production system to be more eco-friendly when we import food from places with worse environmental or animal welfare standards than our own. Many farmers are already struggling with meagre profits, and if we want them to support our environmental ambitions, they need government support to do so. Support that helps rural communities transition from arable monocultures and intensive meat farming to high-welfare, pasture-based livestock, species-rich crop rotations, and chemical-free habitats that can support diversity.

By protecting the countryside from harm, we also allow it to become an asset that can be used for other things. Marginal land taken out of agricultural use and rewilded, for example, could create new jobs in rural communities, including nature tourism, public sector work, research and education, fundraising, ecological restoration and conservation, or wildlife and livestock management. An exhilarating future emerges for the countryside if we attempt to work with nature, not against it. Many of the things that we've talked about in this book also play their part, whether it's reinstating hedgerows, peatlands, wildflower meadows and native woodland or reintroducing native species such as the beaver. Who can guess what the history of the countryside would look like, written in another hundred years? It would be good to know, however, that there was going to be a countryside to write about.

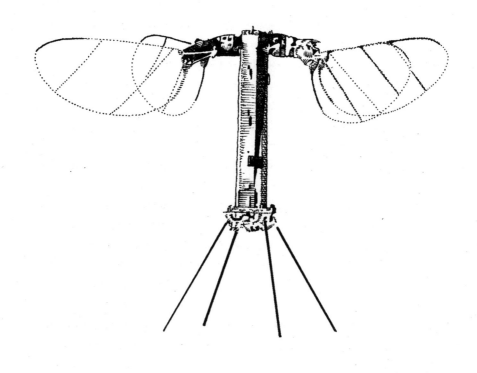

ACKNOWLEDGEMENTS

Jonathan de Peyer, thank you for encouraging me to spend one of the most interesting years of my life on this book. I launched off into the unknown and, to my surprise and delight, the book slowly, magically revealed its own story. Never did I imagine I'd be writing about bear grease pomade and blunt force head trauma but that's the strange, brilliant and totally unexpected history of the countryside for you. Jon, your editorial wisdom is endless, as is your encouragement.

Thanks also to the rest of the fantastic HarperNorth team: Alice Murphy-Pyle, Gen Pegg, Hilary Stein, Megan Jones, Taslima Khatun and all those countless others I've forgotten. Much gratitude to Pa and Ma, too, who generously trawled through my first drafts and always offered penetrating insights and annoyingly accurate spelling corrections. Also to Nicola Stenhouse, for her patient translating of an old, battered French circus poster; Dana Jennings, palynologist and archaeologist par excellence; and Virginia Arrowsmith, possibly the only other person I know who gets giddy with excitement about old farming catalogues and gruesome rural implements. You are all wonderful.

INDEX

Abbots Bromley, Staffordshire 7
Aberdeenshire, Scotland 30, 89
Abergavenny, Wales 96
Aberystwyth, Wales 96
Ach Valley tusk 301
Africa 8, 35–6, 62
Agricultural Revolution 111–12,
    219–20, 239–40, 246, 303
agrochemicals 278–80
Aigle (Eagle, shoe company) 258
Alaska 46
alcohol 42–3, 101, 135, 185–7
ale 42–3
Alfred the Great 123
Alfriston Clergy House, East Sussex
    264
alms and almshouses 209–11
America 9, 26, 70, 240, 297.
    See also North America
Amsterdam 289
Ancient Monuments Protection
    Act, 1882 263
Angles tribe 96
Anglesey, Wales 266
Anglo-Saxons
    agricultural revolution 110–12
    beekeeping 134
    birds 107–9
    cattle 105–6
    farming 129–30

fish and fishing 120–1
forests 98–100
glassmaking 101
grave goods 104
medicine 102–3
Norman conquest 126, 129
pigs and wild boars 117–18
place names 96–8
religion 113–15
swimming 174
Viking occupation 122–4
apples and orchards 68–70,
    185–7, 296–8
aqueducts 231–2
Aran Islands, Ireland 257
ards 62–4
Aristotle 54
Armenia 257
Asia 8–9, 11, 48, 66, 46, 87, 197
Astley's Circus 224–6
Athelberht, King of Kent, 105,
    113–14
Æthelstan, King 105, 123
Augustine 113–14
Aurignacian people 301
Australia 36, 240, 243, 262,
    297
Avon, River 96
axe-hammer 104–6
axes 29–31

baby feeder 38–40
badgers 159
Badger, Shropshire 97
bakers 150
Bakewell, Robert 221–3, 228
Balbridie, Aberdeenshire 89
Bald's Leechbook 101–2
Bales, Peter 171
Baltic region 47, 48
Banffshire, Scotland 214
Bardot, Brigitte 253
barns 112, 198–9
barometers 243–4
Barton Aqueduct, Lancashire 231
baskets and basket making 251–3
Batavi tribe 174
battery cages 282–3
Battle of Hastings 125, 129
Beaker culture 35–7, 42
beakers 101
Beale, John 187
bears and bear-baiting 93–4, 165,
    183–4
Beaufort, Francis 242
beavers 159–60
Bede 120
bees and beekeeping 134–6, 158,
    186–7, 303
Belgium 217
bell beaker 35–7
bells 261–2
Benson, Moses 261
Benty Grange helmet 116–18
Beowulf 118, 135, 174
Bering Land Bridge/Strait 46
Berkshire 60
bestiaries 158–60
Bewick, Thomas 236
Bible 138, 171, 176
billhooks 291–2

biodiversity 292, 298, 305
birds 107–9, 236–8.
    See also chickens; owls
bird scaring 196, 233–5
Birmingham 272
Black Death 36, 141, 155–8,
    161–3, 215, 239
blacksmiths 60–1, 104, 144, 291
board games 163, 182
boats 9–10, 99, 240–3
Boece, Hector 92
bog bodies 50–1, 203–5
bollock dagger 167–9
bone necklace 14–16
boots 257–9
Bordeaux, France 87
Borgwardt, Ronald 47
Botai culture 44–5
bowls 101
boxwood nutcracker 170–2
Bradford 1
breweries 42–3
Bridgewater Canal, North West
    England 230–1, 232
Brindley, James 230, 231
Bristol 155
British Trust for Ornithology 279
Brogdale, Kent 296
bronze 48, 59–60
brooches 121
brown bears *see* bears and bear-
    baiting
buckets 99–100
Buckinghamshire 178
bulls 183
Burton Agnes drum 20–2
Bury St Edmunds, Suffolk 142, 156

Caen Castle, Normandy 126
Caesar, Julius 65–6, 174

Cailleach 146–8
Caithness, Scotland 203–4
Caledonian tribe 85
calendars 56–8, 110–12
Calgacus 85
Calleva Atrebatum, near
    Silchester 54
Calverley, Yorkshire 1–2
Cambridgeshire 52, 75, 147, 147–
    8, 264, 290
Cambridgeshire Fens 179–80
Cambridge University 24, 173, 174
Campaign for Dark Skies 300
Campaign to Protect Rural England
    (CPRE) 294
Canada 9, 240, 266, 297
canals 230–2, 246, 254–6, 261
candles 135–6, 148, 189
Canterbury 111, 114
Cardiff University 293
cars 273, 287, 289, 293–5
Carson, Rachel 280
carts 167, 227, 232
Cashel Man 51
castles 125–7
'castles and roses' folk art 255–6
Catholic Church *see* Christianity
    and the Church
cats 86–8, 177–8, 198
cattle 62, 104–6, 213, 214, 222,
    283. *See also* oxen
Catuvellauni tribe 102
Celtic fields 64, 98, 110
Celtic languages 95–6
Census records 234
Central America 9
Central Asia 87, 197
ceramics 144–5, 228–30, 232.
    See also tiles
chairs 207–8

Chamberlain, Andrew 21
Charlemagne, King of the Franks
    152
Charles I 179
Cheam, London 145
Cheavin's Water Filter 271
Cheshire 261
Chester 96
Chew Valley Hoard 128–30
chicken goggles 282–3
chickens 66, 108, 252–3, 281–3
child labour 168, 233–5, 237, 248–9
chimneys 177, 208, 212
China 26, 86, 197
Chipstable, Somerset 212
Christianity and the Church 67,
    75–6, 102, 113–15, 120,
    135–6, 153, 171, 176–7, 260
churches 67, 75, 113–15, 135–6
    poverty relief 209, 210–11
Church of the Holy Fathers, Sutton
    115
cider 185–7
circuses 224–6
Cirencester, Gloucestershire 65,
    139
Clarke, George Hyde 261
clay tablet 11–13
Cleveland Way National Trail 285
cloth 151. *See also* wool
clothing 203–5
Cnut, King of England 124
coal 230, 232
Coast to Coast National Trail 285
cobnuts 171–2
cockerels 65–7, 108
cock-fighting and cock-throwing
    182–3
coins 91, 114–15, 128–30
Coligny Calendar 56–8

INDEX

collars 164–6
Colman's Mustard 247
colonialism 261. *See also* slavery
Columbus, Christopher 46
Columella 72–3
Communist Party of Great Britain 285
commuting 272–3
conservation 237–8, 279–80, 303–6
Constans, Emperor 91
Constantine, Emperor 75–6
constellations 299–301
Cookham, Berkshire 60
coracles and coracle postage stamp 8–10
Corinium Cockerel 65–7
Cornwall 96, 216
Cotgrave, Randle 171–2
country houses 260–2
Country Houses Committee 264
County Cork, Ireland 264
cows 62, 104–6, 213, 214, 222, 283. *See also* oxen
crafts 251–3, 255–6, 267–8
Cranborne, Dorset 108
Cranham, Gloucestershire 108
Cranwich, Norfolk 108
Croatia 39
crop rotation 111, 219
crosses 156–7
Crufts dog show 249–50
Cuddeson Bowl 101–3
Culpepper, Nicholas 184
Cumbria 96
curfew bells 188–9
Cyprus 78
Czech Republic 62

daggers 59–61, 167–9
Damendorf Man 50–2

Danebury, Hampshire 63
'Dark Sky' sites 300
Darwin, Charles 242
daub 90, 91
DDT 278–80
De Arte Natandi (*The Art of Swimming*) by Everard Digby 173–5
deer and deer headdresses 5–7
Dee, River 231
Delft tiles 179–81
Denmark 29–30, 33, 44, 45, 51, 129
Department of the Environment 280
Derbyshire 118. *See also* Peak District
Derwent, River 96
Devon 96, 155, 290
Dickens, Charles 224
Digby-Curtis, Joseph 222
Digby, Everard 173–5, 300
Dinas Oleu, Wales 264
Dinky toys 287–9
Dishley, Leicestershire 221
Divje Babe flute 27
Dobunni tribe 65
dog food 249–50
dogs 53–5, 164–6, 169, 183, 198
Domesday Book 1, 79, 126, 129–30, 131–3, 134, 138, 153, 227
Dorset 87, 97, 155
Dorvadilla, King 92
Draved Forest, Denmark 29–30
dried cat 176–8
drinking straws 41–3
Druid of Colchester 102
drums, measuring 20–2
Dundee 245

Dunham Massey, Cheshire 261–2
Durrington Walls, near Stonehenge 18, 90
Dutch influence 180–1

eagles 108
earthworms 200–2
East Anglia 96, 104, 123, 129
East Anglian Fens 204
East Hoathy, Sussex 246
East Yorkshire 20
Ecologist, The (magazine) 280
Edgar Ætheling 124
Edinburgh 213, 258
Edinburgh, University of 33
Education Act, 1870 234–5
Edwards, George 233–5
Edward the Confessor, King of England 124, 125
eels 120
Egypt 8, 24, 48, 62, 86
Elizabeth I 261
Ely 120
emigration 240–1
English Channel 10
Essex 96, 108, 115, 180
Eton College 215
Ettmüller, Michael 201
Europe 8, 9, 27, 29, 30, 33, 38, 46, 48, 62, 116
Evelyn, John 171, 172, 185, 218
Exeter 129
explosives 241, 255
Explosives Act, 1875 256

fabric 151, 203–4. *See also* wool
Factory Act, 1844 234
factory farming 281–3
fairs 138–9. See also circuses; markets

falconry 108–9
Farm Animal Welfare Council 283
farming calendar 110–12
fellmongers 248–9
Ferguson, Harry 288
Ferring, West Sussex 147
Fertile Crescent, Near East 8, 11, 12, 15, 59, 62, 86
Fiennes, Celia 216
figurines 47, 48–9, 72, 73. *See also* models
First World War 132, 259, 262, 266, 272, 287–8
fish and fishing 119–21, 168, 237–8, 251–2
Fishbourne Roman Palace, Sussex 78
Fitzroy, Vice-Admiral Robert 242–4
Flag Fen, Cambridgeshire 52
flour 23–5
Flute of Veyreau 26–8
folk art 255–6
Folkton Drums 20–2, 36
food waste 305
Ford, Henry 288
forests and woodland 29–30, 98–100, 132–3
Fortingall Yew, Perthshire 100
four-field rotation 219
foxes 159
France 26, 56, 78, 87, 153, 171, 250, 258, 297
Friends of the Earth 280
Froelich, John 288
frost fairs 194–5
Fulacht Fiadh 43
Fylde coast, Lancashire 207

Galloway bird pin 122–4
Game Research Association
   279
Geoffrey the Baker 155, 156
Georgia 12
Germani tribe 174
Germany 33, 47–8, 50–1, 153,
   278, 301
Gibbs, Jane 216, 217
Glasgow 272
glass 101–3, 153–4
Gloucester 156
Gloucester Candlestick 134–6
Gloucestershire 155
Godwinson, Harold, Earl of Wessex
   later King of England 124,
   125, 128, 129
Goodyear, Charles 258
graffiti 126–7, 155
grain grinding 23–5, 132
Granny Smith first class stamp
   297–8
grave goods 15, 20–2, 39,
   41–2, 65, 93, 102, 104,
   109
graves 33, 35, 141–2, 156
Great Circle, Newgrange,
   Ireland 21
Great Dalby, Leicestershire 270
Great Snoring, Norfolk 95
Greece 8
Greeks 69
Green Party 280
Gregory the Great, Pope 113
Greyfriars, London 156
Gromelski, Tomasz 167
Guazzo, Stefano 170
Guinness 247
Gunn, Steven 167
Gussage All Saints, Dorset 87

Hadow, Grace 267
Hamilton, Edward 237–8
Hampshire 63
handicrafts see crafts
Hardrada, Harald, King of Norway
   124, 125
Harold II, King of England 124,
   125, 128, 129
Harrison, Ruth 282–3
Harrison, William 164–5
Harrying of the North 1–2,
   129
Hartham, Wiltshire 97
Hartley's Jam 247
Harvard University 303
harvests 146–8, 233–4
Hastings 125, 129
Hawk and Owl Trust 294
hawks 236
hazel trees and bushes 171–2
headdresses 6–7
hedgehogs 159, 293–5
hedgerows 290–2
helmets 118
hen baskets 252–3
Henry of Huntingdon 153
Henry VIII 150, 260
herbicides 278–80
herbs 102–3
Herefordshire 187
Herriot, James 275–6
Hertfordshire 140–1, 155
Hesse, Germany 33
Highlands of Scotland 252
hillforts 63, 87
Hill, Octavia 263–4
HMS Beagle 242
Holland 217, 289, 297
Holland, Daniel 197–8
honey 134–5

horns 132–3
horses 44–6, 150, 167, 224–5, 226–9, 231–2, 249, 254, 287–8
Hounslow Dog 53–5
House of Dionysus Mosaic 77–9
housing 272–4. *See also* water: for rural households
Howick, Northumberland 89
Howitt, William 191, 245–6
human fat 201–2
Humber, River 35, 156
Hunter Boot Ltd 259
Hunter, Sir Robert 263–4
hunting 54, 132, 165
Hutchinson, Hiram 258
Huygens, Constantijn 216
Hyde Hall, Cheshire 261

Ilfracombe, Devon 96
India 8, 182
Indonesia 140
industrialisation 2, 230–1, 263–4, 270, 272, 291
Inland Waterways Association (IWA) 256
insecticides 278–80
instruments, musical 26–8
Iona, Scotland 114
Iran 8
Iraq 9, 10, 12
Ireland 9, 21, 42–3, 51, 92, 113, 114, 129, 147, 181, 257, 264
iron 59–61, 83
Isidore of Seville 135
Isle of Skye, Scotland 252
Israel 42
Italy 23, 31, 61, 68, 153

Iverson, Johannes 30
ivory 133

James I 176, 179
Japan 278, 297
Jenner, Edward 243
'Jerusalem' (hymn) 267
jet 93
jewellery 14–16, 108–9, 121, 124
Jordan 84
Judith's Hedge, Cambridgeshire 290
jugs 145
Jutes tribe 96

Kanturk Castle, County Cork 264
Katherine Shearer ship 241
Kazakhstan 45, 68
Keiller's Marmalade 245, 247
Kent 96, 97, 117, 121, 129, 187, 188, 196, 296
Kinder Scout, Peak District 284–5
kingfishers 237–8
Kinsey Cave, North Yorkshire 94
knackers 248–9
knitting and knitting sheaths 191–3
knives 167–9
Krakatoa, Indonesia 140

Lake District 123, 152, 189, 264–5
Lambeth 224
lambs and lambing 206–8
Lancashire 123
Lancaster Canal 261
Land Rovers 287–9
land sparing and land sharing 304–5
Latin 96
Lavant Drum 20–1
Laws of Ine 98–9, 105, 114, 117

Lea & Perrins Worcestershire Sauce 247
lead 83–4, 156–7
Lead Cross 155–7
leather 105, 257–8
Leclerc, Georges-Louis 236
leeches 243–4
Leeds 1, 216, 272
Leicestershire 221, 270
Lewis-Stempel, John 238
lightning 168
light pollution 300–1
Lincoln 96, 126
Lincoln Cathedral 159
Lincolnshire 35, 123, 156, 180
Lindisfarne, Northumberland 114, 122
Liverpool 181, 243, 261
livestock breeding 221–3, 228, 281–2
London 32, 54, 141–2, 145, 154, 156, 181, 194–5, 213, 255–6, 273
Loose, Kent 97
Low Countries 153, 219
Lumbric Alum 201–2
lynx 92

Mabey, Richard 238
Maikop culture 41, 42
malaria 103, 179
Malling, Kent 196
Malton, North Yorkshire 93
Mammal Society 294
Manchester 96, 230, 232, 261, 272, 284
maps 82
markets 138–9, 228, 245–6
Marlborough Downs 17
marmalade 245, 247

Marriage Act, 1653 192–3
Marshall, William 198, 200
mass graves 33, 141–2, 156
Mayhew, Henry 249
mead 135
measuring systems and devices 20–2, 149–51, 243–4
medical treatments and equipment 101–3, 201–2, 277. See also veterinary medicine
Melcombe Regis, Dorset 155
Mendip Hills, Somerset 83
Mercia 123
Mercury 66–7
Merret, Christopher 185
Merrills board 163
Merryweather, George 243–4
Mersey, River 231
Mesopotamia see Iraq
metal 59–61, 83–5
Meteorological Office 243
mice 87–8, 197
Middle East 182, 191
Middlesex 96, 273
Midlands 123, 224
milestones 80–2
milk 38–40
mills 132
Mines Act, 1842 234
mining 83–5, 234
misericords 159–60
models 24–5, 54, 62, 64, 229. See also figurines
monasteries 114, 122–3, 135, 153, 156, 260
Mongolia 197
Moore, Declan 43
Morris, William 263
mosaics 78–9, 87
motte-and-bailey castles 126

mugwort 102
Museum of London 141

National Fruit Collection,
    Brogdale, Kent 296
National Parks and National Trails
    285–6, 300
National Trust 263–5
National Union of Suffrage
    Societies 267
Neanderthals 27
Near East 69, 116, 299
necklaces 14, 15, 16
Netherlands 51, 180–1
Newcastle 195, 300
Newcastle-under-Lyme 224
New Forest 117
Newfoundland, Canada 9
New Zealand 240, 297
Nicholas I, Pope 67
Nicotiana 215–17
Nine-Men's-Morris board
    163
Norfolk 95, 180, 233
Norfolk Broads 204
Normandy, France 126
Normans
    conquest of England 1–2, 78,
        125–30, 174, 188
    land ownership 131–3, 162, 260,
        290
    surnames 143
Norris, Henry Lee 258
North America 45–6, 186–7, 215,
    217, 225, 262
North British Rubber Company
    258–9
Northern Ireland 204
North Piddle, Worcestershire 95
Northumberland 89, 114, 122

Northumbria 123, 129
North Yorkshire 3–4, 93, 94, 195,
    275–6. *See also* Star Carr,
    North Yorkshire
Norway 252
Norwich 126
Nottinghamshire 195
nuts and nutcrackers 170–2

Offa, King of Mercia 152
Old English Martyrology, The 106
Orderic Vitalis 129
Orion 300–1
Orkney chairs 207–8
Orkney Islands, Scotland 14–15,
    21, 214, 252
Ouse, River 96, 195
Owl Misericord 158–60
owls 107, 158, 159, 160, 198, 236,
    294
oxen 62–4, 105, 110, 111, 132,
    227–8. *See also* cattle
Oxford 97, 156

paganism 76, 102, 113, 115
Pakistan 8, 62
Palestine 8
Paris, Matthew 140–1, 142
Parker Pearson, Mike 21
Parmelee, Spencer Thomas 258
Parry, Hubert 267
Peak District 204, 261, 284–5
Peak Forest Canal 261
peat 203–6
Pendle, Lancashire 96
Pennsalt 279
Penryn, Cornwall 96
Penzance, Cornwall 96
People's Trust for Endangered
    Species (PTES) 293

Pepys, Samuel 179
Pershore, Worcestershire 139
Persian Gulf 8
Perthshire, Scotland 100
Peru 9
pesticides 278–80
Peter Rabbit 264–5
Pettie, George 170
Pevensey, East Sussex 125
Piddle, Dorset 97
pig jaw bone 17–19
'pig', lead 83–5
pigs 18–19, 99, 116–18, 132, 188, 283
pike 121
pillories 137–9, 150
pins 124
Pitchford Hall Cup 194–6
Pitt the Younger, William 184
place names 95–8, 108, 123
plague 36, 141, 155–8, 161–3, 215, 239
playing cards 182–4
Pliny the Elder 60, 78, 100, 201
Plot, Robert 7
ploughs 62–4, 110–12, 132, 227
poetry 108, 117, 174
Pompeii, Italy 68
Pontcysyllte Aqueduct, Wales 231–2
Poor Law, 1601 210
Portgate, Devon 96
portraits 221, 223
Portugal 35
postal service 247, 297–8
potatoes 218–20
Potter, Beatrix 264–5
pottery 144–5, 228–30, 232. See also tiles
poverty 209–11, 239–40

Preseli Mountains, Wales 17
Puabi, Queen 42
public footpaths 284–6
Puglia, Italy 23
Purdy Brown, Joshuah 225

Quinn, Billy 42–3
Quintfall Hill, Caithness 203–5

rabbits 78–9
railways 254, 256, 272–3
ramblers 284–6
Ramblers Association 285
rats 197–9
Raveley, Cambridgeshire 108
ravens 108
Ravenscar, North Yorkshire 108
Ravensden, Bedfordshire 108
Rawnsley, Hardwicke 263–4
regenerative farming 305
Regent's Canal, London 255–6
Richard I 153
Rickeby, Sweden 109
Ricketts, John Bill 225
Ring of Brodgar, Orkney 21
rings 108–9
rivers 84, 119–21, 168
roads 80–2, 228, 232, 246, 293–5
Robo-Bee 303
Romans 65–7
    apple cultivation 68–70
    bears 93–4
    buildings 90–1
    cats 87
    fish and fishing 120
    forests 98
    glassmaking 101
    imports to Britain 77–9, 152
    metals 83–5
    place names 96

religion 75–6, 113

roads 80–2

slavery 71–3

swimming 174

wine 74–5

roof tiles 88, 91

Rothman, Benny 284–5

roundhouses 89, 90

Royal Charter ship 243

Royal College of Physicians 215

Royal Commission of Inquiry into Children's Employment, 1840 234

Royal Mail 297–8

Royal Navy 242

Royal Society 185, 243

Royal Society for the Protection of Birds (RSPB) 279

Royal Society of Biology 295

rubber 258–9

Ruislip, Middlesex 273

rush nips and rushlights 188–190

Russia 41

Rutland 270

sacrifices 51–2, 63, 106

saddle quern 23–4

Saffron Waldon, Essex 108

Saint Alban 76

Salcombe, Devon 96

Salisbury Plain 17, 18–19

Samalas volcano, Indonesia 140, 141

Samhain 57, 58

Sandwich, Kent 188

Sanger, George 225–6

Savernake Horn 131–3

Saxons 96

Schleswig-Holstein, Germany 50

Schorn, John 178

Scotland 92–3, 114, 122–3, 147, 181, 203–4, 207–8, 214, 252, 285, 286

Scots 162

Scottish Rights of Way and Access Society 286

seasons 57–8

Second World War 259, 262, 277, 282, 289, 297

servants 261–2

Severin, Tim 9–10

Severn, River 84, 96, 195, 231

sewage and sanitation 270–1

Shakespeare, William 163, 179

sheep 11–13, 152–4, 162–3, 206–8, 212, 214, 222–3

Sheffield 118, 284

shepherds 206–7

Shetland Islands, Scotland 252

ships and shipwrecks 99, 240–3

Shitterton, Dorset 97

shoes 50, 52, 177–8, 257–9

shops 245–7

Shoreditch, London 139

Shrewsbury 115, 126, 195

Shropshire 81, 97, 134, 261

Siberia 46

Sigerslev Axe 29–31

Silchester, Hampshire 54

Silk Road 68, 87

Sinclair, Donald 276

Skara Brae, Orkney Islands 14–15, 36

Skye, Scotland 252

slavery 71–3, 84, 217, 261

Slovenia 27

Smith, George 255

smoking 215–17

Society for the Propagation of Horseflesh 249

Society for the Protection of Ancient Buildings (SPAB) 263–4

Somerset 83, 128, 155, 187, 195, 212, 258

Somerset Levels 179, 204

South Africa 297

South America 26

Southampton 195

South-East Asia 8–9, 66

South-West Asia 11, 48, 197

Spain 35, 78

sparrows 236–7

spiked dog collar 164–6

Spitalfields Mass Burial 140–2

Spratt's dog food 249–50

staddle stones 198–9

Staffordshire 7, 181, 228–30

Stained Glass Roundel 152–4

St Albans, Hertfordshire 140–1

Stamford Bridge, near York 125

stamps 9, 10, 247, 297–8

Star Carr, North Yorkshire 5–6, 7, 29, 89, 93, 160, 302

stars 299–301

Statute of Labourers, 1351 162, 209–10

St Benet's Abbey, Norfolk 180

St Brendan 9

steelyard weight 149–51

Steppes 48

stick chairs 207

St John's College, Cambridge 173

St Leonard's Church, Shoreditch 139

St Mary's Church, Ashwell, Hertfordshire 155, 157

St Mary's Church, York 139

stocks 137–9, 162

Stonehenge 17–19, 21, 22, 27, 36, 160

St Peter 67

St Peter on the Wall, Essex 115

St Peter's Church, Sandwich, Kent 188

St Philibert 171

Strabo 63, 72

strainer 74–6

straw figures/shapes 147–8

straws, drinking 41–3

strong box 209–11

St Swithun's Day, 15 July 146

Suffolk 150

suffrage movement 266–7

Sumerians 12–13, 41–2

Sun Chariot 44–6

Sunderland 275

superstitions and magic 212–14, 258. See also witchcraft

surnames 143–5

Sussex 78, 96, 117, 120, 147, 246, 264

Sutton Hoo 98–100, 104–6, 109

Sutton, near Shrewsbury 115

Sweden 33, 109

Sweyn Forkbeard, King of Denmark 124

swimming 173–5, 242

Swinton 97

Syria 8

Tacitus 85

tailors 150–1

Talbot, Fanny 264

Tasmania 241

taxes 114, 128, 184, 262

Teather, Anne 21

Tees, River 96, 195

Thames Beater 32–4

Thames, River 84, 96, 127, 168, 194, 231
thatched roofs 89–91
Thirsk, North Yorkshire 275
Thoresby, Ralph 216
Thornton Abbey, Lincolnshire 156
three-field rotation 111, 219
tiles 88, 91, 180–1
tobacco 215–17
Tollense Figurine 47–9
tractors 288
Treatise of Cider by John Worlidge 185–7
trees 169–72. *See also* forests and woodland; wood
Trent and Mersey Canal 230–1, 232
Trent, River 96, 195, 231
Trundholm Sun Chariot 44–6
Tuke, John 218
Turkey 8, 69
Turner, Thomas 246
Turnpike Act, 1706 228
Tyne, River 96, 195

universal medicines 276–7
urbanisation 272–4

Vagabonds and Beggars Act, 1494 210
van Hamme, Jan Ariens 181
Varro 57, 78
Vermuyden, Cornelius 180
Veselovsky, Nikolai 41
Vesuvius, Italy 68, 78, 140
veterinary medicine 213, 276–7, 282
Victoria and Albert Museum, London 154
Vikings 122–4, 152, 162, 174

villae rusticae 71, 72–3, 90
village shop 245–7
villages, origins of 112
vineyards 73–5
volcanos 140–2
Vösendorf baby feeder 38–40

Wales 17, 55, 81, 93, 96, 113, 127, 204, 231, 264, 266, 285
Walker, Don 141
Walker's Universal Mixture 277
walnut trees 170–1
Warboys, Cambridgeshire 147–8
Wareham, Dorset 120
Warne, Frederick 264
water 51–2, 119–21, 168, 176, 179–80, 279–71. *See also* swimming
water filters 271
water-mills 132
Water Newton Treasure, Cambridgeshire 74–6
waterwheels 168
wattle 90, 91
Watt, Madge 266
Waugh, Edwin 189–90
weapons 32–4, 59, 60, 61, 104, 167–8
weather forecasting 242–4
weaving 144
Wedgwood, Josiah 230, 232
weights 150–1
wellington boots 257, 258–9
Wessex 123
Wessex, King of 98
West Country 181, 216
Western Isles of Scotland 252
Weston Park Museum, Sheffield 118
West Sussex 20–1

INDEX

Wetherby, West Yorkshire 123
wetlands 179–80
Wharram Percy's church, Yorkshire 115
Wharram Percy, Yorkshire 161–3
whipping posts 137–9
Whitby, North Yorkshire 123, 243
Whiteware Jug 143–5
Wicken Fen, Cambridgeshire 264
Wight, James Alfred 275–6
wild boars 116, 117–18, 158
Wilks, Maurice 289
William the Conqueror (Duke of Normandy) 1–2, 124, 125–7, 128–30, 131–3, 162, 188, 260, 290
willow 252
Wiltshire 132
windmills 168–9, 180–1
Windsor Castle 126–7
wine 73–5, 185
Winnats Pass, Peak District 285
Wintringham, Margaret 268

witchcraft 176–8, 194, 212, 213, 258
wolves 53–4, 92–3, 108, 164, 165
Women's Institute (WI) 266–71
wood 29–30, 98–100, 170–2. *See also* forests and woodland
woodcuts 173, 175
wool 11–12, 152–4, 203–4
Worcester 147
Worcestershire 95, 187
Worlidge, John 186–7
writing, early systems of 12–13
Wulfred, Archbishop of Canterbury 114–15

yew trees 99–100
York 125, 126, 139
Yorkshire 1–2, 115, 123, 129, 147, 161–3, 180, 191, 217. *See also* North Yorkshire; Star Carr
Yorkshire billhook 291–2
Young, Arthur 219

Harper North

BOOK CREDITS

would like to thank the following staff
and contributors for their involvement in making
this book a reality:

Fionnuala Barrett
Samuel Birkett
Peter Borcsok
Ciara Briggs
Katie Buckley
Sarah Burke
Alan Cracknell
Jonathan de Peyer
Tom Dunstan
Kate Elton
Sarah Emsley
Nick Fawcett
Simon Gerratt
Monica Green
Neil Gower
Natassa Hadjinicolaou
Megan Jones

Jean-Marie Kelly
Taslima Khatun
Charlotte Macdonald
Rachel McCarron
Ben McConnell
Petra Moll
Alice Murphy-Pyle
Adam Murray
Holly Ovenden
Genevieve Pegg
Amanda Percival
Florence Shepherd
Matthew Richardson
Eleanor Slater
Emma Sullivan
Katrina Troy
Daisy Watt